The Lord's Prayer in the Early Church

Also by Dr. Roy Hammerling

Previous Publications:

Roy Hammerling (*editor*)

A HISTORY OF PRAYER: The First to the Fifteenth Century, 2008.

The Lord's Prayer in the Early Church

The Pearl of Great Price

Roy Hammerling

palgrave
macmillan

THE LORD'S PRAYER IN THE EARLY CHURCH
Copyright © Roy Hammerling, 2010.

First published in 2010 by PALGRAVE MACMILLAN® in the
United States - a division of St. Martin's Press LLC, 175 Fifth Avenue,
New York, NY 10010.

Where this book is distributed in the UK, Europe and the rest of the
World, this is by Palgrave Macmillan, a division of Macmillan
Publishers Limited, registered in England, company number 785998,
of Houndmills, Basingstoke, Hampshire RG21 6XS.

Palgrave Macmillan is the global academic imprint of the above
companies and has companies and representatives throughout the world.

Palgrave® and Macmillan® are registered trademarks in the United
States, the United Kingdom, Europe and other countries.

ISBN: 978–0–230–10589–8

Library of Congress Cataloging-in-Publication Data

Hammerling, Roy.
    The Lord's prayer in the early church : the pearl of great price / by
Roy Hammerling.
        p.   cm.
    ISBN 978–0–230–10589–8 (alk. paper)
    1. Lord's prayer—History.   2. Church history—Primitive and
early church, ca. 30–600.   I. Title.
    BV230.H365 2010
    242'.72209015—dc22   2010007923

Design by Integra Software Services

First edition: September 2010

10 9 8 7 6 5 4 3 2 1

Printed in the United States of America.

Special thanks to Brill Publications for granting permission to reprint three previous
articles that have been revised and are included as parts of Chapter 3 in this book.
The first is entitled in this volume as "The Lord's Prayer in Baptismal Catechesis,"
which previously appeared under the title "The Lord's Prayer: The Cornerstone of
Early Baptismal Catechesis" in a slightly different form in Roy Hammerling, ed.,
A History of Prayer: The First to the Fifteenth Century (Leiden: Brill, 2008),
pp. 167–182. The second is a part of the section in this work entitled "The Lord's
Prayer in Theological Education," also found in the aforementioned volume,
pp. 183–200, in which it is entitled "St. Augustine of Hippo: Prayer as Sacrament."
And finally, the section in this book called "The Lord's Prayer in Polemics" is also
found in the aforementioned work, pp. 223–244, in which it is in a slightly
different form and called "The Lord's Prayer in Early Christian Polemics to the
Eighth Century."

For Peggy

In Memory of Pamela Jolicoeur
October 21, 1944—June 9, 2010

"Prayer is intimacy with God and contemplation of the invisible. It satisfies our yearnings and makes us equal to the angels. Through it good prospers, evil is destroyed, and sinners will be converted. Prayer is the enjoyment of things present and the substance of things to come. Prayer turned the whale into a home for Jonah (Jonah 2:1ff.); it brought Hezekiah back to life from the very gates of death (2 Kings 20:1ff.); it transformed the flames into a moist wind for the three children (Daniel 3:19ff.) . . . Past history furnishes thousands of other examples beside these which make it clear that of all the things valued in this life, nothing is more precious than prayer." Gregory of Nyssa, *On the Lord's Prayer*.

"Dearly beloved, you have received the faith by hearing; now listen to . . . the Lord's Prayer . . . The angels stand in awe at what you are going to hear today. Heaven marvels, earth trembles, flesh does not bear it, hearing does not grasp it, the mind does not penetrate it, all creation cannot sustain it. I do not dare to utter it, yet I cannot remain silent. May God enable you to hear and me to speak . . . " Peter Chyrsologus, Sermon 67.

Contents

List of Tables

Acknowledgments

Fortunate are they who need to acknowledge so many that they will sadly leave someone out, and this is my case. So numerous are those who have helped me over the years with this manuscript that I am indeed indebted to a host of scholars, friends, and family members— and alas, some who will go unnamed. Thanks to you all.

First of all, I am grateful to the publishers, editors, and their staff for their careful work and help on this volume. I am especially thankful for the expert readers at Palgrave Macmillan who gave numerous useful suggestions and for the help of Burke Gerstenschlager, Afrin Kabir, Samantha Hasey, Rachel Tekula, and Kristy Lilas in shepherding this project to completion.

I would like to thank all those who have given me clear, sound advice and careful counsel and encouragement. In particular, I cannot show enough appreciation to John Van Engen, who taught me to be a critical scholar and student of what he calls "low-flying," in-depth scholarly analysis of texts. Likewise, I offer my sincere gratitude to Lisa Wolverton, Paul Savage, Karlfried Froehlich, Daniel Sheerin, William Dohar, David Fagerberg, Kathleen Biddick, John Cavadini, and numerous paper respondents at various conferences over the years.

Those who have been worthy models for my scholarly life are the faculty and administration at Concordia College. My colleagues and friends who have supported me and at times read parts of this work, providing critical and kind emendations, include Jim Aageson, Somaya Abdullah, Ahmed Afzaal, Per Anderson, Jim Egge, Sam Giere, Jim Haney, Stewart Herman, Pam Jolicoeur, Joan Kopperud, Basit Koshul, Hilda Koster, Mark Krejci, Tammy Lanaghan, Les Meyer, Jan Pranger, Ernest Simmons, Elna Solvang, and Matt Stith, but especially Larry Alderink, Shawn Carruth, Rene Clausen, Nick Ellig, Michelle Lelwica, and David Sprunger. My deepest thanks to you all.

My students at Concordia College have often provided inspiration and valuable insight. I thank them all, especially Sarah Rohde, Phil Abrahamson, and Michelle Urberg. Special thanks to those who helped with editing this book: I am deeply indebted to Kayla Goetz and her tireless, professional, and expert work reading over this manuscript and to the wonderful Mary Thornton and the religion department secretarial staff. Also, my deepest appreciation goes to Sharon Hoverson and the Concordia College library staff, who helped me get so many obscure books in dead languages through interlibrary loan.

Of those who inspire me to seek after the good in life and to leave the rest, as William Caxton once said, I thank Ralph Quere, Ken Christopherson, Walt Pilgrm, Mark Bigott, Ted Kleinman, Kyle Pasewark, Mike Root, and the good people and staff of St. John Lutheran Church. Similarly, I would like to thank PACODES for their work in Sudan, especially Machien Justin Luoi and Gatkier Machar, Joan Kopperud, Mike Bath, Rick Chapman, Ron Twedt, and BethMarie Gooding, as well as Endless Eye Productions, especially Tom Clayton, Sean Fahey, and Jeremiah Hammerling.

Finally, to my family—in particular my dear wife, Peggy; my remarkable children, Jeremiah, Rachel, and Josh; my mother, Nelly; my father-in-law, Bill Ekberg; my sister, Evelyn, and her sons, Jon, Aaron, and Kevin—and to my whole extended family—especially Dan Tynan and David Turner; to all of you, my most humble and heartfelt thank you.

Abbreviations

ACCS	Ancient Christian Commentary on Scripture Series
ACW	Ancient Christian Writers Series
ANF	Ante-Nicene Fathers
CCCM	*Corpus Christianorum, Continuatio Mediaevalis*
CCSL	*Corpus Christianiorum, Series Latina*
CIL	*Corpus inscriptionum latinarum*
CPL	*Clavis Patrum Latinorum*
CSA	*Corpus Scriptorum Augustinianorum*
CSCO	*Corpus Scriptorum Christianorum Orientalium*
CSEL	*Corpus Scriptorum Ecclesiasticorum Latinorum*
EEC	*Encyclopedia of the Early Church*
FC	Fathers of the Church Series
GCS	*Die griechischen chrislichen Schriftsteller*
IGR	*Inscriptiones graecae ad res romanas pertinentes*
ILS	*Inscriptiones latinae selectee*
LXX	The Septuagint
MGH	*Monumenta Germaniae Historica*
MGH AA	*Monumenta Germaniae Historica: Auctorum antiquissimorum*
NPNF	Nicene and Post Nicene Fathers
NRSV	New Revised Standard Bible
OGIS	*Orientis Graeci Inscriptiones Selectae*
PG	*Patrologia cursus completes: series graeca.* Ed. J.-P. Migne, Paris, 1857–1866.

PL   *Patrologia cursus completes: series Latina.*
            Ed. J.-P. Migne, Paris, 1841–1864.
SBLSBS   SBL Sources for Biblical Study
SC   *Sources Chrétiennes*
SSRM   *Scriptores Rerum Merovingicarum*

Introduction

The Mystery and Power of the Lord's Prayer

Two Central Points of View

The Lord's Prayer (LP) is the most important prayer in the history of Christianity. Early authors down to the sixth century argued that the LP was full of mystery and power, a treasure of immeasurable wealth, and a pearl of great price. As a result, any thorough examination of how Jesus' prayer was actually prayed, used, and understood in the history of the early church is daunting because of the numerous and diverse types of sources with which a scholar must contend. Nevertheless, an in-depth survey of these texts is able to provide valuable insights into various aspects of the life, practices, beliefs, and exegetical concerns of early Christian churches. This book examines all the major sources of the LP in the early church through the fifth century from two central points of view, namely, historical and theological. It does so, however, by applying these scholarly disciplines in a variety of ways. First of all, it reads theological texts—biblical commentaries, sermons, and the like—with historical eyes in order to discover the development of early church attitudes and practices regarding the LP; at the same time, it also closely examines these texts in a more straightforward, traditional way, that is, by carefully analyzing the religious and intellectual implications of these early works. It also carefully sifts through the historical contexts of the early sources in order to discover theological insights. By considering the theological texts historically and the historical events theologically, an interesting picture of the first five centuries of Christianity emerges. Sometimes these historical and theological vantage points affirm other scholarship on the LP about this era; at times they help to bring previous scholarly views into clearer light, and still at other times they confuse matters even further, often requiring new interpretations of old texts and contexts concerning the LP. Nevertheless, generally speaking, an examination of the historical events and theological views encompassing the pious practices and theological attitudes toward the LP in the early church reveals a picture of early Christianity that is more complicated and richly diversified than has often been imagined.

Chapter 1 elucidates how an overarching reverential attitude of mystery and power concerning the LP during the earliest centuries of Christianity profoundly affected both its use and interpretation. Chapter 2 analyzes the wondrous origins of the LP down to the third century. Since source material is scarce from this time, this chapter further develops the themes of mystery and power, as well as sets up the major issues that surround the life, ritual, and teachings of the LP throughout the period of the early church. Chapter 3 discusses the historical and theological use of the LP in the early church during the fourth and fifth centuries, looking specifically at how it developed in poetry, baptismal catechesis, theological education, polemics, and monastic theology. What results is an examination of a group of churches and people who struggled with the great questions of life and what it meant to be faithful followers of God and compassionate people in a world full of trouble and change. The historical and theological methods clarify insights into the life, practices, and beliefs of early Christians, especially with regard to the most distinctly Christian activity of the time, praying the LP.

CHAPTER 1

The Pearl of Great Price

Ambrose, the renowned fourth-century bishop of Milan, passionately loved the church and what he considered to be its immeasurable treasures. The great wealth of the church for Ambrose, of course, did not reside in the tangible possession of magnificent buildings, gold-plated crosses, and other ornaments of the worship space, but in Jesus and his priceless words.

The heart of Jesus' teaching, for Ambrose, as it was for many early authors, was the LP. Ambrose even likened the LP to a "pearl" of great value. After all, the gospels (Matthew 6 and Luke 11) suggest that the mystery and power of the LP were in part due to the fact that the prayer came directly out of Jesus' divine heart and mind, flowing forth from his holy mouth and eventually passing straight into the ears of his loyal disciples. They in turn faithfully handed it over to their spiritual descendents, the people of the church. In this manner, the LP developed into the most widely known, identifiable, and precious prayer in Christianity. No other text from the Christian scriptures was as cherished or even as jealously guarded as this gem of Christian worship, doctrine, education, and daily devotional practice.

Early Christians around the fourth and fifth centuries were so enamored of this fine jewel that they even safeguarded the LP with a notable affection. Ambrose, like many before him, refused to teach the LP to anyone who had not been baptized. This was largely due to his understanding of Matthew 7:6: "Do not give what is holy to dogs; and do not throw your pearls before swine, or they will trample them under their feet, and turn and maul you."[1] Ambrose considered the mysteries of the church (e.g., baptism, the Eucharist, the Apostles' Creed, and the LP) to be precious pearls that were the sole property of the faithful. Only believers who had been properly adopted as true children of God through the rite of baptism, argued Ambrose, had the right to call upon the Creator of the universe with the lovingly intimate address of the opening words of the LP, "Our Father." In other words, only the baptized had the proper inheritance, and therefore, the honor or even the ability to experience the true mystery and power of these remarkable words.[2]

Those outside the church, the unbaptized, around the fourth century were not allowed to learn, read, or hear this most holy of all prayers until they had been fully incorporated into the body of Christ through their watery initiations. Those inside the church cherished their Savior's prayer, their pearl of great price, as if it were a valuable heirloom to be carefully guarded by the family from any who might falsely or accidentally seek to lay claim to it by either thieving intent or ignorance. Ambrose and others believed that if an uninitiated person prayed the LP, it would somehow become besmirched with the dirty fingerprints of unworthy hands. The address "Our Father" was a wondrously mysterious, self-limiting declaration for the bishop of Milan. If the people speaking the words "Our Father" were not truly adopted children of God, their declaration made them usurpers of a relationship that they were unworthy of or without the power to claim. They were like slaves claiming to be princes or princesses. The LP was only for those who possessed baptized ears and mouths, even if they intended to join the church but had not done so yet.[3]

The Awe-Inspiring Lord's Prayer

Early Christian writers who turned their attention to the LP approached it with a deep sense of awe, and they likewise tried to instill this feeling in other believers, particularly in recently baptized converts. The amount of praise that early Christian authors showered upon the mystery and power of the LP is indeed at times something that strikes the modern reader as unexpected. Peter Chrysologus, a fifth-century bishop of Ravenna, exemplifies this early reverence toward the LP. On the occasion of teaching the LP to some converts, Peter preached:

> Dearly beloved, you have received the faith by hearing; now listen to the formula of the Lord's Prayer.... The angels stand in awe at what you are going to hear today. Heaven marvels, earth trembles, flesh does

not bear it, hearing does not grasp it, the mind does not penetrate it, all creation cannot sustain it. I do not dare to utter it, yet I cannot remain silent. May God enable you to hear and me to speak.... It is indeed more awesome that the earth is transformed into a heaven, that a person is changed by a deification, and that those whose lot is slavery get the rights of domination.... For, He who has changed from a judge into a Father [in baptism and in the words of the "Our Father"] has wished to be loved, not feared.[4]

Bishop Chrysologus' moving comments on the LP and his respect for a great mystery of the faith clearly point out that the LP is instrumental in revealing a central reality of Christianity, namely, God has retired from a fearsome occupation as heavenly Judge and chosen instead to take on the remarkably intimate title of Father in relation to baptized humanity. For Chrysologus, a truly mysterious transformation occurred in baptized believers, who were born again as children of God, even though they were nothing better than slaves to sin. They now not only had the right but also the power and ability to utter those wondrous words, "Our Father."

Likewise, Gregory of Nyssa (ca. 335–394) bowed before the nobility of the LP's wisdom in a slightly different but no less awe-inspiring and respectful manner:

...the Lord said to His disciples, "When you pray, say, 'Our Father, who art in heaven.'" "Who will give me wings like a dove," said the great David somewhere in the Psalms [54:7]. This I, too, would say, boldly using the same words. Who will give me those wings that my mind may wing its way up to the heights of these noble words? Then I would leave behind the earth altogether and traverse all the middle air; I would reach the beautiful ether, come to the stars and behold all their orderly array. But not even at these would I stop short, but, passing beyond them, would become a stranger to all that moves and changes and apprehend the stable Nature, the immovable Power which exists in its own right, guiding and keeping in being all things, for all depend on the ineffable will of the Divine Wisdom. So first my mind must become detached from anything subject to flux and change and tranquilly rest in motionless spiritual repose, so as to be rendered akin to Him who is perfectly unchangeable; and then it may address Him by this most familiar name and say, "Father."[5]

The veneration of the early church given to the celestial mystery and power of the LP helped to promote it as "the" most frequently discussed text of the Christian scriptures down through the Reformation.[6] Almost every Christian scholar of the early and medieval church believed that the LP was worthy of special place among the scriptures, not only because of its divine origins, but also because it was nothing less than a perfect "summary of the entire gospel."[7]

A Perfect Summary of the Gospel

Tertullian, in the early third century, boldly declared that all the writings of the prophets, evangelists, and apostles as well as all of Jesus' sermons, parables, examples, and precepts are "touched on in the brief compass of a few little words," namely, the LP. He then mused, "Yet, why be surprised? God alone could teach us how he would have us pray. The homage of prayer, then, as arranged by Him and animated by His Spirit at the very moment it went forth from His divine lips, because of the prerogative granted to Him, ascends to heaven, recommending to the Father what the Son has taught."[8] For Tertullian, the LP's divine origin, brevity, and ability to aid its petitioners all point to the depth of the mystery of the prayer. The power of the LP, argued Tertullian, lies in the animating force of the Holy Spirit, who empowers those who pray it to have direct access to the very presence of God. The LP has the awesome ability to aid those who pray it in attaining what they seek; namely, they might keep God's name holy; might seek God's kingdom; and will receive daily bread, be forgiven, and ultimately be freed of temptation and evil. Indeed, Tertullian suggests that the LP not only helps Christians understand what they ought to focus their lives upon, that is, God and honorable Christian lives, but it also assists in the impartation of every good gift worthy of God's granting.

Cyprian, the great bishop of Carthage, in his commentary entitled simply *On the Lord's Prayer* (written ca. 252) concurred with Tertullian. Though brief in words, said Cyprian, the LP abounds "spiritually in power,"[9] so that nothing at all is omitted which is not included in our petitions and in our prayers in a compendium of heavenly doctrine!"[10] Even much later, Paschasius Radbertus (ca. 790–865), a Benedictine monk during the Carolingian era, quoted these words of Cyprian and added that Christ offered this prayer in order to bring salvation "to every sex and age."[11] Another earlier monastic writer,

Cassian (ca. 365–435), in his *Conferences*, called the LP "the fullness of perfection"[12] and "an example and a rule" for all prayer.[13]

Early Christian authors assumed that the LP was both a summary of the essence of gospel teaching, which includes essential Christian doctrines, and a worthy summation of ethical and virtuous behavior. Gregory of Nyssa in the fourth century, for example, called the LP a "guide to the blessed life," by which he meant a life dedicated to God through virtuous deeds.[14] The individual petitions of the LP urge worthy practices, such as keeping God's name holy, doing God's will, seeking God's kingdom, and forgiving others as God had forgiven them. Thus, though short, this prayer encompasses all that one needs to know and do concerning God and a noble Christian life.

Cyprian fascinatingly notes that Christ put forth in the LP a "great compendium of His precepts, so that the memory of the learners might not be burdened in heavenly training, but might learn quickly what was necessary to a simple faith."[15] The mystery and power of the LP are in part revealed for Cyprian in its simple succinctness, which is able to communicate great wisdom in such an intelligibly abridged manner that even the simplest souls are able to memorize easily the LP and grasp the profound complexity of the faith.

The prophet Isaiah, Cyprian continued, even prophesied about the holy brevity of the LP when he said, "[God's will] completes and abbreviates His word in justice, since God will offer an abbreviated word in the whole earth."[16] The "abbreviated word" Cyprian equated with the LP, which was an important part of God's grand plan to offer divine loving-kindness to a woefully needy world.[17]

Tertullian and two Greek authors, namely, his contemporary Origen (ca. 185–254) and the later Gregory of Nyssa (ca. 330–390), understood the brevity of the LP to be a way of guarding against the sin of the "heaping on of empty phrases"[18] in prayer. Tertullian declared that people ought to avoid drawing near God with an "army of words" because "brevity rests upon the foundation of a great and fruitful interpretation, and in proportion as it is restrained in wording, so is it copious in meaning."[19]

Origen and Gregory of Nyssa accused both Jews and Gentiles of multiplying the words of their prayers in the hopes that God might more readily be willing to grant their petitions. In this manner, these early fathers accused Jews and Gentiles of seeking what God forbids them: earthly wealth as opposed to heavenly treasure, of the kind that is in the LP. Gregory of Nyssa, however, noted that in contrast to these phrase heapers, the faithful ought to gradually learn from their experience of praying the shorter petitions of the LP. God more willingly hears succinct supplications, and as a result, those who pray aright "may rise to the desire for the higher gifts which are more worthy of God."[20] The small number of words in the LP communicated for early authors a mysterious depth of meaning and power that helped petitioners to obtain the spiritual riches that God desired to bestow.

A Heavenly Prayer

Tertullian noted in his commentary *On Prayer* that "[e]verything which belongs to the Lord Christ is heavenly, as is also this training in prayer."[21] He explained that the heavenly prayer of Jesus stood in sharp contrast to John the Baptist's prayer (Luke 11:1). Tertullian believed John's prayer was good, but it was not to be considered a heavenly, eternal prayer. He argued that the Baptist's "earthly" prayer has been lost and has passed away into oblivion: if it had been heavenly, it would still remain and last forever within the prayer life of the church. God alone, however, is able to teach the faithful how they ought to pray. That is why Jesus taught his disciples the mysteriously powerful, and heavenly, LP in the first place. When children of the heavenly Father pray the LP, it swiftly returns to the One from whom it came, God.[22] The LP offers God's baptismal children a mysteriously direct, effective, and prompt access to the power of God. Also, God readily desires to grant the fulfillment of all the petitions of the LP to everyone who prays it, in part because God is indeed the loving Father who is addressed in the prayer. Therefore, as a divine parent, God wishes to meet the needs of those faithful children who pray the LP in a proper manner.

The mystery and power of the LP also led some early commentators on it to emphasize its eschatological tone.[23] Raymond Brown has noted that the eschatological emphasis of the LP arose out of its place within early liturgies. The juxtaposition of the LP and the Eucharist led Cyril of Jerusalem (d. 386) to include the LP as a part of his commentary on the Eucharistic liturgy.[24] Early churches often prayed the LP immediately before the Eucharist, a practice that remains intact even today in many denominations, for example, in Roman Catholic and mainline Protestant churches. Early and present-day theologians often interpret the Eucharist as a foretaste of the great heavenly feast yet to come. Therefore, the LP as the prayer that prepares the faithful for the feast also naturally takes on eschatological overtones, because it prepares the faithful for the eschatological meal.

Brown, commenting on the early church Eucharistic connection, concludes, "The prayer given them by Jesus was an expression of their yearning for His return and for the ultimate fulfillment of the things He had promised."[25] The desire of early Christians for the end times, virtuous lives, and salvation thus was seen to be an essential part of the message of the LP from the earliest days of the church.

The Lord's Prayer and the Future of the Church

A work attributed to the German missionary Boniface (d. 754), which probably dates close to his day, admonished Christians to memorize the LP because "in it in brief form is contained every need of the present and the future life." The author argued that not only ought Christians to pray this prayer regularly, but they must also be ready to hand it over faithfully to future generations, because the prayer anticipates life in heaven itself.[26]

The very future of the church, therefore, in some ways depended upon the LP being handed over, in order that it might be properly practiced and taught. The power and mystery of the LP made it an invaluable text for the life of early Christian community. As a result, the LP, the pearl of great price in early Christianity, came to influence every aspect of the Christian faith, from communal worship to private piety down to the present day. A close examination of how the LP was specifically used and interpreted in the early church reveals that of particular interest is how the LP developed in the poetry, baptismal catechesis, theological education, polemics, and monastic theology of the early church. However, before we can explore these aspects of the LP, we must first look at how early Christians delighted in the wondrous origins of the LP, and how they incorporated it into the very fabric of every aspect of Christian living in the first three centuries of the church.

CHAPTER 2

The Wondrous Origins of the Lord's Prayer

The Lord's Prayer in the First Three Centuries

Christian authors throughout the early and medieval church delighted in the wondrous origins of the LP despite some obvious difficulties with what the original wording of the LP actually was. A close examination of the only two biblical passages that record the entire LP (Matthew 6 and Luke 11) reveals that the Bible preserves two slightly different versions of Jesus' prayer. Shortly thereafter, even more diverse versions of the prayer appeared. While modern scholars have pored over this problem rather extensively, early authors ignored, simply dismissed, or even explained away the differences in rather straightforward ways. Modern scholars essentially have concluded that the two renditions of the LP developed within two different cultural, geographic, and literary contexts, whereas almost all ancient authors simply considered the two to be versions of the same prayer given to the disciples by Jesus. Here we will focus on the historical issues and largely leave the modern debate over the origins of the LP in other capable, scholarly hands, even though we do need to make a few brief remarks in this regard. With respect to the earlier writers, however, every aspect of the LP, including its origins, was wrapped in wondrous mystery.

Two Biblical Versions of the Lord's Prayer: A Brief Comment on the Views of Modern Scholars

Luke 11:1–4 recounts how the disciples asked Jesus, "Lord, teach us to pray, as John [the Baptist] taught his disciples." Jesus responded simply by giving them a five-petition prayer in the context of what some scholars have called the Sermon on the Plain. Matthew 6:9–13, on the other hand, placed Jesus' presentation of a seven-petition LP in the midst of the Sermon on the Mount and a broader discussion concerning prayer among an apparently sympathetic crowd of followers, which happened to include the 12 apostles. A brief look at the texts of Matthew 6:9–13 and Luke 11:1–4 reveals their differences:

Table 2.1   The Lord's Prayer in Matthew and Luke

Matthew 6:9–13:

Introduction/Address	Our Father in heaven,
First Petition	Holy be your name.
Second Petition	Your kingdom come.
Third Petition	Your will be done, on earth as it is in heaven.
Fourth Petition	Give us this day our daily (or supersubstantial) bread.
Fifth Petition	And forgive us our debts, as we also have forgiven our debtors.
Sixth Petition	And do not bring us to the time of trial (or into temptation).
Seventh Petition[1]	But rescue (or deliver) us from (the) evil (one).[2]

Luke 11:1–4:

Introduction	Father,
First Petition	Holy be your name.
Second Petition	Your kingdom come.
Third Petition	(Not in Luke)
Fourth Petition	Give us each day our daily bread.
Fifth Petition	And forgive us our sins, for we ourselves forgive everyone indebted to us.
Sixth Petition	And do not bring us to the time of trial (or into temptation).[3]
Seventh Petition	(Not in Luke)

Recent scholars have tried to explain the differences between the two versions by suggesting that they developed in two separate contexts and were a part of gospel writings that were directed at two specific groups of people: Matthew wrote primarily for Jewish converts to Christianity and Luke for Gentile Christians. Ernst Lohmeyer takes this one step further by suggesting that these two texts reflect the two separate geographical locations that the authors of Matthew and Luke were associated with. Lohmeyer suggests that Matthew was connected to Jerusalem, whereas Luke was associated with Galilee.[4]

Joachim Jeremias argues that the two different audiences and cultural contexts for these gospels also reflect two different catechetical emphases that are associated with the preceding audiences of the two gospels. The LP and the surrounding context of the Sermon on the Mount in Matthew, says Jeremias, indicate a teaching situation in which the audience, who comes out of a context of Jewish traditions, has already learned to pray as children. The problem for the Jewish converts to Christianity was that they were in danger of making their prayers routine and meaningless, suggests Jeremias. The LP and its commentary in Matthew 6 therefore address this problem. In Luke, on the other hand, the LP is directed at Gentile converts, or people who are just learning how to pray, and they need encouragement to persist in their newly adopted religious practice.[5]

Hans Dieter Betz has affirmed this analysis but has further clarified that the LP has its own unique brand of "Jewish Theology" that underlies the literary and cultural contexts of both versions. Betz states,

> Therefore, we can conclude in regard to the Lord's Prayer that the ascription of this prayer to Jesus may indeed be historically correct, but that Jesus created the prayer out of traditional elements by giving it the form and content he wanted. This method must have been the same as that of consciously formed prayers at the time.[6]

Although modern scholars puzzle over which of these versions is more authentic, ancient authors rarely considered the point worthy of parchment. Jeremias concluded that Matthew's version has a style and poetic feel characteristic of a liturgical context and tradition. Luke's shorter version, which Jeremias argues is less developed and rhythmic, is probably the older of the two, because it is difficult to imagine that anyone would dare shorten the LP for whatever reason. On the other hand, it is conceivable, says Jeremias, that someone might slightly alter and expand upon an original version in order to turn it into a more easily remembered and/or spoken text, which could be used in a public worship setting where such things mattered.[7]

Betz, however, also notes that liturgical communities often show a remarkable amount of flexibility and willingness to accept new forms of prayers, as long as they "reflect a traditional language and form."[8] James Charlesworth, another modern author, has demonstrated that other early prayers and liturgical texts have abbreviated important documents over time to increase their liturgical and educational appeal.[9] Therefore, it is possible that Matthew might be the older and more authentic version of the LP.

Jeremias himself notes that the some parts of Matthew's LP are older than the same parts in Luke, but taken as a whole, Luke's LP offers readers the oldest complete version of the LP. For example, Jeremias states that the fourth petition in Matthew, "Give us *this* day our daily bread," is actually the shorter version of the petition. Luke instead explains the word "this" by expanding it: "Give us *each* day our daily bread." Therefore, with regard to which version is the oldest, Jeremias finally decides that "the Lucan version has preserved the oldest form with respect to *length*, but the Matthean text is more original with regard to *wording*."[10]

The moderately different tones of the two early versions of the LP have led the modern biblical scholar Ulrich Luz to promote a theory that is now commonly held, namely, that the Matthean rendition of the LP has a fuller and more liturgically rich language with a more obvious rhythm than the Lucan version. Matthew's Greek LP with its clearer poetic rhythm reflects a prayer that lends itself better to a worship context. Poetry is easier for individuals to memorize and for people to recite alone in private devotions or collectively in worship. The preceding arguments might lead some to conclude that the less poetic Lucan version is less liturgical or a prayer that was not used in a worship setting. In reality, however, this is an argument by comparison. That is, Luke compared with Matthew appears less liturgical, and therefore Luke is not liturgical. But such thinking does not take into account the poetic cadence of Luke's wording. Simply because it is less poetic does not mean it is nonpoetic, and indeed, Luke's LP does share some poetic similarities with Matthew in the original Greek as well. For example, the first two petitions, about hallowing God's name and seeking God's will, have a pleasant rhyme and rhythm in both Matthew and Luke. Hence, Luz ultimately argues that both Matthew's and Luke's versions of the LP appear to reflect prayers that were used in worship, or at the very least, were liturgically friendly.[11]

The original liturgical context of the LP is very significant. Willy Rordorf has concluded that "even if the LP can be prayed in private or in small groups, we must always remember that, by virtue both of its form and even of its very content, *it is a prayer of the church*. Its essential *Sitz im Leben* is the *worship* in which the baptized Christians of a local congregation are gathered to honor God, to hear his word and to administer the sacraments."[12] The corporate emphasis reflected in the LP does indeed indicate that the prayer was meant primarily for the church as a body of believers first and foremost, and then secondarily as a means of private devotion. Even when the LP is prayed privately, the emphasis upon "our," "us," and "we" in the prayer always reminds individuals of their corporate connections and responsibilities to the church as a whole. In fact, all interpretations of the LP down through the Middle Ages constantly remind those who pray or study its words that the focus of this prayer is primarily upon the community of the church. Rather than a prayer that asks for one's private needs, it unabashedly always seeks the good of all faithful worshippers.

In any case, the cultural, geographic, and literary contexts of the LP in both Matthew and Luke strongly support the conclusion that the LP developed early on within a variety of early worshipful and educational contexts.[13] Prayers do not simply provide words that the faithful as individuals or groups utter with a rote and an unthinking manner to God, but rather, they are theological statements of faith that teach those who pray them how to believe, think, and act—in other words, the basics of Christian doctrine, practice, and morality.[14] The LP played an essential role in the lives of the earliest Christians, because it was a crucial part of their liturgical, educational, and private devotional experience of the faith. Before we can elaborate on this point, however, it is important to first look at how the early church viewed the LP as a prayer in and of itself.

The Lord's Prayer as Understood by Ancient Scholars

Early Christian authors almost always assumed that the two biblical versions of the LP were one and the same prayer. However, Origen, the third-century Greek author, was the only one who took issue with this idea. He argued that the two biblical versions of the LP were offered on two distinct occasions, and therefore must be considered two separate prayers. Origen stated logically: "On the whole, it is better to suppose that the prayers are different, even though they have certain parts in common."[15] After coming to this conclusion, he puzzles over the question, why would Jesus hand over two distinct yet similar prayers? Origen noticed that Luke 11 records that Jesus taught the LP to his disciples in a more private setting than the more public setting of Matthew 6. Since they were his students, they didn't require a detailed explanation of the prayer. Therefore, Luke's version was short and to the point, with an economy of words. Matthew, on the other hand, recounts the story of Jesus presenting the LP to a multitude of common folk on a mount: the less astute masses required a longer and better-developed LP in order to understand it more fully. The two prayers were certainly similar, but ultimately different because they uniquely reflected their intended audience and the specific occasion when they were handed over. This duplication was not a problem for Origen, but he also was not willing to say the two prayers were one and the same either.[16]

The North African scholar Augustine of Hippo (ca. 354–430), unlike Origen, believed that Luke simply recorded a more succinct version of the same prayer in Matthew. In this, he reflected the attitude of all other authors in the early church. The third petition, concerning God's will, was deliberately omitted by Luke, argued Augustine, for the purpose of emphasizing that it merely repeats the ideas of the first two. For a similar reason, the Lucan LP left out the words "but deliver us from evil" in order to show that Christians have deliverance from evil when they are not led into temptation. After all, Augustine noted, Matthew wrote, "*but* deliver" and not "*and* deliver" to point out that the final petition is expressly connected to the previous one. Augustine simply considered Luke to be the type of author who preferred to avoid repetition. Note that Augustine assumed that the longer Matthean version was the more complete and authoritative, while Luke's was merely a short version of Matthew's prayer. Likewise, all early scholars suggested that Matthew's LP took precedence over Luke's shorter text, whereas modern scholars have been divided on this issue. Indeed, ancient scholars presumed that Matthew's LP, being the more complete of the two versions, must be the more authoritative.[17]

Also, all other early Christian writers, unlike Origen, were unwilling to concede that these two biblical versions of the LP were in fact two different prayers. Since Origen himself came under doctrinal scrutiny later on and his orthodoxy was in question, many were able to dismiss his ideas rather easily. Since Augustine's theology emerged later and was revered as the height of orthodoxy, his views often held sway over later authors.

Early Christian writers simply assumed, like Augustine, that scripture was its own best interpreter *(scriptura sui ipsius interpres)*, and they therefore used the Bible to minimize textual difficulties rather than enhance them, especially if there were two versions of the same text.[18] The interpretation of the fourth petition, concerning daily bread, is a case in point. Augustine, like others, reconciled the two prayers by interpreting them in light of each other. The spiritual tone of the word "supersubstantial" in Matthew, noted Augustine, was best understood when viewed in comparison with the more earthly tone of "daily" in Luke. By combining the "supersubstantial" (i.e., those necessities that are spiritual or "above substantial/earthly matters") with the "daily" (or ordinary, everyday bread), Augustine and others interpreted both Matthew and Luke to mean "daily spiritual needs."[19] A hybrid interpretation of the two LP texts developed simply because authors assumed the two versions must both somehow go back to Jesus: therefore, the two versions of the LP were interpreted in light of each other, creating a collaborative explanation of the LP's meaning.

The Earliest Commentary on the Lord's Prayer

No comprehensive commentary dealing with the entire LP can be found before the year 200. Nevertheless, some comments on individual petitions of the LP do exist, even if they are short in length and on content. The earliest explanations of parts of the LP actually come from within the Bible itself. For example, the gospels themselves offer some commentary on the introduction, the third petition (on doing God's will), and the fifth petition (on forgiveness).

Luke 11:5–13, or the verses immediately following the LP, offers two parables on prayer. The second parable reads, "Is there anyone among you who, if your child asks for a fish, will give a snake instead of a fish? . . . how much more will the heavenly Father give the Holy Spirit to those who ask him!" The introduction of the LP, and especially the word "Father," is therefore further explained. Children of God need not fear that their heavenly Father will refuse them what they need, but they can trust in a God who will present to them what no one else can give, the Holy Spirit. This earthly and heavenly father/Father contrast would become one of the most important ways of explaining this text in the future.

Matthew 6:14–15, immediately following the LP text, directly comments upon the fifth petition: "For if you forgive others their trespasses, your heavenly Father will also forgive you; but if you do not forgive others, neither will your Father forgive your trespasses." The author of Matthew feels it necessary to explain how a petition of the LP actually suggests that God might refuse to forgive one of God's adopted children should they not obey their Heavenly Father. The blame is not to be placed upon the Father for not answering prayers, but on the unforgiving child.

Other second-century scholars saw the difficulty of the fifth petition as well. For example, the fifth petition, on forgiveness was a popular text to comment upon; Clement of Rome (ca. 96),[20] Ireneaus (ca. 130–200),[21] *The Epistle of Polycarp to the Philippians* (chs. 7 and 8), and Clement of Alexandria (ca. 150–215) are cases in point.[22] In each mention of this petition, the authors sought to encourage Christians to be more forgiving of others, in part because this is a concept that is not only at the heart of the LP but also the Christian faith itself. Indeed, Christian authors throughout the centuries often focused upon the particular importance of the fifth petition in the LP, making it the central concern of the entire prayer.

Similarly, other passages in Matthew's Gospel, outside of the immediate context of the LP, also refer to the prayer. Jesus in Matthew 26:36–46 offers two prayers which further emphasize the nature of God as Father, as well as the third petition. They read, "Father, if it is possible let this cup pass from me; yet not what I want but what you want," and "My Father, if this cannot pass unless I drink it, your will be done." Some ancient and modern scholars have argued that these verses are directly related to the introduction of the LP and the third petition, "Your will be done on earth as in heaven."[23] The idea of Father is clarified in this context in relation to actions that seem harsh or inconsistent with a loving God. In this case, the necessity of Jesus' death on the cross is resolved when the gospel writers show that Jesus borrows from his own prayer and focuses upon doing God's will as opposed to avoiding the cross. One early extra-biblical reference makes a similar point about martyrs doing God's will. Facing martyrdom, Polycarp (ca. 69–155) prayed for strength in order that he might do God's will: his words clearly hearken back to the third petition of the LP.[24] Clement of Alexandria likewise encourages Christians to pray that they might do God's will on earth as it is in heaven.[25]

Elsewhere in the gospels, a few other passages bring to mind the opening address of the LP. In John 17:1–5, Jesus addresses God as Father, and Mark 11:25 speaks of the "Father in heaven." Both Mark and John do not record the full text of the LP, but the fact that they hint at it is interesting. The concept of God as Father receives the greatest attention in biblical texts that hearken back to the LP, and even texts outside of the gospels see this idea as a central theological concern early on.

In the Pauline epistles, two verses provide an important clue as to how the LP was used in some early churches: Romans 8:15 and Galatians 4:6 both connect the introduction of the LP with baptism. These passages call God "Abba," which is the same Aramaic word for Father that scholars generally agree is the origin of the word for Father in the LP for both Matthew and Luke. They state that Christians have a right to call God by the name and title of "Father," because they have received the spirit of adoption in baptism and are true, adopted children of God. They have been freed by this adoption from slavery and therefore are no longer fearful servants but heirs of the most high God. This idea is ubiquitous in complete LP commentaries throughout the Middle Ages.[26]

The preceding point is significant. Throughout the history of the church, and even in its earliest days, the LP has always been closely associated with the rite of baptism. The two Pauline verses suggest that the LP may have been the first prayer of believers as they emerged from the baptismal waters. Rordorf notes that John 3:3ff. and Titus 3:5, which mention that baptism is a second birth, indicate that "[the LP] becomes as it were the first utterance of the stammering infant's unloosed tongue."[27] These biblical passages show that the earliest layers of LP commentary were particularly concerned with the relationship between God and Christians. The word "Father," specifically, revealed the radical nature of this new relationship, and therefore early biblical authors were not afraid to emphasize its importance. The situation in which the relationship of a convert to God changed from slave to heir of the Kingdom of God was the act of baptism. The text that most clearly revealed this reality was none other than the LP.[28]

One other New Testament verse, 2 Timothy 4:18 ("The Lord will rescue me from every evil attack and save me for his heavenly kingdom. To him be the glory forever and ever."), also deserves mention. Note that this verse echoes both the second petition of the LP (about the kingdom of God) and the sixth petition, concerning evil. What is equally important here is the reference to a brief doxology, that is, "to him be the glory forever and ever." There is a strong similarity between this doxology and another doxology that is added to the LP very early on. The late first- or early second-century work entitled the *Didache* includes at the end of the LP the phrase, ". . . for yours is the kingdom and the power and the glory forever and ever." Timothy's verse may well be the source and origin of the later doxology. Since the author of Timothy adds the doxology to texts that are reminiscent of a few petitions of the LP, such a suggestion seems within the realm of possibility.

Early extra-biblical sources that briefly mention the LP during the late first and second centuries are scarce, but a few brief references to individual petitions of the LP remain. Almost all of the specific or strong allusions to the LP have been mentioned earlier in this chapter. A close look at these references indicates that individual petitions of the LP were quoted from time to time in the context of broader theological arguments. Commentary on the LP specifically, therefore, may be considered to be sparse during the first few centuries, especially since we don't have a complete commentary on it until about the year 200.[29] Even other early church prayers that have survived offer almost no comparisons with the LP in either their form or content.[30]

Outside the Bible, only two other complete versions of the LP exist from the first and second centuries, namely, the one found in the *Didache* and another in Tatian's *Diatessaron*.[31] Neither of them, however, is identical to either of the previous biblical versions. During the third century even more unique versions appear, and finally, commentary on the LP as a whole becomes available.

More Versions of the Lord's Prayer and the Earliest Commentary on the Prayer

The problem of different forms of the LP was not limited to the two different biblical texts. Early records indicate that every full text of the LP that we possess (with one possible notable exception) from the first through the end of the third century has at least some slight variation in wording or phrasing. Therefore, scholars have a puzzle to solve: why were there so many different versions of the LP from this period of history?

The only other complete version of the LP that may date from the first century is in the Greek work entitled the *Didache* (aka, *The Teachings of the Twelve Apostles*).[32] A note of caution: some scholars place the date of this text in the early second century. Either way, this very early version of the LP departs only in a few minor ways from Matthew's LP. What is most important about this version is that it is the first adaptation to add a doxology at the end: ". . . for yours is the kingdom and the power and the glory forever. Amen."[33] Why did the *Didache* add a doxology? Both gospel LP versions end without a doxology and with the rather stark word "evil." Some pastors and congregations may have desired to conclude the prayer on a note of praise to God rather than with the word "evil" as the last word falling off their lips. A doxological ending, such as the one the *Didache* employs, helps to make the prayer more attractive in both worshipful and private devotional settings. The addition of a doxology is not unusual when we remember that liturgical communities had no problem changing prayers for liturgical reasons, so long as the change kept the spirit of the prayer and worship in mind.

A close look at the entire text of the *Didache* indicates that its version of the LP, like Matthew's and Luke's versions, reflects a liturgical context and an educational focus as well. The *Didache* includes three major sections: chapters 1–6 deal with the moral behavior required of catechumens (i.e., converts seeking baptism), chapters 7–10 discuss liturgical and ritual practices, and chapters 11–15 talk about church organization and life. The *Didache* records its version of the LP in Chapter 8, or in the liturgical section of the work.

The *Didache*'s liturgical chapters discuss the liturgical rite of baptism for "pagan" converts, and they reveal how its version of the LP was intimately connected to the ceremony of baptism. Chapter 7 mentions how baptismal candidates *and* those who are going to baptize them are both required to fast before any watery initiation occurs, in order to be properly prepared for this momentous event. The author of the *Didache* then reveals those places that are preferable for baptisms (e.g., a baptism in the running water of rivers is better than a baptism in a pool of still water) and in what manner the ceremony ought to be conducted. Chapter 8 instructs the newly baptized on how they ought to fast on Wednesdays and Fridays, a practice that runs counter to the example of those who are called "hypocrites," and for the *Didache* author this refers more specifically to the Jews. Christians are not to pray as the hypocrites do, but rather with the words of the LP "three times a day"; the specific times for prayer, however, are not mentioned. Paul Bradshaw has noted that "the absence of any specific directions as to when these three prayers were to be offered does not mean, as some have supposed, that no particular hours were intended but rather that the times were traditional and unchanged, and so needed no specific mention." Bradshaw points to Acts 10:9 and Peter praying at the sixth hour of the day (or noon), which may reflect the middle of the three prayer times. Or, suggests Bradshaw, it may simply signal a literary device of the author of Acts and Luke, who has a tendency to associate important moments in his writings with prayer.[34] The *Didache*, however, clearly indicates how the LP was closely linked with what was known as "mystagogical" training (i.e., the training of converts shortly *after* their baptisms) in a liturgical context.

Immediately following the *Didache*'s LP discussion, chapters 9 and 10 explain the Eucharist and how only the baptized may partake of the heavenly bread and wine. These chapters end with some recitation of early blessings for the Eucharistic cup and bread. Hence, there is even a loose connection between the LP and a central part of the worship ceremony, the Eucharist. The relationship between the LP and the Eucharist will continue to be important in the future. Today, this connection is still important in Roman Catholic and many mainline denominational liturgies, in which the LP is spoken immediately before the congregation comes forward to partake in the Eucharist. The *Didache* supports Rordorf's previously mentioned argument that the LP in the earliest texts developed primarily in a liturgical context from the earliest days of the church, especially in the first century.

When and where the Greek LP was first translated into Latin is unknown.[35] Some scholars have suggested that the earliest evidence for a Latin LP may be found in the ruins of Pompeii (ca. 79 AD), where the now famous "magical" square, SATOR AREPO TENET OPERA ROTAS, was discovered in four places. The square looks like this:

Table 2.2   The Sator Rotas Square

SATOR
AREPO
TENET
OPERA
ROTAS

The square can be read from top to bottom, backward bottom to top, from left to right top down, and upside down right to left. Some scholars point out that the letters of the square can be unscrambled as a cryptogram to form the words Pater Noster (or "Our Father," the first two words of the LP in Latin) twice, with an A and an O left over. If one arranges these letters in the Christian symbol of a cross with the N used once in the middle and with the A and the O on either sides of the cross bar, one will have the following image of the Sator Rotas Square Cross:

Table 2.3   The Sator Rotas Square Cross

```
                      P
                      A
                      T
                      E
                      R
        A PATERNOSTER O
                      O
                      S
                      T
                      E
                      R
```

Some believe that the square and the cryptogram indicate that Christians had a Latin LP in Pompeii during the latter part of the first century. Advocates of this theory also propose that the Latin letters A and O stand for the first and last letters of the Greek alphabet, Alpha and Omega, and that they refer to Revelation 1:8, in which Jesus speaks in a vision to John on Patmos: "I am the **A**lpha and **O**mega, the beginning and the end, says the Lord God, who is, and who was, and who is to come, the Almighty." This theory holds that early Christians developed the squares in order to hide the words *Pater Noster* from unsuspecting eyes; Christians, however, who were in on the game recognized the square as a secret code which revealed that those who scratched the square on their walls were in fact Christian.

The coincidence is certainly striking. There is evidence that Christians may indeed have been secretive with regard to the LP early on, and as a result, the suggestion that this was some sort of secret code has some appeal. However, Karlfried Froehlich has noted that the main difficulty with the overall Sator Rotas argument is that the Roman church at this time was still Greek, and it is very unlikely that the early Roman believers would have had a Latin LP.[36] Likewise, it is hard to reconcile the fact that no Latin Patristic or medieval writers I am aware of refer to the square cryptogram in connection with the LP. In any case, first and foremost, it must be remembered that only two words of the LP are hidden here. Thus, this square in the end tells us little or nothing about how or when the LP may have come into Latin or how it may have been used in the early church. Perhaps the most that can be said is that the connection between the square and the LP is most likely a modern invention of scholars who have creatively noticed a most striking coincidence.

After the first century, new versions of the LP continued to appear. However, outside the two gospels and the *Didache*, there is no other written text of the entire LP in the first century that scholars are aware of.[37] During the second century there is only one complete LP reference. Tatian's *Diatessaron*, written ca. 172, attempts to harmonize the discrepancies between the various gospels by synthesizing them into a single paraphrased text. Tatian's *Diatessaron* essentially follows the structure and content of the Gospel of Matthew, and as a result incorporates an essentially Matthean version of the LP with a slight variation on the fourth petition, which reads, "Give us the bread of the day."[38]

Tatian's version of the LP is worthy of note. Tatian was born (ca. 110–120) in the land of the Assyrians but later on traveled west (to Rome in particular), learning Greek in the process. About the time he wrote the *Diatessaron* (ca. 172), Tatian had returned home to the east. Whether he wrote it before or after this journey took place is difficult to ascertain. Partial editions of the *Diatessaron* exist in both Greek and Syriac, which makes it the first non-Greek version of the LP.

The *Diatessaron* was especially popular in the east, where its compact size, harmonization of the gospels, minimization of textual problems, and "rigorous interpretation of the Christian faith" were well received by the ascetically minded Eastern church.[39] The Syrian linguistic connection has been regarded as significant among modern scholars because of the similarity of Syrian to Jesus' own language of Aramaic. Carmel McCarthy has noted, "Indeed it has been suggested (by some) that the form of the Lord's Prayer used in the Syrian churches today cannot be all that different from the word that Jesus himself must have uttered in first-century Galilean Aramaic."[40] While this is a significant point, it must be noted at this juncture that the earliest versions of the LP that we possess are in Greek. Also, the issue of the various versions of the LP still remains a quandary.

The earliest extant Latin version of the LP is a part of the first full commentary on the LP, a work entitled simply *On Prayer,* by Tertullian (ca. 160–225, with the commentary being written ca. 200).[41] Before this time, early Latin writings that contained what would later come to be known as the New Testament included the LP in early versions of Matthew and Luke. Copies of these texts have not been discovered as of yet, but are presumed to have existed. The document called the *Acts of the Martyrs of Scilli* (the oldest Latin document of Christian Africa, ca. 180) provides evidence for a Latin translation for parts of the New Testament, specifically Paul's writings.[42] Tertullian hints at the existence of a Latin version of the Bible that he used, but unfortunately it has not survived. Nevertheless, we assume that Tertullian's version of the LP in *On Prayer* at least in part reflects this Bible. Tertullian's LP is a hybrid liturgical version of the LP that draws from both Matthew and Luke. Late in his life, Tertullian also refers to another version of the LP that he may have used. The two versions read as follows:

Table 2.4 Tertullian's Version of the Lord's Prayer

Introduction	Father,[43] in heaven,
First Petition	Holy be your name.
(NB: Tertullian later in life quotes another version of the first petition, which reads, "Holy Spirit, come upon us and cleanse us.")	
Third Petition	Your will be done on earth as in heaven,
(NB: the third petition comes before the second)	
Second Petition	Your kingdom come.
Fourth Petition	Give us today our daily bread.
Fifth Petition	Forgive us our debts, as we also forgive our debtors,
Sixth Petition	lead us not into temptation,
Seventh Petition	but take away from us (the) evil (one).[44]

A quick glance suggests that the uniqueness of Tertullian's version has five elements. Tertullian's version lacks the word "Our" at the beginning (which is similar to Luke's version, but it also adds "in heaven," which echoes Matthew); the first petition has a strikingly different reading in a later version of the LP; the second and third petitions have been inverted; and the fourth petition uses the more common liturgical "daily" *(quotidianum)* of Luke, rather than the more cumbersome *supersubstantial* of Matthew. Also, Tertullian has the word "take away" *(devehe)* instead of "deliver us" *(libera)* in the final petition.

The genre of Tertullian's commentary has been debated. Ernest Evans has argued that the work is a sermon preached during worship.[45] Timothy Barnes also feels the work is a sermon, but he suggests that it was presented outside of a worship setting at a communal meeting or gathering.[46] William Harmless has argued that Tertullian's *On Prayer* is a sermon and that it, and other works like it, may well have been primarily directed at recently baptized catechumens.[47] Some scholars believe that Tertullian did indeed hand over the LP to pre-baptized believers.[48] In fact, the document suggests that its audience was primarily mature members of the church, with an occasional emphasis upon recently baptized believers. The text, therefore, was preached or taught to an audience in which both mature and probably newly baptized members would have been present.

Tertullian offers a verse-by-verse explication on the entire LP, and then he presents some general practical advice on prayer. Should people wash their hands before they pray (chapter 13), raise their hands in prayer (14), take off their coats to pray (15), sit or stand in prayer (16), be subdued in voice while praying (17), withhold the kiss of peace after certain prayers (18), partake in the kiss of peace on fast days (19), dress modestly in church for prayer if a woman (20), be veiled for prayer if a virgin woman (21–22), or kneel while praying (23)? Tertullian concludes with discussions about the appropriate place and time[49] of prayer (24–25), the benefit of praying with visitors in one's home (26), and the fruitful practice of adding the "Alleluia" and psalms to one's prayers.

Most of the aforementioned recommendations could easily be applied to anyone within the church, even catechumens preparing for baptism, but chapters 18 and 19 clearly suggest that the sermon was for mature baptized Christians. Tertullian in these chapters disdains a recent trend among some who had begun to refuse the kiss of peace during worship on designated fast days. Tertullian argued that the Bible forbids making a show of any act of piety (fasting included), and so he advocated that these Christians partake in the kiss and not draw attention to their fasting by abstaining from the kiss. From what we know of early church practices, unbaptized catechumens were not allowed to offer, or even know about, the kiss of peace until after they had been baptized. Tertullian would not have instructed unbaptized converts in the practice of the kiss of peace, from which they were excluded. Therefore, *On Prayer* was probably written to educate a more established Christian audience in basic Christian prayer practice.

Tertullian's *On Prayer* is best understood if it is interpreted as being directed at the newly baptized. The theme of "newness" in this work, for example, hints that part of this sermon may have been specifically directed at recently baptized converts. Tertullian opens *On Prayer* with a discussion of how Jesus, who is Spirit, Word, and Reason, offers to his new disciples (the 12 apostles) a new covenant and a new form of prayer (the LP). This new prayer is like new wine in new wineskins or a new patch on a new garment. The old practice of circumcision has been transformed; a new grace, which has been made available, transforms the lives of baptized believers.[50] Later on, Tertullian added that those who confess their faith by praying the words "Our Father, who is in heaven" enter into a new relationship with God. In fact, when Christians pray "Our Father," they declare that they are really sons and daughters of God, siblings of Christ, and children of their mother, the church.[51] The assumption is that this new relationship is one that begins in baptism. Unfortunately, says Tertullian, some have refused the call of the Holy Spirit and these are identified as the Jews. More on this later.

Tertullian's newness theme clearly refers to baptism and is especially appropriate for those who have been recently baptized, although it applies to all Christians as well. In Christ, the old covenant of circumcision was replaced with the new covenant of baptism, in which catechumens were made new creatures. Indeed, in baptism, Christians have been adopted by God, their heavenly Father; Christ has become their brother and the church their mother. Once this baptismal adoption has taken place, they are truly able to pray the words "Our Father," because God in fact has become their heavenly Father. Thus, the new prayer (i.e., a new wine and a new patch) is given over to the newly baptized believers (i.e., placed into new wineskins or on new clothing). Ultimately, the power and mystery of the LP for Tertullian was that the prayer itself participated in making believers "candidates of the angels"[52] and helped bring them to salvation.

Even though the LP brings some into a closer relationship with God, it also reveals, for Tertullian, how others are excluded from this relationship. In a dialogue that would make many modern readers uncomfortable, Tertullian argues that those who are not baptized do not have the right to call God "Father." The Jews, Tertullian asserts, were once chosen by God in the past, but they rejected the Father when they refused to accept His Son, Jesus, as the Messiah. Tertullian chides them, saying that they wash every day according to their ritualistic practices but they are never clean—and here comes the difficult part for modern readers—because their hands are stained with the blood of the prophets and Jesus. Tertullian quickly moves from this to the idea that the "wordy" prayers of the Jews, in contrast with the brevity of the LP, also demonstrate how the Jews have forfeited the truth of the gospel. Instead of praying short prayers, like the LP, they heap their prayers with empty phrases. The prayers of the Jews condemn them, says Tertullian. As a result, Tertullian concludes that the prayers of the baptized are a "bulwark of faith," a defensive and an offensive weapon against the enemy, i.e., the Devil.[53]

To be fair to Tertullian, he does admit that God heard some of the ancient Jewish prayers in the Old Testament: God, for example, heard the prayers of the Israelites and delivered them from "fire and wild beasts." Tertullian adds that recently, however, Christ has replaced these prayers with a new kind of succinct way of calling upon God.[54] The LP is a new covenant that has superseded the old covenant with the Jews. The divine brevity of the LP has replaced the lengthy prayers of old, the new spiritual sacrifices wipe out the sacrifices of long ago, and the new priests and worshippers of God have established a new order. Tertullian's commentary, which was very popular and frequently referred to throughout the Middle Ages, thus became one of the first documents with a reasoned argument of the superiority of Christianity. No doubt this contributed to an attitude of anti-Judaism at best and anti-Semitism at worst, if indeed the two concepts can be separated. The inescapable conclusion is that since the LP was so popular in the life and teachings of the church, a corresponding reality emerged, namely, that the use of the words "Our Father" came to be identified with the truth of Christianity and the falsehood of other religious traditions, especially Judaism. Later authors likewise turned to the LP in order to reject various aspects of Judaism. More will be said about this in the section "The Lord's Prayer in Polemics."

The LP, for Tertullian, besides condemning the Jews, also revealed the depravity of heretics. Tertullian in *Against Marcion* (written ca. 207–212) refers to yet another version of the LP in order to counter

Marcion's view of God.[55] The Marcionites apparently replaced the first petition, "Holy be your name," with a petition that read something like "Holy Spirit, come upon us and cleanse us."[56] Jeremias translates the entire text of the Marcion LP as "Father, Thy Holy Spirit come upon us and cleanse us. Thy kingdom come. Thy bread for the morrow give us day by day. And forgive us our sins, for we also forgive everyone who is indebted to us. And do not allow us to be led into temptation."[57]

Modern study on this Holy Spirit petition has led to considerable scholarly debate. Some believe that the Holy Spirit petition is not only authentic, but actually represents the earliest and most original version of the LP.[58] Interestingly enough, two later medieval biblical manuscripts include a similar variant in Luke's version of the LP, while Gregory of Nyssa (ca. 330–395) and Maximus Confessor (ca. 580–662) likewise refer to this petition.[59] Gregory points to both versions of the third petition and gives them each equal time in his LP commentary and does not seem to be bothered by the variance. He simply notes that the version of Luke included the words "May your Holy Spirit come upon us and purify us" instead of Matthew's "Your kingdom come." It is impossible to say, however, if the Lucan version of Gregory's Bible may also have been a part of the liturgical version he and others prayed in his area. Nevertheless, the main reason he commented on this version was because he wrote frequently and fervently about the nature of the Trinity. Since the LP was a summary of the gospel for Gregory, and since one of Gregory's most important writing themes was the Trinity, the Holy Spirit petition enabled Gregory to bring up the topic of the Trinity in his commentary on the LP. Without this Holy Spirit petition, the LP mentions only two of the three persons of the Trinity, but with the Holy Spirit petition the entire Trinity and the nature of God are fully present in the LP—hence the appeal for Gregory.[60]

Other scholars argue that the Holy Spirit petition was in Marcion, but does not represent the original version of the LP.[61] For example, F. C. Burkitt has suggested that the Marcionites prayed the LP as a prayer of consecration and therefore added the Holy Spirit petition as an *epiclesis* (or a petition to call down the Holy Spirit to aid and cleanse the one who prays the prayer).[62] Jeremias has concluded that this petition originates out of an old baptismal prayer of the Marcionites and that it was added to the LP when it was offered in the baptismal ceremony.[63] Jeremias concludes, "One may compare the fact that the Marcionite version of the Prayer . . . has, in the petition for bread, 'Thy bread.' This is probably an allusion to the Lord's Supper, thus Marcion has both sacraments in view: baptism in this first petition and the Lord's Supper, which followed baptism, in his phrase 'Thy bread.' "[64]

Some modern scholars doubt that the Holy Spirit petition was ever in Marcion's version. Vokes contends that the Spirit emphasis has strong Old Testament connections, and since Marcion disdained the Old Testament, he would not have prayed this way.[65]

Jeremias, however, has suggested that Tertullian himself may have used the Holy Spirit version of the LP in his own private or public prayer life; after all, Tertullian first mentions this petition later on in life after he had already become a Montanist; this particular sect was known to have had a "special fondness for texts pertaining to the Holy Spirit." Perhaps Tertullian used this petition himself as a liturgical or communal version of the LP.[66] Indeed, Tertullian does not treat the Holy Spirit petition of the Marcionites as a problem: he simply points to the Holy Spirit petition as having an authority in and of itself, which thwarts Marcionite dualistic tendencies. Tertullian attacked Marcion's notion that the Old Testament had two gods—an evil god, who created the wicked physical world, and a more loving god, who was "just" and sent Christ to save it. Tertullian asked quizzically, "To whom can I say, 'Father?' To him who had nothing to do with making me, from whom I do not derive my origin? Or to Him, who by making and fashioning me, became my parent? Of whom can I ask for His Holy Spirit? Of him who gives not the mundane spirit; and whose Spirit was it that in the beginning hovered upon the waters?"[67] Therefore, the LP and its central idea of God as Father, for Tertullian, condemned both Jews and heretics like Marcion and his followers. Tertullian may well have used this Holy Spirit petition toward the end of his life, and if so, the petition would have fit well in a worship setting in which an *epiclesis* would have been appropriate, quite possibly in a baptismal setting.

Tertullian's rearrangement of the second and third petitions also deserves some mention at this point. Marcion's view of the nature of God moved Tertullian to appeal to the heavenly petitions, albeit with a Holy Spirit version as the first petition, to counter Marcion's heretical ideas. Tertullian's reversal of the second and third petitions has the effect of emphasizing the second petition, "Your kingdom come," by placing it last.[68] Overall, Tertullian's LP has a decidedly eschatological tone in which God comes down to Christians by means of the Holy Spirit in order that God's kingdom might come in the end. This theme was consistent with his later Montanist ideology and the anti-Marcionite debate.

Later Christian authors throughout the Middle Ages continued to use the LP to both include the faithful and exclude the Jews and the heterodox authors and their flocks. Few scholars have explored this element of the interpretation of the LP. The fact that the LP was central to Christian catechesis made it the perfect text to counter heretical ideas as well. The LP for early authors encompassed the essential doctrines and moral teachings of the church; therefore, those who had wandered away from their baptismal heritage, which is reflected in the LP, were called back to the faith by means of the LP. In this way, the LP was the path by which the lost could find their way back into the church.

In the end, Tertullian's verse-by-verse explanation of the LP was written for the purpose of educating baptized converts and for the edification of the congregation. The necessity to educate created the need for a full commentary on the LP, so that the faithful might understand the essentials of Christian doctrine and practice. However, beyond this, Tertullian also explained the LP in other writings not only to edify the faithful, but as a means by which to call the unorthodox back to the truth of pure Christian teaching.[69]

Cyprian, the bishop of Carthage, wrote the second earliest complete commentary on the LP, appropriately entitled *On the Lord's Prayer* (*De Dominica Oratione*, ca. 252), and in it we find yet again another version of the LP.[70] This LP mostly follows the more common Matthean form (but rather than the Matthean "supersubstantial" bread, he, like Tertullian, used Luke's word for "daily," or *quotidianum,*[71] bread). Cyprian also includes a variant of the sixth petition, which reads, "And do not allow us to be led into temptation."[72] Ambrose in the late fourth century likewise preferred a similar "do not allow us" (or *ne patiaris*), probably because it clarified the ambiguity of the more traditional wording "and lead us not into temptation." The latter version could be read to mean that God leads people into temptation. "Do not allow us," however, suggests that God "allows" people to be tempted by the Devil or their own desires, but does not actually tempt them directly. Hence, a problematic theological issue is avoided.[73]

Cyprian's commentary borrows heavily from Tertullian, but it is more of a treatise for clergy than a sermon for the baptized congregation. The purpose of Cyprian's work was to educate pastors, who in turn were to use it in their sermons and in the education of their flocks. Therefore, the end result of both Tertullian's and Cyprian's commentaries is similar, namely, the education of recent converts and the faithful.

Cyprian's *On the Lord's Prayer* derives its overarching threefold structure from Tertullian's work *On Prayer*. Both texts begin with an introduction; however, Cyprian's is more finely crafted and much longer. Both discuss the LP in a verse-by-verse fashion, but again, Cyprian's comments are more detailed. Finally, both offer extensive practical advice on how to pray, but Cyprian's advice differs considerably from Tertullian's. Cyprian, rather than being concerned about posture and the like, spends most of his time discussing the importance of praying continually (Chapter 29); how prayer unites believers as a community (Chapter 30); how Christians should not be slothful but alert in prayer (Chapter 31); how prayer is good when accompanied by fasting and alms (Chapter 32) and how these good works aid the speedy ascent of prayers to God (Chapter 33); the importance of praying at terce, sext, and none (or at 9 a.m., noon, and 3 p.m., chapters 34–35); and how prayer turns the dark, night-like human existence into day.[74] Among these themes, the emphasis upon unity is of particular importance.

Cyprian probably wrote his commentary after he finished his famous treatise, *On the Unity of the Church* (*De Ecclesiae Unitate*, ca. 251). The central theme of unity found in Cyprian's earlier work carries over to his discussion of the LP. Cyprian was deeply concerned with creating a more unified group of believers out of a divided, troubled, and persecuted church.[75]

Cyprian's emphasis upon unity and the LP is most clearly laid out at the beginning of his discussion of the words "Our Father." Cyprian argues that Jesus, "the Teacher of peace and the Master of unity," does not desire Christians to pray only for themselves or privately. Instead, true Christian prayer ought to be public and in common; believers ought to beseech God with the words "Our" Father and not "My" Father. When the faithful speak to the Father in this plural rather than singular way, they pray not for themselves individually, but for the whole people of God. Therefore, they all stand united in a familial bond as children of the same heavenly Father. To use the LP in solely a private or individualistic way is to miss the point of the prayer, says Cyprian. This last comment may well indicate that a problem had arisen concerning the LP in the middle of the third century, namely, the LP had come to be used in a more private and personal way, and as a result, Cyprian tried to curb some sort of individualization of the faith. This abuse, believed Cyprian, could only be corrected by returning to the original meaning and intent of the LP as a liturgical and communal prayer. Thus, a central function of the LP was to bind the church together in unity.

Biblical examples such as Shadrach, Meshach, and Abednego; the apostles and the female friends of Jesus; the Virgin Mary; and the whole company of disciples all revealed for Cyprian that these ancient models lifted their voices to God with one mouth and one mind, ". . . continuing steadfastly in prayer, declaring alike by their constancy and unity in prayer that God, who makes people of one mind to dwell in a home, does not admit into the divine and eternal home any except those who are of one mind in prayer."[76] The LP handed over by Christ, therefore, helps all Christians to unite their voices, hearts, and wills with that of God's will. The church needed to be united in God—the Father, Son, and Holy Spirit—who is, was, and always shall be One and completely united.[77]

For Cyprian, the LP reveals that those who are baptized are united into one home and family as adopted sons and daughters of God and siblings of Christ.[78] The "mysteries of the LP" (sacramenta orationis dominicae) are great, many, and collected into a few words, but they are offered only to whomever is reborn by the grace of God, the true Father.[79] Cyprian, therefore, was the first to offer a detailed rationale for why the LP should be kept from the unbaptized. The LP is not to be prayed by converts until after they have been baptized, because unbaptized sinners have no right to call God "Father." The newborn children of God have a right to pray the LP on account of the "birth of spiritual grace" (nativitas gratiae spiritualis), which declares God to be a loving parent. Therefore, it is completely inappropriate to teach the LP to those who are not yet baptized. Whether or not this is a change in attitude or an affirmation of what went on before Cyprian's day is very difficult to say, but at least there is now a theological argument to support the practice of keeping, and in some cases even hiding, the LP from non-Christians.

More on this in the section "The Lord's Prayer in Baptismal Catechesis."

Cyprian also expands upon Tertullian's argument against the Jews.[80] The Hebrew prophets, noted Cyprian, foretold Jesus' coming, but still the Jews did not recognize him when he came.[81] The Jews, by refusing to acknowledge Jesus as the Messiah, despised their true heavenly Father, who had given them every opportunity to recognize Jesus once he came. Therefore, the Jews rejected their inheritance and in turn embraced the Devil as their parent, said Cyprian. Christians were and are sanctified in the baptismal font and therefore have the right to pray with confidence to God as Father, notes the bishop of Carthage.[82] Cyprian, on the other hand, does not use the LP to counter heretical teachers.

Cyprian also further developed the idea that the LP helps the children of God to persevere in the faith unto eternal life. Discussing the first petition, Cyprian notes, ". . . we petition and ask for this (that we be made holy as God is holy), so that we who have been sanctified in baptism may persevere in what we have begun. For we have need of daily sanctification, that we who sin daily may cleanse our sins by continual sanctification."[83] Christians need perseverance for two reasons. First, they need to persevere against sin and therefore should pray the fifth petition of the LP every day to find forgiveness for their daily sins. Also, the church of Cyprian's day was under the threat of oppression and as a result needed a good measure of perseverance, which comes from the grace of baptism and the LP, in order to remain faithful. Therefore, believers ought to pray for perseverance daily in the words of the LP.[84]

Cyprian believed that the LP played an important role in the "daily" process of sanctification as well. Christians are saved from sin and able to call upon God in the LP as Father all because of their baptismal adoptions, but they similarly are able to seek forgiveness in its words. These two acts of sanctification sought in the LP (baptism and forgiveness) are intimately connected for Cyprian. Baptism brings Christians into a right relationship with God and the LP, and the fifth petition keeps them in this promise, because "He who taught us to pray for our debts and our sins promised that mercy and forgiveness would follow."[85]

Unfortunately, like Tertullian before him, Cyprian in *On the Lord's Prayer* does not reveal much about how the LP was actually used in catechesis or liturgical practices.[86] Cyprian's comments do, however, clearly connect baptism and the LP, and these references help to clarify the baptismal-catechetic context of the LP in Carthage during his time. Likewise, Cyprian connects the LP to his need to seek unity in the church and his desire to distinguish Christians from Jews.

We must not forget that Tertullian was also from Carthage, and thus it is significant to note that the two earliest full-length commentaries on the LP were produced in the same city. In the extant written evidence, commentary on the LP was first written down and explained more openly in North Africa around Carthage than it was anywhere else. Tertullian began a trend that continued in the local Christian community and eventually spread to other parts of Africa and the Middle East. The remarkable popularity of Cyprian's commentary especially encouraged later authors to follow his example and develop their own commentaries on the LP to speak with relevant voices to their own contexts.[87]

The apocryphal *Acts of Thomas*, which scholars date from the early to mid-third century, includes a version of the LP that is basically the same as Matthew's LP with one variation. The fourth petition of this work has puzzled scholars because it reads, "...give us the constant bread of the day,"[88] or some have translated this same phrase as "give us constantly our daily bread."[89] The exact meaning is a bit obscure. Nevertheless, the version is recognizable, if slightly different.

Although the origins of *Acts of Thomas* are difficult to ascertain, scholars generally feel that the work comes from Syriac-speaking lands out of a group whose Christian worldview was considered "Gnostic" and as a result would have been heretical in the third century. The text exists in Syriac, probably the original, and in Greek, most likely a later translation of the earlier version. This work is the second version of the LP in Syriac, after Tatian's *Diatessaron*'s LP. Both the *Diatessaron* and the *Acts of Thomas* had Greek versions as well. Again, we see that the LP texts are grouped in similar areas, but this time the language and general location of Syriac-speaking Christians are the focus. The community of the *Acts of Thomas*, however, was considered to be beyond the fringes of Christian orthodoxy, and therefore the text was rejected within most Christian circles.[90]

The LP appears late in the text of the *Acts of Thomas*. According to the *Acts of Thomas*, Thomas, aka the apostle Judas Thomas, was the twin of Jesus, and not only looked like Jesus, but also had the same "destiny and redeeming work."[91] Following the diaspora of Christians, and especially the disciples, from Jerusalem after Jesus' death, the *Acts of Thomas* says that its title character traveled to India to spread the gospel. Unfortunately, as was often the case in such stories, he offended a local king with his Christian teachings. The king's son and some others, however, were sympathetic to Thomas' message, which in the *Acts of Thomas* includes many typical elements of other Gnostic works of the time.[92] Confronted by the king, Thomas is told that he will die for his convictions and so in a typical trope of such literature, Thomas preaches a long sermon. In the midst of his declaration of the mysteries of the faith, he recites the LP, adding that he has given it to them because Christ had commanded him to do so. The implication is that as Thomas faces death, this prayer is particularly important and appropriate. Its importance is threefold. First, Thomas perceives the LP to be a central teaching of Christianity. By reciting it, he reveals a great mystery, or secret wisdom, to his audience. Second, the recitation near his death also ensures some grace or power for Thomas in his time of need. Third, the LP has a profound effect upon those who hear it, namely, the son of the king and others who are converted to Thomas' view of the truth. Outraged by the conversions, the king has Thomas martyred.

What is unusual in this case about the presentation of the LP is that Thomas appears to have no qualms about praying, or at least reciting, the LP before unbaptized Asian Indians. The only other text that has no such difficulty is the Gospel of Matthew, which relates how Jesus teaches the LP to the multitude on the mount. In both instances, the LP presumably enlightens and encourages the conversion of those listening. All the other texts we have from the first to third centuries indicate the LP is for those who have already converted to the faith, or at least are in the process of coming to baptism. The *Didache*, Cyprian, and Tertullian clearly suggest that the LP is meant only for baptized ears. During the fourth century in the Latin-speaking world, however, the LP became a text exclusively for baptized converts.

Whether or not the *Acts of Thomas* is historical in part or as a whole does not matter in the end. The text reveals that at least its author, and probably the author's religious community, believed the text could be used in this way. Was this perhaps a reason why those who considered themselves to be more orthodox Christians rejected it? Were they offended by the fact that the LP was given out publicly? We have no

record of anyone saying so and as a result, this idea is pure specu-
lation. What can be said is that orthodox Christianity rejected the
Acts of Thomas, and hence it had little influence in more traditional
circles.

The last third-century work that included a full text of the LP is
Origen's Greek treatise, *On Prayer*. Origen wrote this lengthy, and
apparently hurried, exposition for his friends Ambrose and Tatian
(ca. 233). In general, it is a philosophically sophisticated analysis of
prayer that includes a fascinating section on the LP. Origen mentions
Tatian and even criticizes what he calls Tatian's imperfect translation
of the LP in one place.[93] Some believe that Origen may have been
familiar with Tertullian's commentary on prayer as well.

It was noted earlier in this book that there was one exception to the
rule that all versions of the LP down through the third century were
different in wording: Origen is that exception. As a biblical exegete,
Origen simply discussed without variation the Greek biblical versions
of the LP found most commonly in Matthew and Luke, and therefore his discussion of the LP is the only early text that does not reveal
a new variant of the LP. Given his scholarly concerns, however, this
makes sense.

We do not know which version Origen may have prayed, however,
or even if he favored one over the other. He clearly gave both versions
equal weight with regard to authority, and he readily commented on
both, even though his commentary focuses more on Matthew's version
due to its length. As has been noted, Origen argued that these two texts
were actually two separate and distinct prayers that had been offered
by Jesus on two different and unique occasions; Origen is the only one
to make this argument in the early church.[94]

Origen's commentary is very sophisticated and interesting on a
number of levels. Philosophically speaking, Origen deals with top-
ics that none before and few after him were interested in. This is in
part due to the fact that he desired to answer the intricate questions
of his friends, who asked him to write the treatise. An example of
his philosophical concern comes when Origen discusses the objection
that prayer is superfluous because God has foreknowledge and knows
what believers will pray even before they ask. Origen's response is a
sophisticated answer that concludes that foreknowledge is not to be
equated with foreordaining, and that people still have free will and the
need to pray even if God knows what people will pray before they

open their lips. It would not be until the later part of the fourth century that these more Origen-like questions would be taken up again.[95]

Another question Origen tries to answer is, "To whom is prayer properly addressed?" His answer, that all prayer should be directed toward God the Father because Jesus prayed to the Father, led to much debate. Some felt that Origen's emphasis upon the Father in this and other instances lent itself to the idea that Christ, and perhaps even the Holy Spirit, were subordinate to the Father.[96] Origen's Christology, therefore, came under suspicion, along with a few of his other ideas. The Fifth Ecumenical Council of Constantinople in 553 challenged the orthodoxy of some of Origen's writings; it condemned some of his ideas and this had the effect of reducing his popularity after this time, even though he still continued to be read up until the thirteenth century in Latin translations in the West.[97]

The tone of the treatise is decidedly didactic. Even though Origen at times mentions baptismal adoption and the Eucharist as being important to his discussion, for the most part his words focus less on liturgical matters than other contemporary works do. Nevertheless, Origen still hints at the important connection of the LP to worship and early theological training of mature Christians and converts. Compared with other early texts, however, Origen spends very little time discussing these matters. His concern is to address his friends' questions, so he provides them with reasoned argumentation on why, where, how, and what believers ought to pray. The LP fit into a broader discussion he was engaged in, but his main point was to present some clear teaching on prayer in general.[98]

Origen concluded that prayer helped those who pray to access true knowledge, or wisdom concerning God in the person of Christ Jesus. While absolute wisdom is unattainable in this life, said Origen, God's grace can impart and reveal aspects of true wisdom nonetheless. God created the world by wisdom and God continues to create wisdom in those who seek Jesus, who is God's wisdom. The righteousness, sanctification, and redemption of the faithful come through Christ and the wisdom he imparts. Truth nourishes and empowers humans and even angels, both of which engage in prayerful contemplation. Without this wisdom, believers are not only unable to pray, but are without revelation and incapable of true understanding. God's sovereignty reigns over all creation, even reason. Therefore, when people pray for "daily bread" in the fourth petition of the LP, they actually pray for what Origen called soul bread, wisdom, or eternal truth.[99]

The unique flavor of Origen's commentary on the LP suggests that the LP in the early days of the church proved to be a flexible and resilient text: early Christians had no qualms about constantly adapting the words of the LP to a variety of worship, educational, devotional, and now even philosophical contexts. Hence, the wording of the LP was in a constant state of flux, even if the basic ideas of the prayer remained intact. The fact that there were two varying biblical versions of the LP may have contributed to this phenomenon. Without a definitive text in the scripture that was more authoritative, neither the wording of Matthew nor of Luke took ultimate precedence over the other. As a result, early Christians felt free to create hybrid versions of the two LP texts in Matthew and Luke for the purpose of worship and education. Only Origen, a gifted biblical exegete, commented on the texts as he found them in their scriptural contexts as unique prayers. The slight variations in the two gospels and later LP texts didn't bother scholars or congregations. Origen did express some frustration with Tatian's version of the LP, but his comments reflect the quibble of one scholar berating another for having made a mistake in translation. In general, the LP was always perceived to be the prayer of Jesus and a precious possession of the church. It was always one prayer despite its many versions, or at the very least, two prayers, both offered by Jesus for the benefit of the church. As such, the LP was the Truth and the very wisdom of the Creator.

One Prayer in Two Parts

With the exception of Origen, early scholars assumed that the LP was simply one prayer from the mouth of Jesus, even if it existed in two biblical versions and a host of variations. Still, most were quick to point out that the LP itself could be divided into two convenient parts, or what they liked to call the heavenly or eternal petitions (1–3) and the earthly or temporal petitions (4–7). Tertullian was the first to make this distinction. In his discussion of the fourth petition, Tertullian writes, "How gracefully has divine wisdom drawn up the order of the prayer, that after heavenly things, that is after God's name, God's will, and God's kingdom, it should make place for petitions for earthly necessities too."[100] Augustine later on summed up this view:

> Accordingly, in the Evangelist Matthew the LP seems to embrace seven petitions, three of which ask for eternal blessings, and the remaining four for temporal; these latter, however, being necessary antecedents to the attainment of the eternal. For when we say, "Hallowed be Thy name: Thy Kingdom come: Thy will be done in earth, as it is in heaven: . . ." we ask for blessings that are to be enjoyed forever; which are indeed begun in this world, and grow in us as we grow in grace, but in their perfect state, which is to be looked for in another life, shall be a possession forevermore. But when we say, "Give us this day our daily bread: and forgive us our debts, as we forgive our debtors: and lead us not into temptation, but deliver us from evil," who does not see that we ask for blessings that have reference to the wants of this present life?[101]

Augustine adds that like bread, which requires breaking and chewing, the scripture feeds the soul on earth only after the biblical texts have been opened and discussed. Drink, on the other hand, can be taken into the body directly, without chewing. Augustine concludes, "Thus in the present time truth is bread . . . ; but then it will be drink when there will be no need of laborious discussions and disputations—as it were, breaking and chewing—but only of drinking the clear, limpid waters of truth."[102] When the last day finally arrives, then God will teach Christians directly, but until then, says Augustine, the faithful are to pray all the petitions of the LP, "so that we may reach that life; and here let us beg, in order not to be cut off from it."[103] The LP for the early church was a scriptural text worth chewing on: its words nothing less than nourishment for the church not only in this life, but also as eternal truth, the draft of salvation.

Conclusions: The Versatile Lord's Prayer

The LP during the first three centuries of the church was a remarkably adaptable prayer, and as a result it existed in a splendid variety of versions in various places and times. As the prayer filtered through a variety of languages and locales, slight changes occurred. The LP spread from the East (Jerusalem, Palestine, Syria, etc.) toward the West (North Africa, Greece, Rome, etc.) as Christianity spread. However, there was no uniform manner of praying the LP among Christian communities, just as there was no single standard version of the LP early on. Rather, local traditions developed around variations in liturgical and private prayer practices that involved the LP and according to what authoritative texts were available to them. The fact that Matthew and Luke had two versions of the LP contributed to uncertainty about one authoritative text, and therefore a number of slightly different versions of the LP existed from very early on. The fact that there were local variations to its wording nearly everywhere did not bother early Christian authors, believers, or communities. They merely took for granted the idea that the LP had been handed over by Jesus directly to his disciples and that the text had been given over by them to the church. No matter which version they used, the LP remained not only recognizable, but true to a basic content and form.

A look at the modern English use of the LP in the United States, as an example, suggests similar continued development of the LP even today. For example, the Evangelical Lutheran Churches in America (ELCA) printed various versions of the LP in both their Lutheran Book of Worship (Minneapolis, 1977) and the Evangelical Lutheran Worship Book (Minneapolis, 2008) at the same time. Sometimes two versions exist side by side. Neither prayer is identical to the Matthew or the Luke texts. All the versions are hybrid liturgical versions that draw on Matthew for the most part, but they also use some of Luke and they add the *Didache's* doxology. One version has a more traditional older English language feel (it still uses phrases like "Thy will be done"), and the second is more contemporary in its wording ("Your will be done"). The contemporary version of the sixth petition, ". . . save us from the time of trial," avoids the problem of blaming God (not unlike the sixth petition found in Cyprian and Ambrose), which is a hazard of the more traditional wording, ". . . lead us not into temptation."

The ELCA offers various prayers for their congregations, but congregations are free to pray whichever version they like. Some congregations even alternate versions. No one that I am aware of has ever suggested that the denomination should be more biblical and pray either Matthew's or Luke's version. Rather, the liturgical LPs of the ELCA are perceived as two versions of one prayer handed over by Jesus. Roman Catholics sometimes use the doxology and sometimes they do not, but generally, like Lutherans, they have a variety of liturgical versions of the LP that they draw upon in worship.

Some congregations maintain a more archaic wording out of loyalty to tradition and the past and may even see the new versions of the LP as a part of the eroding of tradition within a particular church or denomination. Others feel freer to adapt to more contemporary language, while still others switch back and forth as a concession to both sides that may exist in one congregation. Why one congregation uses one version and another uses a second, even in the same town and denomination, occurs for a variety of reasons, not least of which has to do with pastoral preference, lay leadership, congregational sensitivities, views concerning tradition, and a host of other concerns, some of which are more obvious than others.

At present, other denominations (e.g., some Baptists and Pentecostals) adhere to more traditional versions of the LP because of a strong loyalty to what they consider to be the most authoritative version of the Bible. Some of the earlier English versions of the LP, which echo the style of the King James Version of the Bible from 1611, are still used quite commonly in modern churches, even though some of the words are archaic and strange to modern youth. Some denominations and congregations consider the first major English translation of the Bible to be authoritative and therefore prefer a version of the LP that reflects this sensitivity, even if the version of the prayer they are using is not identical to either of the biblical versions of the LP. This phenomenon is true in other languages as well. Therefore, sometimes the wording of the LP adapts as the language changes over time, and at other times congregations cling to older, more traditional versions as a form of protest against change. A similar sensitivity to language and a liturgical desire for poetry and ease of recitation allow for either a traditional adherence to earlier versions of the LP or a desire to make the wording more contemporary; the evidence suggests that such concerns were at play in the early church as well.

The different versions of the LP that exist from the first centuries of the church reflect early biblical variants of Matthew, Luke, and different liturgical contexts. A desire for a more standardized LP emerged as the church grew in popularity and as authorities in the church were able to enforce, or at least strongly encourage, one version over and against another. For the sake of Christian unity, churches in the West and the East eventually moved toward more standardized prayers as they at the same time adopted more standardized liturgies. Still, as time went on, the LP adapted when language changed and developed new nuances. A similar concern is at play in the ELCA. While the denomination as a whole wanted to provide some consistency in the versions of the LP they included in their Lutheran Book of Worship and Evangelical Lutheran Worship Book, it at the same time desired to be sensitive to both traditionalists and to those wanting a more contemporary version of the LP. When the Lutheran Book of Worship was first put into congregational pews in the late 1970s, lay people debated over much of the liturgy, but the one area perhaps least commented upon was the new version of the LP, because the traditional version remained in the text. If congregations moved to a more contemporary version of the LP, they often did not do so lightly. Those that stayed with the older version did so consciously, deliberately, and perhaps even dogmatically, even if few noticed any change at all.

Some early versions of the LP in the Gospel of Matthew have variants, which were either intentionally or unintentionally altered by replacing the word "supersubstantial" with the more common liturgical version of Luke's "daily."[104] The manuscript variations probably occurred due to the copier's familiarity with the liturgical versions of the LP. Either they changed the texts deliberately to reflect liturgical sensitivities, or they did it accidentally by copying from memory, rather than from the text in front of them. The earliest commentators on the LP, like Tertullian, Cyprian, and later Ambrose, even preferred to comment on the liturgical versions of the LP in their commentaries. This makes some logical sense. After all, their churches used a liturgical LP rather than the biblical LPs of Matthew or Luke. Many later authors did the same. Only writers through the third century, who specifically wrote biblical commentaries quoting directly from Matthew or Luke (like Origen), did otherwise.

By the end of the fourth century in North Africa and Italy, a hybrid Latin version of the LP developed which essentially became a type of standard LP for the much of the rest of the Middle Ages. Since Matthew's LP was perceived to be more complete than Luke's and since it was the gospel most often used for the lessons in the liturgy in the West, this may account for why Matthew's longer version became standard, except for the word "daily" from Luke and the doxology that was sometimes added.[105]

The earliest churches lifted up the LP as a model of prayer in both communal (i.e., worship)[106] and private (i.e., perhaps three times a day[107]) practice. The LP was especially associated with the baptismal rite and the new relationship that converts had with God as "Father." A few versions (Matthew and the *Acts of Thomas*, for example) present the LP in a context in which non-Christians heard the prayer. In the case of Thomas, the written context suggests that the prayer was important in helping convert some to Christianity. Other texts (e.g., the *Didache*, Tertullian, and Cyprian) discussed the LP in the context of the education of neophytes (i.e., those who had been recently baptized). These suggest that the LP was kept from the uninitiated. Once baptized and completely within the church, believers said the LP regularly within the context of worship and in particular as a preparation for the Eucharist. Some early Christians made additions to the LP, like the doxology (e.g., the community of the *Didache*), in worship settings in an effort to improve its liturgical tone and perhaps its communal and private appeal.[108] The LP became not only one of the central elements of worship, but it was also an important text used in the theological education of the mature faithful (e.g., Cyprian and Origen). Early writers pointed to the LP as the most excellent model of prayer, which was superior to other prayers, especially those uttered by the Jews and Gentiles. Perhaps most importantly, however, was that idea that these churches and authors always stood in awe of the LP, a prayer which was considered to encompass Christian truth and wisdom in a way no other prayer or short text could. These were the wondrous words of Jesus, the pearl of great price, and a treasure worth polishing and contemplating daily. As a result, any sort of analysis or actual praying of the LP had a tendency to take on an air of mystery and awe.

In the end, the LP continued to be a precious primary text of the church in the coming centuries, but its significance as it settled into an even more standardized form continued to increase. In the centuries that followed, churches discovered even more uses for the marvelous LP that helped it permeate every aspect of Christianity.

CHAPTER 3

The Flowering of the Lord's Prayer Tradition

The Lord's Prayer in the Fourth and Fifth Centuries

Some churches during the fourth century slowly surrounded the LP with a comfortable, yet firm, desire to be cautious with their precious pearl, which is to say that they sought to keep the LP from outsiders and to expand its importance throughout the life of the church. A furtive attitude toward the prayer may have already existed for some time in places like Tertullian's and Cyprian's Carthage in North Africa, as has been shown earlier. However, by the end of the fourth century, some notable authors developed what some scholars have called a discipline of the secret (*disciplina arcani*). The fourth century came to an end with some strong bishops, such as Ambrose of Milan, promoting a definite secrecy with regard to the LP. This teaching held that, along with other sacred mysteries of the church, like the Eucharist and the Creed, the LP was to be known by Christians alone and hidden from non-Christian outsiders, even those seeking to be baptized. The pearl of great price in any case was to be carefully handled and reverently cherished.

For some, there emerged a special concern for offering appropriate esteem to the Lord's Prayer; they kept the LP pure by seeking to house it completely within the life and theology of the church. The teachings of Ambrose of Milan represented a high-water mark for such respect, which manifested itself in an unsurpassed concern for preserving the

LP within Christian circles. The majority of commentary upon the LP from the late second until the early sixth century dealt primarily with the education of adult converts. The customs of teaching the LP to neophytes in a mystagogical context included a tension between offering it to either the already baptized or to those still awaiting their baptisms.[1] Converts were given the Latin names of *competentes*, "those who seek"; *electi*, "those who have been chosen"; or *illuminandi*, which the Greeks referred to as *photisomenoi*, "those who are to be enlightened."[2] Slowly, whatever *disciplina arcani* attitudes that existed surrounding the LP became less rigid, and a period of transition can be observed in Christian literature in certain places with regard to the LP. During the fifth century, there was a more widespread move away from secretive attitudes concerning the LP to allowing catechumens to learn it before baptism for practical reasons; this shift in some areas required a clear theological defense. Augustine of Hippo, for example, reflected this transitional, new attitude regarding the use of the LP in baptismal catechetic training.

Augustine wrote more about the LP than any author before him and almost every author after him down to the time of the Reformation. In fact, it can be argued that the LP was one of Augustine's favorite scriptural texts by virtue of the fact that he was so fond of quoting it throughout every phase of his life and teachings.[3] Augustine's attitude of awe toward the prayer developed out of his view that the LP was a sacrament, or what some have called a sacramental.

Still, the fourth century did not necessarily start out being entirely guarded about the LP. Juvencus, the great fourth-century poet, wrote the first poetic paraphrase of the LP, which made its ideas available to a wide audience, even the uninitiated. The LP, nevertheless, continued to be the primary prayer of the church during the fourth and fifth centuries. The LP became a central part of the lives of Christians, because it was used in worship, daily devotional practices, baptismal-catechetic training, and the theology of the church in general. Likewise, it also became a key text in polemical arguments and in monastic theology. Because of a perceived intrinsic aesthetic beauty, the LP even came to be a part of literary works, where it was transformed into poetic meter for the benefit of telling epic stories.

The Lord's Prayer as Poetry

An innovative kind of LP exposition appeared at the beginning of the fourth century when Caius Vettius Aquilinus Juvencus, a priest and Christian poet of noble birth from Spain, wrote a Latin hexameter versification and harmonization of the gospels, entitled *The Four Books of the Gospels* (*Evangeliorum Libri IV*, aka *The Evangelical History*, *Evangelica Historica*, ca. 330). Of Juvenus' life we know little, but Jerome believed him to be a significant enough writer to warrant mention in his work *On Famous Men*.[4] *The Four Books of the Gospels* is both uniquely innovative in form and firmly grounded in the historical traditional content of LP interpretations. Juvencus either borrows from or echoes Tertullian and Cyprian in his poetic explanation of the LP, yet his means of presenting the LP as poetry was a wholly new, innovative, and creative way of explaining the LP to Christians and non-Christians alike.

For the most part, *The Four Books of the Gospels* follows the order and content of the Gospel of Matthew. In the midst of this gospel harmonization, Juvencus includes a poetic versification of the LP within the section "On the Sermon on the Mount" (Matthew 5–7), which of course is where the LP is presented in Matthew's Gospel (Matthew 6). The Roman literary world of Juvencus' day was full of wondrous stories and glorious epic poetry about the gods and goddesses, heroines and heroes. However, the Spanish poet considered what he believed to be the truth concerning the life, death, and resurrection of Jesus to be superior to fictitious Roman mythology. Thus, in a simple and unadorned style reminiscent of the great Latin poet Virgil, Juvencus hoped to expose the inferior nature of the mythological narratives of old by offering a new and more compelling view of life based on the life and teachings of Jesus.[5]

Why did Juvencus offer a versified version of the gospels, and the LP in particular, to readers who might include both Christians and nonbelievers alike? While it is impossible to say, a close examination of Juvencus' LP demonstrates that Juvencus explained some of the basic teachings associated with this prayer without actually disclosing the specific wording of the text. By placing the LP into a poetic form that paraphrases the LP, the text itself remains essentially hidden to anyone who doesn't already know the prayer. A look at the poetic prayer itself, which puts in bold the words of the LP, makes this point:

Table 3.1 Juvencus' Poetic Version of the Lord's Prayer

Juvencus' Latin Poetic Pater	English Translation
Sidereo Genitor residens in vertice coeli,	O Creator, who dwells among the stars in the highest heaven,
Nominis, oramus, veneratio **sanctificetur** in nobis, **Pater** alte, tui	O Most High **Father**, we pray that our veneration of your **name** may be made **holy** in us:
tranquillaque mundo **Adveniat, regni**que **tui** lux alma patescat.	may the peaceful and bountiful light of **your kingdom come** and shine forth in the world.
Sic, **coelo** ut, **terris** tua **fiat** clara **voluntas,**	May **your** manifest **will be done on earth as in heaven**.
Vitalisque **hodie** sancti **substantia panis** Proveniat nobis,	May the sustenance of holy life-giving **bread** be provided for us **today**
tua mox largitio solvat Innumera indulgens erroris **debita** pravi;	and may your **forgiving** largess release us soon from the innumerable **debts** of our evil misdeeds.
Et nos haud aliter concedere fenera fas est.	It is right for us likewise **to forgive the debts of others**.
Tertri saeva procul **tentatio** daemonis absit,	Remove far away from us the fierce **temptation** of the vile demon,
Deque **malis** tua nos in lucem dextera tollat.[6]	and may your right hand lift us up into the light away from all **evil**.

Certainly, anyone who did not already know the LP would not have been able to reconstruct it from this poem, because Juvencus only used key words and phrases of the LP intermittently, at times even in a scrambled order. Juvencus was more concerned with presenting the teachings of the LP rather than preserving the actual text of the LP. Perhaps he did this intentionally in order to keep the actual wording of the LP from non-Christians. Who knows? Still, Christians who knew the LP would have readily recognized how the prayer had been integrated into the poem. In other words, for Juvencus, the wisdom of the LP could be made known and available to outsiders, while the prayer itself lay hidden within the poem. Insiders also would have benefited from the paraphrase, which acts as a lyrical commentary on the famous prayer.

Juvencus probably believed that the teaching of the LP, along with the rest of the gospel story, might aid in the conversion of non-Christians from Roman myths to Christian truth. This fits with two earlier documents, namely, the Gospel of Matthew and the *Acts of Thomas*, which placed the presentation of the LP in the context of educating non-Christians about the faith for the sake of teaching them the truth about Christianity.

Juvencus introduced the paraphrased section of the LP by reiterating the same concerns preceding the LP in Matthew's Gospel: people ought not to pray with an abundance of words or pompous public fanfare. Prayer to God is to be done in secret and without longwinded effort. Juvencus' paraphrase of the LP offers his readers an example of how this might be done. Clearly, the tone of the paraphrase suggests that it might be a prayer in and of itself. It is addressed specifically to God the Creator and Father, and it asks in a pleading tone that the various petitions might be granted. Nevertheless, in the end, his primary concern is to convince people of the greatness and truth of the gospel, even if he offers them a specific and unique way of praying the LP.[7]

What motivated Juvencus to paraphrase the LP? First of all, the prayer is in Matthew's Gospel and he is simply following his plan to present the prayer in its paraphrased biblical context. He may also have felt free to do so because there were a variety of biblical versions of the LP already available, as has been mentioned earlier in this book. Perhaps he felt the freedom to paraphrase this most holy prayer because so many other versions of the LP were a part of the Christian tradition and because there was an openness with regard to the actual wording of the prayer.

Juvencus also used paraphrase to eliminate some of the more troubling aspects of the LP. For example, the first petition, "Holy be your name," is rephrased by Juvencus in a way that removes ambiguity. Tertullian and Cyprian had already recognized that some might have a problem with this petition because it could be read to imply that God's name is not holy or that it is lacking in some way and therefore needs prayers to make it so. But both Carthaginian authors cautioned against such a reading and argued that those who pray this petition are really asking that God's name might be made holy in them. God's name, after all, is indeed holy in and of itself. Juvencus makes the same point. Given this similarity, and a few others, it seems very likely that Juvencus knew the teachings of either or both Tertullian and Cyprian.

The originality of Juvencus regarding the content of the LP comes in his interpretation of the sixth and seventh petitions, "Lead us not into temptation, but deliver us from evil." In his version, the Spanish priest avoided the difficult wording of the LP, which could be read to imply that God leads people into temptation. He did this by changing the words to "Remove far away from us the fierce temptation of the vile demon." Juvencus clarifies beyond any shadow of a doubt from whom temptation originates, namely, the Devil. The paraphrase of the final petition, "And may your right hand lift us up and into the light away from evil," further indicates that Juvencus believed that God does not tempt people and that God seeks instead to rescue humanity from all evil.

The primary significance of Juvencus' commentary rests on two issues. First, his work was the first time any extant Latin written commentary on the LP appeared outside of North Africa. It is also important to note, however, that of extant writings, little else comes down to us on the LP in Spanish lands for some time to come. Second, his poetic treatment is the oldest extant versification or paraphrase of the LP. Juvencus' rephrasing of the LP inspired many later authors to produce similar poetic versions of the prayer.

One of the most prominent authors who followed Juvencus' example was Coelius Sedulius (ca. fifth century). Coelius Sedulius[8] (not to be confused with the ninth-century writer Sedulius Scotus) wrote his poetic interpretation of the LP in the fifth century. Juvencus inspired many others as well; a few of these include Proba's *Cento* (ca. 360–380) and Prudentius' (late fourth or beginning of the fifth century) hymn *Cathemerinon*, both of which are poetic versions of the life of Jesus. In a similar manner, Paulinus of Nola (ca. 353–431) wrote about the birth and ministry of John the Baptist; the sixth century Italian poet Arator produced a poetic work called *On the Acts of the Apostles*; and Cyprian the Poet (aka Cyprian of Gaul, ca. 360–430) and Avitus of Vienna (d. 518) produced biblical epics out of some of the books of the Old Testament. Others, like Jerome, Fortunatus, Isidore of Seville, Theodolphus of Orleans, and Rabanus Maurus, had a great deal of admiration for Juvencus' poetry.[9] Despite the fact that all of these works were inspired by Juvencus, none, save one, mention the LP. Coelius Sedulius was perhaps the author most influenced by Juvencus, and as a result, Sedulius relied heavily upon *The Book of the Four Gospels* when he paraphrased the LP in his writings.

About the life of Sedulius we know little other than that he probably converted to Christianity and was baptized by a Greek presbyter named Macedonius after having spent his earlier life in the secular study of philosophy and poetry (*grammaticus*).[10] Some believe he was a priest who wrote during the reigns of Theodosius II and Valentinian II (425–450). He probably lived in both Italy and Greece at some time in his life.[11]

Sedulius' own hexameter epic poem on the life of Christ is similar to Juvencus' *The Book of the Four Gospels*, but it is also more detailed and thematically consistent. The five books of Sedulius' work the *Paschal Song*[12] (probably written before 431) recounts the life, and especially the miracles, of Jesus. Unlike Juvencus' writings, the first book of the *Paschal Song* serves as an introduction that refers back to Old Testament materials. Like Juvencus, Sedulius put forth the story of the four gospels by essentially following the order of events in the Gospel of Matthew. Both Juvencus and Sedulius placed their poetic paraphrase of the LP after the call of the 12 disciples and before some miracle stories.

The intended audience of Sedulius' and Juvencus' poetry was essentially the same. Sedulius presumed that part of his audience had some detailed knowledge of the scriptures. As a result, Sedulius often explained biblical episodes with veiled allusions that only educated Christians would grasp. For example, it is difficult to imagine that a non-Christian would understand Sedulius' comparison of the flood of Noah's day to baptism (an allusion to 1 Peter 3:20–22).[13] Juvencus also used a similar method at times.

In other passages, Sedulius appealed to the learned nonbeliever, as his preface makes clear. Sedulius actually compared himself to the Apostle Paul and portrayed himself as a latter-day apostle to the Gentiles;[14] for example, Sedulius encouraged the "Athenians" (i.e., non-Christians, cf. Acts 17:16–34) to exchange the "barren wasteland" of their philosophies for the "green fields of paradise" (i.e., Christian truth).[15]

Juvencus' retelling of the gospel stories eventually came to be used as a text in Christian education. Sedulius himself composed the *Paschal Song* with the hope that his work might also be used in a similar way. Sedulius revealed this when he mentioned in his prefatory letter to the *Paschal Song* that part of his audience was a group of ascetic Christians who associated themselves with Macedonius.[16] Sedulius' work did in fact become a popular textbook.

The historical context of Sedulius was slightly different from the days of Juvencus. First of all, Christianity had become much more popular in parts of the Roman West, and the *disciplina arcani* that surrounded the LP in parts of the Christian world had nearly disappeared by his time. Sedulius appears much freer to speak openly about the LP than Juvencus had been.

Juvencus made no mention of baptism within the context of his LP paraphrase, but Sedulius connected them in his introductory section on the LP. In a manner reminiscent of Cyprian and Augustine, however, Sedulius stated that God desires to confer salvation upon all those who pray with few words and in an attitude of forgiveness toward others. Then he said, "Thus [Jesus] says we may pray to the Father, we on account of our baptism, and he on account of his own right."[17] This phrase suggests a Christian audience. Sedulius returned to this idea again in his explanation of the words "Our Father"; he explained that Christians are called brothers and sisters of Christ because of their baptismal adoption. However, in the rest of his discussion on the LP, the baptism theme is absent.

Sedulius' *Paschal Song* though indebted to Juvencus, is much longer; he offered more of his own commentary and provided a more coherent overarching theme. Juvencus streamlined the stories in order to focus on the life of Christ, while Sedulius was more interested in specifically talking about Christ's miracles. For Sedulius, the miracles of Christ displayed the heroic nature of the Messiah; thus, the emphasis on the miracle-worker Jesus helped to create the epic atmosphere Sedulius wanted.

Like Juvencus, Sedulius distinguished Christ's work from that of the heroes of pagan epics by avoiding stories of battles, erotic love, great feats, and heroic people. In his introduction, Sedulius warned his readers of this difference and noted that he was simply offering "vegetables on common earthenware" in comparison to the more flamboyant luxurious diningware of earlier epics.[18]

Carl Springer has noted that one of the main differences between the authors of Greek and Roman classical epics and the authors of Christian epics has to do with the relationship of Christian authors to their sacred subject matter.[19] Whereas classical authors realized their stories were flights of fantasy that conveyed truth, Christian authors strongly believed in the truth of their message and in the power of that message to change lives and offer salvation. No doubt this was the reason both of these poets included the LP; they believed in the power and mystery of its words to help transform people into children of God.

Sedulius also appears to have borrowed from earlier commentaries on the LP and he also felt free to add his own particular emphases. Juvencus preserved a concise and reverential tone when discussing the LP and added a unique theme of light imagery in the second and seventh petitions. Sedulius, on the other hand, chose to explain the LP with a more detailed interpretive emphasis. A comparison of the interpretation of the first petition by both Juvencus and Sedulius will help to make the preceding point. Juvencus' paraphrase of the first petition simply reads, "O Most High Father, we pray that our veneration of your name may be made holy in us."[20] Sedulius, by contrast, noted, "Where is the Lord, the one who makes all things holy by creating them, made holy? Where, indeed, unless in the loving or the spotless heart? In order that we might be made holy with our worship of him, he himself first grants and likewise commands that we bless him, the one by whom we all are blessed."[21]

Sedulius in his explanation of the first petition essentially followed the argument of Tertullian, Cyprian, and Augustine; but the wording and structure of his version is strikingly different than his poetic mentor's poem. Sedulius puzzled over the odd wording of this petition, but then concluded that God is holy when God is made holy in believers who worship God correctly. However, Sedulius omitted any mention of God's "name" being made holy, perhaps because he felt that God's name was always holy in and of itself. Thus, although he borrowed Juvencus' ideas, he often did so with very different wording.

The poetic imagery that Sedulius included in the section on the LP at times was completely unique; for example, when speaking of God's kingdom, he noted that in heaven there is no rest or sleep in death; no time, no night, but only a place of continuous day.[22] He called original sin the tomb of ancient evil (2.40) and he declared that good and evil are as far apart "as the stars are from the earth, fire from water, light from darkness, harmony from war, and life from the tomb" (2. 290–293).

Sedulius also appealed to the central overarching themes of his *Paschal Song* in order to explain the LP. Sedulius often referred to evil as a snake: the snake is Satan in the Garden of Eden (2.1–6), Satan tempting Jesus in the wilderness (2.185–188), the enemy of humanity in the third petition of the LP (2.259), and in numerous other places (4.94–97, 4. 145–9, 5.226, 5.217ff., 5. 283–4, 5.332–3). The serpent is not only Satan, but anything connected with him, such as false doctrine, lies, or any danger that threatens the sheep of the shepherd, Christ. Anything that seeks to destroy Christianity is also a threat to the teachings of the LP, which embodies the truth.

In contrast to Satan the snake (or the wolf, as Sedulius was also fond of calling him), the source of all good for Sedulius was the good shepherd, Christ. Carl Springer has pointed out that Sedulius made the good shepherd theme central to the work by placing it at the very center of the *Paschal Song* (book 3.158–175, and specifically line 3.167). For Sedulius, Christ's greatest miracle, and therefore his most heroic act, was to rescue humanity though his death on the cross, in the same way that shepherds rescue their sheep when they are willing to lay down their lives for their sheep who are in danger.[23]

The climactic line of his poetic analysis of the LP also referred to Christ, the good shepherd. It reads, "Therefore this is the sole will and good liberty of God for his sheep and lambs, to escape the fierce mouth of the bloody wolf and to enjoy life in the pastures of Christ."[24] The work of the LP, which brings about salvation more quickly than any other prayer (2.231–236), is one way that the good shepherd saves his sheep.

Another significant recurring image that Sedulius used in his poem was that of the Christian life as a "narrow path" that is seldom trod and full of danger (2.80ff., 2.293–297, and 3.330–333). Perhaps the most telling of these path passages is Sedulius' explanation of how the Magi went home by another way because they were warned by the angel not to return to King Herod; in so doing, they followed the narrow path to salvation and avoided doing evil.[25] In his comments on the sixth petition, dealing with temptation, Sedulius encouraged his readers to follow "the narrow path which leads through the narrow gate to the celestial kingdom."[26]

Sedulius' theme of Christ as the "bread of life" fits perfectly with the fourth petition. Like most commentators before him, Sedulius equated Christ with the daily bread. Christ feeds and nourishes the faithful not only with the bread of his own body but with the bread of doctrine, which is sweeter than honey in the mouths of those who eat it.[27] This theme occurs throughout the *Paschal Song*: Christ is the bread of the fourth petition, the manna in the wilderness in the story of the Exodus (1.159), the bread of the Eucharist meal (5.401–404), and even in the bread at the feeding of the four thousand (3.257–272).

These examples demonstrate that Sedulius deliberately integrated some of the main themes of his work into his interpretation of the LP. By doing this, the poet revealed how the LP embodied the essential truths of the Christian faith. Whereas Juvencus was satisfied to expand the LP with only a brevity of words and poverty of imagery, Sedulius interpreted this prayer in light of the central ideas of the *Paschal Song* and what he considers to be the great truths of the faith.

Sedulius rarely dealt with any of the sayings of Christ in his *Paschal Song*. Rather, he spent most of his time on the deeds and miracles of Jesus. Why then does he go into such detail in his description of the words of the LP? Sedulius makes an exception of the LP because he believed it to be central to his understanding of Christianity and the life of the church.

Carl Springer, who has also puzzled over Sedulius' uncharacteristic explanation of the words of the LP, has suggested that Sedulius may believe that the LP is a miracle; Springer's insightful point suggests then that the LP materials would be a logical extension of Sedulius' overall thematic emphasis on the work of Jesus.[28] Springer, however, does not mention how central the LP is for Sedulius on a thematic level. Since the LP includes the most important themes of the *Paschal Song*, it must also be considered to be a summary of Sedulius' doctrinal teachings, or a compendium of the faith. The LP is both a miracle and the wondrous word of Christ—both of which deserve comment. As a miracle, it comes from Christ's mouth to offer faith and salvation; as a word, it embodies the essence of truth. The LP is then for Sedulius nothing less than a miraculous word.

The *Paschal Song* also needs to be compared with Sedulius' prose writing, the *Paschal Work* (*Paschale opus*). Some scholars have speculated that after the *Paschal Song* became popular, Sedulius' friend Macedonius encouraged him to write another work in order to offer more doctrinal clarity and detail to his poetic treatment of the gospels. Macedonius indeed made such a request in a letter to Sedulius, but the exact motive for doing so is unknown. The date is also uncertain, but it probably was written some time after 431.[29]

The practice of turning poetic works into prose was common in Sedulius' day.[30] The *Paschal Work* is much longer than the *Paschal Song*, but it follows the same structure and order of the original epic very closely (it too has five books) without any significant changes of the central themes.[31] The content is clarified in places and slightly expanded upon in other spots. The section on the LP is a case in point.

The section on the LP in the *Paschal Work* once again appears after the calling of the 12 disciples at the conclusion of book 2. In the *Paschal Song*, a brief discussion on how those who have been baptized may call God "Father" comes after the LP discussion. The same discussion occurs in the *Paschal Work*; however, rather than mentioning baptism explicitly, the *Paschal Work* states that it is on account of "grace"[32] that believers are able to call God "Father." No doubt, baptism should be inferred in the notion of grace as it is used here, but the fact remains that the word "baptism" is not a part of the *Paschal Work* version. Sedulius was satisfied with simply assuming that his audience would know what he meant. Perhaps this provided theological clarity for Macedonius, but if so, it is hard to see how this was accomplished. Only a more theologically sophisticated audience would be able to make this connection, whereas in the *Paschal Song* the reference is clearer for the educated non-Christian. Thus, educated Christians best understood the prose of the Paschal Work.

Sedulius then launched into a fairly lengthy explanation of the words, "Our Father, who is in heaven." Sedulius marked off the various petitions of the LP by setting forth the exact words of each petition in his text. Both Juvencus and Sedulius refused to offer the exact words of the LP in their poetic treatments, perhaps because they were partially directed toward a non-Christian audience. But Sedulius showed no such hesitation in his prose work setting out a version of the LP. This strategy may have been borrowed from other earlier LP commentators such as have already been discussed. In any event, this is further evidence that the intended audience was mature believers.

Sedulius clearly wanted his *Paschal Work* to clarify certain doctrinal issues for Macedonius, and, by extension, for other Christian readers. In the *Paschal Song*'s description of God as "Our" Father, Sedulius noted that the LP indicates that Christians are brothers and sisters of Christ and the adopted children of God. In the *Paschal Work*, however, Sedulius added Jesus' words from John 20:17, "I go to my father and your father" to this discussion in order to indicate how God is "our" (or the believers') Father by an adoptive grace, but Jesus is a son by his nature. Although the explanation of the *Paschal Work* does not change the meaning of the *Paschal Song* version, it does provide a more refined theological statement that is backed by more frequent biblical references. Also, this explanation closely echoes Augustine, and thus, he may also have sought clarity by referring to the teachings of the great church father.[33]

A similar use of scripture may be discerned throughout the *Paschal Work*. In the explanation of the first petition, Sedulius once again quoted from the Gospel of John (10:17) to support his belief that God is glorified when the faithful properly worship God. God is honored in his disciples and makes them holy, while God continues to remain holy. Sedulius also appealed to the biblical story of Shadrach, Meshach, andAbednego, who did not burn in the fiery furnace because of their honorable worship of God. Cyprian also referred to this trio in his commentary.[34]

Sedulius actually clarified his reason for appealing to scripture more often in the *Paschal Work* in the midst of his discussion of the LP. Sedulius specifically noted, like others before him, that the scripture has a threefold meaning: literal, moral, and spiritual.[35] The actual context in which Sedulius brought up the threefold meaning of scripture was in the discussion of the fourth petition. Sedulius argued, like Cyprian and Augustine, that the spiritual meaning of bread is more important than the literal meaning. Daily bread means "divine bread"—that is, Christ, who offers salvation to those who eat this bread. For Sedulius, this was more nutritious than bread eaten simply for daily, bodily sustenance.[36]

Besides being longer, the *Paschal Work* is also much more difficult to read. In the *Paschal Song*, the poetic form moves the interpretation of the LP (and various stories) along, but in the *Paschal Work*, the text at times becomes ponderous and difficult to follow. Sedulius may be attempting to demonstrate a sense of profundity with this style, but an analysis of his LP section does not readily imply that he succeeded in making his explanation any easier to read or understand.

The influence of Sedulius may be judged by the fact that the authors in the second half of the fifth century already spoke of him with respect, such as Paulinus of Perigueux, Avitus, Dracontius and Ennodius, among others.[37] Around the year 494, Turcius Rufius Apronianus Asterius, the consul of Rome, edited editions of the works of both Virgil and Sedulius. This perhaps suggests that Asterius considered the two authors to be of equal stature with the finest examples of pagan and Christian poetry. The *Paschal Song* had become a classic in a very short time.[38] Other later authors such as Cassiodorus (ca. 485–580), Fortunatus (ca. 600), Isidore of Seville (ca. 560–636), Ildephonsus of Toledo (ca. 667), Gregory of Tours (d. 594), and Bede (d. 735) all speak of Sedulius with respect. Sedulius was also enormously popular among Carolingian authors such as Alcuin (d. 804), Theodulphus of Orleans (d. 821), Smaragdus (d. after 825), Jonas of Orleans (d. 843), Rabanus Maurus (d. 856), Notker Balbulus of St. Gall (ca. 840–912), Eulogius of Cordoba (ca. 810–859), Paschasius Radbertus (ca. 785–860), Gottschalk of Orbais (ca. 803–869), Hincmar of Reims (845–882), and Remigius of Auxerre (ca. 840–908), who even wrote a commentary upon the *Paschal Song*.[39] Remigius' commentary, though interesting in and of itself, does not add new detail to the *Paschal Song*, but merely offers explanations of troubling words and phrases.[40] Thus, the *Paschal Song* eventually proved itself to be one of medieval Europe's most popular and influential poems. This was due in part to the fact that it became required reading in the schools and was widely circulated among monastic libraries in particular. Sedulius himself became known as a curriculum author.[41] Sedulius was honored as a true father of the church by Dante, the Renaissance (a period where Sedulius encountered his first critics), and the Reformation (Luther called Sedulius the most Christian poet—*christanissimus poeta*).[42] And thus Sedulius' influence was tremendous, and by extension, his interpretation of the LP became widely known and one of the most popular ways of reading the LP throughout the Middle Ages.

Sedulius' works indicate how he was freer to talk openly about the LP to a non-Christian audience than Juvencus was. Sedulius also had another advantage. By the mid-fifth century, the *disciplina arcani* had softened considerably: it was a time when the LP could be taught to catechumens before baptism. Even so, he did not reveal the actual wording of the LP, except to the Christian audience in the *Paschal Work*. In both works, he demonstrated a tremendous respect for the LP, considering it to be a miraculous word that not only summarized biblical truths, but that also had the power to lead the faithful down the narrow path away from the serpent Satan to Christ, the good shepherd. The medium of poetry and paraphrase proved to be an enormously popular method of interpretation of the LP, and many later authors emulated Sedulius' example. Out of the poetic context in particular, the LP became widely known in and outside of the church. A few other notable examples of later poets who were influenced by Juvencus and Coelius Sedulius, and who also refer to the LP, are the anonymous author of the alliterative gospel poem called the *Heliand* (ninth century),[43] Francis of Assisi (1182–1226),[44] David of Augsburg (OFM, 1200–1272),[45] Dante Alighieri (1265–1321),[46] Ludolf of Saxony (Carthusian, d. 1378),[47] and still others.[48]

The Lord's Prayer in Baptismal Catechesis

Two of the most important bishops in the world during the mid-to-latter part of the fourth century were Cyril of Jerusalem (ca. 315–386) in the East and Ambrose of Milan (ca. 339–397) in the West.[49] Theirs and other writings from the period reveal that early Christian communities benefited greatly from the remarkable leadership of these strong bishops. Many fourth-century churches were able, due to the vision of talented clergy, to become more fully defined doctrinally and liturgically. Churches became more organized and institutionally focused as a result of the leadership of strong, creative bishops and the direction of councils, despite the numerous divisions that plagued the early church. Slowly, more regularized forms of worship and theology began to spread and define these churches.

What is also true of the fourth century is that bishops and the churches at times became more furtive about the mysteries of the church. In other words, at the same time congregations became more organized and defined, they also became more secretive about their most precious teachings and religious practices. Ambrose, for example, eagerly promoted the instruction of the LP but was careful to keep it from the unbaptized. For Ambrose, the prayer of Jesus should be kept from the ears and even the eyes of all non-Christians, and this included catechumens involved in Lenten training, who had not yet received baptism. This careful attitude toward the LP can be traced back to the Bible itself and may have been a part of the worlds of Tertullian and Cyprian as well. However, the forceful admonitions of Ambrose and the complicity by his churches to carry out such practices reflect a tone and an attitude that are unique in the history of the church prior to this point.

Ambrose of Milan in his *On the Sacraments* argued that unbaptized catechumens should not even dare to turn their faces toward heaven in order to seek God's favor: they are sinners and not true children of God. However, if their sins are forgiven through the waters of baptism, then they are changed from slaves into truly adopted sons and daughters of God. Begotten in the grace of baptism, notes Ambrose, they may indeed lift their eyes to God in devotion, not out of some prideful desire for earthly gain, but because they are honestly children of God, who indeed is their "Father," as the LP teaches.[50] Those who might pray the LP before their baptisms would be arrogantly presumptuous; for Ambrose, they usurp the title of heirs of God, when in fact they are only unworthy paupers trying to steal noble names.

Ambrose only briefly mentioned the LP in a few places; nevertheless, he represents the culmination of the *disciplina arcani* tradition with regard to the LP. His comments offer the clearest and most forceful justifications for applying a rule of secrecy to the mysteries of the church that may be found in the early church.

Ambrose specifically stated that the LP was to be taught in a mystagogical manner to the newly baptized on the Friday following the Easter of their baptismal initiation. This placement of the instruction of the LP following the Lenten season and Easter once again demonstrates how the interpretation and use of the LP was often intimately connected to baptism.[51] It must be remembered that the mature members of the Milanese church would also have heard these teachings along with the neophytes within a liturgical setting. Cyril likewise offered his explanation of the LP in his fifth sermon on *Mystagogic Catechesis*. If these sermons were offered one at a time each day after Easter, as some have suggested, then Cyril's instruction on the LP, like Ambrose's teaching, would also have occurred on the first Friday after Easter as well.[52] Alexis Doval has noted that the *Mystagogic Catecheses* have for some time been believed to be the earliest source in the East for the LP being a part of the Eucharist.[53] What is not clear in Cyril's work is whether or not he held the same sort of concerns as Ambrose with regard to being secretive about handing over the LP before the initiates were baptized. What is clearer is that he did appear to preach about the LP after they had been washed in baptism.

During the season of Lent, Ambrose handed over the Apostles' Creed (aka, the *symbolum*) to those preparing for baptism on the Sunday before Easter (sometimes called Palm or Passion Sunday). Converts needed to know this one mystery of the church before their baptisms because the Creed was used as an integral part of the baptismal ceremony, which required that those seeking initiation into the Christian faith repeat the text as they were baptized.[54]

In Cyril's case, we do not have specific evidence in his works that tell when he presented the Creed to those seeking baptism. Cyril himself considered catechumens during Lent to be in a special category known as the "faithful" or "enlightened ones." Nevertheless, a work commonly attributed to a pilgrim nun, Egeria, says that it was the regular practice in Jerusalem at this time to hand over the Creed during the fifth week of Lent, or two weeks before Palm Sunday (Egeria describes a Lent of eight weeks). Cyril admonished the faithful, when he gave them the Creed, with the following words: "I want you to memorize [the Creed] word for word, and to recite it very carefully among yourselves. Do not write it down on paper, but inscribe it in your memories and in your hearts."[55] These words may indicate that Cyril appears to be careful with the Creed because he doesn't even want copies of it lying around that might accidentally fall into the hands of non-baptized folk.

Later on, Peter Chrysologus in Ravenna (d. 450) also believed that learning and memorizing the Creed and LP were essential for converts so that they might gain an understanding of the basic elements of the Christian faith. Chrysologus similarly cautioned those who were learning the Creed that they were not to put it down in writing, even to facilitate the memorization process.[56] Peter's concern, however, may not have been the same as Cyril's. For Peter, the physical paper and actual written letters might be deterrents to the faith, because they can remind those seeking baptism of earthly objects to be cared for, and thus detract from the grace of Christ. Quoting Romans 10:10, Chrysologus said that it is only through the heart and mouth that profession of the faith should be made.[57] Whether such a restriction was applied to the LP is not mentioned by Chrysologus, but if it in fact existed, then in this one instance Peter kept a remnant of the *disciplina arcani,* albeit for different reasons. For Peter, the emphasis was not upon keeping the LP, or the Creed, from unworthy eyes, but upon the concern that the physical paper might lead the youthful catechumen astray. In fact, as we will see in the next chapter, Peter Chrysologus did teach the LP to unbaptized converts in order to prepare them for their baptismal initiations. The question here, however, is what attitude did Cyril take toward the Creed, and perhaps the LP? Why did he not want the Creed to be written down? In the end, it is impossible to say. The two options represented by Ambrose and Peter appear to be the main options available to scholarly analysis of these comments. Cyril may have had the same concerns as Peter, but he unfortunately did not leave us any written record to clarify his position.

A monk known as Didymus the Blind (ca. 313–398 from Alexandria in North Africa), in his work entitled *On the Trinity*, states specifically that the LP was to be kept from non-Christians and was only to be prayed by and given to the baptized.[58] Given Didymus' and Cyril's cautionary comments, it may well be that early educators presented their comments on the LP to recent converts and to the faithful in worship almost exclusively in an oral fashion. This might explain why some scholars have wondered about the relatively few written commentaries on the LP, especially during the fourth century. Some works from the East and West clearly indicate a desire and practice that presents the mysteries in an oral fashion during Lent. Therefore, much of what might have been known about views of the LP simply has not come down to the modern day.[59]

Ambrose, like Didymus, argued more forcefully for a *disciplina arcani* when he said, "A vow or a prayer is commendable to the extent that its substance is not divulged. We should keep intact the hidden mysteries just as Abraham did when he caused loaves to be baked under the ashes."[60] This rather strange allusion refers to an ancient practice of baking bread within warm ashes. Ambrose suggested that to the untutored eye, all seems to be ash and dust; to the trained students, however, the hidden bread of life appears from amidst the cinders. This was especially true of the two great prayers of the church, and so Ambrose warned, "Beware lest you carelessly disclose the mystery of the Creed and the Lord's Prayer."[61]

For Ambrose, Cyril, and Didymus, the cautious handing over of the Creed and perhaps the LP grew out of four concerns. First, as has been noted in the opening chapter, Ambrose's notion of secrecy was based on his understanding of Matthew 7:6: "Give not that which is holy to dogs; neither cast your pearls before swine, lest perhaps they trample them under their feet, and turning upon you, they tear you." Thus, Ambrose desired to keep the LP from those who might not reverence it in an appropriate manner, or even worse, might abuse it in some way. An example of abusing the LP would be to call God "Father" before God was indeed a Father through baptism.[62] For Ambrose, the LP was the pearl of great price, which required protection, lest it be spirited away by unworthy thieves. The LP was full of power and mystery, despite its brevity, and the words of Christ were not to be taken lightly. Didymus agreed with the notion of keeping the mysteries from unworthy hands. How far these authors went beyond this is hard to say.

Second, Ambrose wanted to hand over an appropriate text (the LP) to the suitable people (the baptized): the LP needed to be presented in the proper context (after baptism and in a liturgical setting) and place (in the church).[63] This notion of appropriateness helps to clarify a problem that some modern scholars have puzzled over—that is, the difference and similarity between Ambrose's works *On the Mysteries* and *On the Sacraments* (both written ca. 390–392[64]). Ambrose composed both writings for the purpose of catechesis. Although very similar in content and form, one of the key differences between them is that *On the Mysteries* has no explanation of the LP, while *On the Sacraments* does. Internal evidence suggests that Ambrose intended *On the Mysteries* to be read by a broader audience, and as a result, it is a more polished treatise and avoids talking about the LP. *On the Sacraments*, on the other hand, is a collection of sermons probably written down by a stenographer (*a notarius*) at a time when only the baptized were present in a liturgical setting. Srawley argues that *On the Mysteries* was intended for a catechetical audience that included unbaptized catechumens, and therefore Ambrose did not include the LP section, because it was an inappropriate audience for the teaching of the LP. Srawley's thesis holds if one simply looks at the use of the LP in this text.[65] However, a closer examination of *On the Mysteries* reveals that Ambrose also discusses the Eucharist at some length, and this mystery would not have been appropriate for the unbaptized catechumens in Ambrose's view. Perhaps Ambrose did not include the LP in *On the Mysteries* because it could be used both in and outside of a liturgical setting. Since it was not specifically focused toward the newly baptized, it does not include the LP. *On the Sacraments*, however, may have been sermons that instructed newly baptized Christians. The issue, then, may be one of appropriate message for appropriate context. Even though Ambrose could have easily included the explanation of the LP in *On the Mysteries*, he chose not to: the reason appears to be that the text was not directed at the right context and audience for the LP. In other words, Ambrose didn't want the LP presented to neophytes except during the Easter season.[66]

Ambrose's caution concerning the LP may even have kept him from including a discussion of the LP in his commentary on Luke.

First, it must be noted that Ambrose left out a few other important Lucan passages in his commentary, so he did not single out the LP per se. Some think that stenographers copied Ambrose's sermons on the subject over a period of 12 to 15 years (finishing them before 390), and therefore, the absences may simply be a matter of chance.[67] But given Ambrose's hesitance in writing down commentary on the LP, it may also have been done intentionally, because the sermon commentary may have been heard, or perhaps even read, by an audience that included catechumens who had not yet been baptized.

Third, the attitudes and actions of Ambrose and others concerning the LP and other mysteries of the church surely aroused a certain curiosity and awe among catechumens and outsiders, whether intentionally or unintentionally, through the preservation of secrecy regarding certain texts and teachings. With regard to Cyril, Edward Yarnold beautifully describes how awe may have been incited in parishioners, especially those seeking baptism, during the Easter Vigil service in Jerusalem. Says Yarnold,

> Cyril seems to have striven to create a dramatic effect on the candidates like that of the pagan mysteries...he used the same terms to express religious awe as they did, and he practiced the same techniques. There have been preliminary mysterious hints, the effects of protracted fasts and sleeplessness, daily moral exhortations and exorcisms, constant prompting by the godparents, all of which have conspired to raise the candidates to a pitch of expectation. Finally, at the Easter Vigil after prolonged prayers, they are lead into a corner, where a voice comes out of the darkness commanding them one by one to turn on the devil, point at him, and reject him to his face, then to turn to Christ and swear allegiance to him; they remain only half comprehending as they find themselves stripped, anointed from head to toe, pushed three times under the water; then, after fragrant oil has been poured on their heads, they are dressed in white and led to the tomb of the risen Lord, then into the Martyrium, the church which is the witness to the Passion, where they are greeted with joy and for the first time take part in the secret rites of the Mass, and receive for the first time the bread and wine...[68]

Egeria states that the bishop of Jerusalem explained the mysteries of the faith to the neophytes and they responded by applauding so loudly that the noise could be heard outside the church.[69] Since the mysteries required explanation, converts were generally eager to learn about the faith they had been initiated into, as the previous example illustrates.

The secrecy had the effect of creating curiosity in those who were unaware of what the mysteries were or meant. At about the same time, John Chrysostom actively promoted this interest by calling baptism, "the holy and awesome rite of initiation."[70] An emphasis upon involvement in the secret practices encouraged unbelievers to become active members of the church. Because Christianity was in part defined by participation in baptism, in eating bread and drinking wine at the altar during the Eucharist, listening to preaching and teaching, and praying the Creed or the LP, believers remained faithful to God through active involvement in worship. Also, since a sense of mystery was a familiar element in the Hellenistic mystery religions, some converts may even have expected a similar type of secrecy in Christianity.[71]

Fourth, an initiation process, which handed over the great mysteries of the church, created solidarity within the community of the faithful, who alone were privy to the wonders of God. This especially was true of the LP, whose words suggested that whoever was allowed to pray it became a daughter or son of God, sibling of Christ, and fellow member of the body of Christ.[72]

The concern for secrecy surrounding the LP reached its peak in the late fourth century, and this is clearly seen in Ambrose and Didymus, perhaps in Cyril. After Ambrose, however, whatever *disciplina arcani* existed surrounding the LP loosened, and the LP slowly became a more public document, even if it was still primarily a prayer solely for the church.[73] During the day of Ambrose, however, the LP was a precious treasure of the church, a carefully guarded heirloom, and a pearl of great price.

The turn of the fifth century proved to be a time of transition away from such secretive treatments of the LP. The evidence for this transition comes in the writings of John Chrysostom, Theodore of Mopsuestia, Cyril of Jerusalem, Augustine, Chromatius of Aquileia, and Peter Chrysologus.

John Chrysostom (d. 407)[74] exerted a great deal of influence on both the Greek-speaking East and the Latin authors of the West. Anianus of Celeda translated 25 sermons of Chrysostom's larger collection of late fourth-century homilies on Matthew (dated to ca. 390) into Latin around 420. Among these, Sermon 19 discusses the LP specifically. Chrysostom's homilies on Matthew are his most complete commentary on an entire book of the Bible that is extant.[75] Chrysostom's explanation of Matthew is typical of the Antiochene School of exegesis, that is, it is literal, clear, and well organized. Chrysostom was in Antioch when he preached these sermons, and so they reflect the situation at this place and time.

Sermon 19 on the LP is a part of a series of sermons intended for mature members of Chrysostom's own congregation, and there is no indication that the sermon is directed at neophytes or catechumens. Still, there are a few brief mentions of baptism that provide valuable, if ambiguous, insight into the connection of the LP to baptismal catechesis at this time.

Chrysostom opened his discussion of the LP in Sermon 19 by stating that all of God's bounty is given to whoever prays the words "Our Father." Christians receive forgiveness of sins, sanctification, and righteousness in these words because people are not allowed to call God "Father" unless they have already received these blessings. Chrysostom assumes that it is in baptism that believers are first given this grace.

When he comes to the discussion of the fifth petition, on forgiveness, Chrysostom refers back to his opening comments, arguing that the fifth petition is the key to understanding the entire LP. Chrysostom, like Ambrose and Augustine, noted that only those who believe in God have the right to have the LP explained to them; nonbelievers especially ought not to pray to God as "Father." At first glance, such a comment seems to suggest that Chrysostom does not want the LP taught to the unbaptized and perhaps not even to catechumens until after their baptism. Given what we have seen earlier in this chapter, this seems a likely explanation. Still, Chrysostom's point is primarily that even after people are baptized, they continue to sin, and therefore Christians need the fifth petition, which brings God's forgiveness even when they fall after baptism. However, believers only attain forgiveness if they forgive others first. Only then will the disease and madness of sin be removed and only then will the faithful become like their Father in heaven, whose most gracious acts are those of offering forgiveness.[76] However, it must be noted that Chrysostom's views on when to teach the LP are not clear in these passages.

Chrysostom's other explanations of the LP and baptism unfortunately only shed a diffused light on this matter. His baptismal-catechetic sermons, which are directed at both pre-baptismal catechumens and neophytes, do not mention the LP or any of its individual petitions.[77] The handing back of the Creed (redditio symboli) by neophytes during Lent appears to be alluded to in one sermon, but modern scholars debate whether this is actually the case. In the end, it is not clear whether Chrysostom taught the Creed before baptism.[78]

Chrysostom's commentary on Colossians (ca. 399, written while Chrysostom was Patriarch in Constantinople), however, may indicate how he used the LP in baptismal catechesis at a different place and time. Note that this commentary was written nine years after the homily on Matthew was written in Antioch. One verse in the Colossians commentary states, "For immediately when he comes up [from the baptismal waters] he pronounces these words, 'Our Father, who is in heaven, . . . Your will be done, as it is in heaven, so on earth.'"[79] These words are significant, but they remain ambiguous. Evidence from other authors, however, may help to clarify this matter.

A contemporary of Chrysostom, Theodore of Mopsuestia (ca. 350–428) preached a series of catechetical homilies that consisted of two parts: part 1 on faith and part 2 on the sacraments. This textbook for catechumens, according to Mingana, was originally written in Greek around 388–392, or about the same time Chrysostom's Sermon 19 was written. Later, the work was translated into Syriac shortly after Theodore's death. What is most important to note is that the text was used by the Greek church in Antioch as a part of their catechetical training program. The chapters on the LP in part 2 of the book offer pre-baptismal instruction on the LP, requiring catechumens to memorize the prayer before they are baptized. The assumption here might be that neophytes were meant to emerge from the sacramental waters and pray the LP immediately, and therefore they needed to learn it before they had actually been adopted into the faith. But the text is ambiguous on this point. If there is some truth to this notion, then the reluctance of Ambrose did not apply to Theodore and to those he was preaching to in Antioch. The liturgical need to train candidates made it necessary to hand over the LP during Lent in order that the baptismal ceremony might be properly carried out. If indeed the baptized prayed the LP upon emerging from the baptismal font, they would need to learn it during Lent in order to be ready for the ceremony.

Theodore's writings may indicate that Chrysostom's silence on these matters suggests two possibilities. First, there was a handing over of the LP to catechumens during Lent in Antioch just before the turn of the fifth century and Chrysostom does not mention the practice. This

seems the most likely explanation. Second, there were two practices
going on simultaneously in Antioch. In either case, a firm conclusion
must wait for more complete evidence to be revealed. What may well
be the situation, however, is that what we see in these texts is a time of
transition and some ambiguity. Chrysostom later on in Constantinople may have handed over the LP to catechumens, but again, firm
conclusions are difficult if not impossible to make.[80]

For Theodore, the LP is a brief text that contains all one needs to
know concerning good works, love, and Christian duty. Prayer calls
forth virtuous deeds and moves people to pray: these are insepara-
ble and circular acts in which one leads to the other. That's why it is
essential to pray at all times, as Paul suggests (Ephesians 6:18), says
Theodore, because this is what Jesus did in his own life. The LP is a
prayer of perfection that comes out of and increases one's zeal for a
good Christian life. Therefore, theologically speaking, if good works,
love, and duty can move the individual to prayer, it would be appropriate to conclude with regard to Theodore that people who lead godly
lives already in some way have God as their Father. Their devotion to
God moves them to lead good lives and to be baptized. As Theodore
begins his explanation of the introduction of the LP, "Our Father, who
is in heaven," he notes that it is essential for him to explain to his
audience what their relationship is to God. To the unbaptized catechumen, Theodore declares that God's great gift of baptism will make
them all adopted sons and daughters of God. Therefore, they will be
able to have confidence when they call upon God as Father. The Holy
Spirit will set them free and they will be citizens of heaven and free
to live out of that freedom. Although he does not say so specifically,
Theodore implies that the unbaptized who seek God are already free to
do so because their good works, love, and sense of duty, which already
make them children of God. Even in the first sermon on the LP, he
orders them to call God "Father" as if they are reluctant to do so;
indeed, they may be hesitant because they have not yet been baptized,
and given other previous practices that forbid such prayer, one would
be hard pressed to blame them. Clearly there is something going on.
Theodore justifies his reasons for giving catechumens the LP before
baptism, and the catechumens aren't quite sure what this all means.
Still, Theodore believes it is appropriate that they pray, or at least recite
the LP before they are actually baptized, so that on the occasion of
their baptisms they may pray the LP as they emerge dripping from the

font. Theodore makes no distinction between reciting and praying the LP, but Augustine will. In fact, the move to allow the unbaptized to at least recite the LP before baptism, will be fully developed by Augustine in Northern Africa.[81]

Augustine's examination of the LP in a baptismal-catechetic setting builds upon the fathers of the past, hearkening back especially to the explanations of Cyprian. Nevertheless, Augustine's writings on the LP are strikingly innovative. This is most noticeable in his sermons (see especially, sermons 56–59,[82] written ca. 410–412), where Augustine presents the explanation of the LP primarily to *competentes* preparing for baptism during Lent.[83]

The baptismal-catechetic writings of Augustine reveal that some North African churches during the late fourth and early fifth century prepared candidates for baptism by leading them through a series of Lenten worship services. In this formal rite of preparation, *competentes* were questioned, or "scrutinized," with regard to certain central teachings of the Christian faith. At the very least, the scrutinies included the instruction of the Creed and the LP.[84] Augustine handed over (*traditio*) both the Creed and the LP to *competentes* during Lent in order to teach (*explanatio*) its meaning to them. These catechumens in turn had to demonstrate that they knew these texts by reciting them from memory a week or so after they had received them. In Latin, this was called *redditio*, or literally a returning of the LP to those who had handed it over (*traditio*) in the first place.[85]

Augustine and Theodore of Mopsuestia are the earliest authors to teach the LP to *competentes* before they had emerged from the baptismal font; whether Augustine or Theodore originated such a practice is highly doubtful. The tone of their writings suggests that they are merely discussing a practice that is already in place, or at least recently emerging, in the practice of some churches. Nevertheless, Augustine and Theodore still considered the mystery and power of the LP to be wondrous, so they only presented the LP to those who were about to be baptized. Thus, in their own way, they too guarded the precious pearl of a prayer from outsiders. Many previous authors, however, would have had a great deal of difficulty with Augustine's openness in this regard.

Fortunately, Augustine's writings are much more revealing about what happened in the churches he served. *Competentes*, according to Augustine, received the LP on the Saturday before the fifth Sunday of Lent; this was also the same day that they had for the first time recited the Apostles' Creed and demonstrated that they had at least a basic understanding of their new faith.[86] Then, and only then, did Augustine teach them the LP. First, he taught converts about the nature of God, and after that, he offered them a prayer that explained the relationship of the believer to God. Sermon 58, preached on the occasion of the recitation of the Creed, states:

> You have given back the Creed, which contains a brief summary of the faith . . . So fix [the LP] as well firmly in your minds, because you are to give it back in a week's time. As for those who did not give back the Creed very well, they have some time yet to get it by heart; because on Saturday, with everyone present listening, they are going to give it back again—that is the last Saturday, on which you are to be baptized. But in a week from today [i.e., the Saturday before Palm Sunday] you are going to give back this prayer which you have been given today.[87]

Augustine, the pragmatic pastor, believed that handing over the Creed before the LP made sense. In North Africa around the time of Augustine, the recitation of the Creed occurred during worship only three times a year: it was first handed over to the *competentes* during Lent; then it was heard again at the returning of the Creed (*redditio symboli*) by the *competentes*; and finally, it was spoken at the profession of faith during the baptismal ceremony. Since such scant use was made of the Creed in worship—as opposed to the regular and frequent daily liturgical and private praying of the LP—Augustine felt it necessary to teach the Creed in a more thorough manner than the LP. By teaching the *competentes* the Creed first, they had more time to learn it before Easter, when they would need to repeat it from memory during their own baptismal ceremonies. The bishop of Hippo even counseled them not to worry if they were not able to memorize it right away, but they should strive to commit it to memory by the time of their baptismal washing. Augustine, in Sermon 58, is more lenient when it comes to learning the LP:

> When you have been baptized, you will have to say [the LP] daily. For the Lord's Prayer is said daily in Church at the altar of God, and the faithful hear it. We are not therefore disturbed by any fear, wondering whether your minds have grasped it with less care: for if any of you have not been able to grasp it perfectly, yet by a daily hearing you will grasp

it. That is why, on the day of the Sabbath, before we keep vigil and wait on the mercy of God, it is the Creed and not the Lord's Prayer of which you are to make return. For unless you have a firm grasp of the Creed, you do not hear the Creed daily in Church among the people. So when you have grasped it, say it daily, so as not to forget it; when you rise, when you lie down to sleep, make return of your Creed, return it to the Lord, remind yourselves of it, do not tire of repeating it.[88]

The recitation of the Creed at the moment of their baptisms was the *competentes'* declaration of faith in the Trinity. Through baptism and this declaration, they are then free to call upon the Creator of the universe with the words "Our Father."[89]

Augustine recognized that there might be a theological problem with what he and the North African church were doing: by presenting the LP to *competentes* during Lent, he was teaching them to pray the LP, and call God "Father," before they had been adopted in baptism. Augustine cautiously put forth the question that was no doubt on their minds: he wondered out loud in a sermon what they were really doing if they recited the LP at least a week before they entered the font. Were they not claiming a relationship with God that they did not presently have? Perhaps, said Augustine. But he quickly made an important distinction: Augustine claimed that the mere memorization and recitation of the LP was very different from the act of actually praying it. Indeed, the full benefit of praying the LP was not fully conveyed to the *competentes* until they were born again in baptism. But if this is true, then what, if anything, happened when the catechumens learned the LP during Lent? Augustine boldly suggested that the LP had a transforming power over those who memorized it, even before their baptisms.

The act of learning the LP was like the act of conception, said Augustine; *competentes* who committed the LP to memory were actually being "conceived" in the womb of the church. The seed that brings about this conception is none other than the LP itself. Augustine said in Sermon 56, "With these words [of the LP], you, as you can see, have begun to have God as your Father. You certainly will have Him as such, when you have been born [in baptism]—although even now, before you are born, you have already been conceived by his seed, to be duly brought forth from the womb of the Church,[90] so to speak, in the font."[91] And so, Augustine theologically justified the practice of handing over the LP to *competentes* outside of a mystagogical setting.

In doing so, Augustine did not lessen the connection between baptism and the LP, but he strengthened it.

Augustine presented a similar idea in what modern scholars call Letter 130 to a woman named Proba. In the midst of his discussion on the LP, Augustine recalled the verses in Luke 11:11–13 (the text shortly after the LP in Luke's Gospel), which read, "Which of you, if he asks his father for bread, will he give him a stone? or if he asks for a fish will give him a serpent? or if he asks for an egg will hand over to him a scorpion?" Augustine explained the verse allegorically and noted that the fish signifies faith, because it lives in the water, just as Christians live in the waters of their baptism. Believers, like fish, remain unharmed by the waves of this world because they live underwater, that is, in baptism. The serpent is opposed to the fish, and therefore represents the evil that the Devil seeks to do to the faithful. Second, the egg symbolizes hope, because the chick is not yet alive, but waits in anticipation of its birth. The scorpion, that is, the Devil, is opposed to the egg, or what Christians' hope for in life. Finally, the bread symbolizes love, and the stone represents the stonehearted, who cast love out of their lives.

The comparison of the egg with hope is striking, even if Augustine did not specifically mention the LP in these lines, because Augustine intimately connected the virtue of hope with the LP in a number of his other works, saying specifically that the LP is hope.[92] Thus, one might infer that the LP is an egg that has not hatched, but that waits in anticipation of the birth of the chick (the baptized Christian). Augustine, therefore, compared the LP with both a seed and an egg because it helped him to explain why catechumens were allowed to learn the LP even before they were born out of the watery womb of the church.

Augustine's justifications and influence upon later authors helped to bring an end to an emphasis on a *disciplina arcani* surrounding the LP, like the one his teacher Ambrose advocated. Likewise, Augustine's interpretation of the LP, which was intimately connected with the Creed and baptism, strongly influenced commentaries throughout the Middle Ages.

How the handing over of the LP took place elsewhere in the fifth century is more uncertain. Concerning the development of the rite of baptism itself, Nathan Mitchell has noted, "Indeed, one could defend the thesis that through the entire period (from 500–1274) there exists no single western rite of initiation, but rather a collection of local rites similar in structure yet divergent in significant details."[93] Before 500, the problem was no different. Today, modern scholars wonder about the development of the scrutiny process and have a variety of theories about it.

Jean-Paul Bouhot has noticed that the available liturgical documents of the city of Aquileia in Italy, for example, down to the ninth century do not mention that the LP was a part of the Lenten baptismal scrutinies. According to Bouhot, the *Capitulary of the Gospels* (an early ninth-century work that makes no mention of the handing over of the LP) and the *Order of the Scrutinies of Catechumens* (a mid-ninth-century writing that includes the LP in its scrutinies) demonstrate that the LP became a part of the formalized baptismal liturgy during Lent in Aquileia in the mid-ninth century.[94]

On the other hand, Pierre Puniet has argued that the LP was a part of the Lenten interrogation process in Aquileia by the fifth century. Puniet connected Chromatius (d. 407), the bishop of Aquileia (the acquaintance of Jerome and Ambrose and a defender of John Chrysostom), to a catechetical homily on the LP found in the late sixth-century or early seventh-century Gelasian Sacramentary.[95] Puniet suggested that the Gelasian sermon on the LP was actually written by Chromatius.[96] This sermon proved for Puniet that a scrutiny process included the LP and was a part of church practice in Aquileia when Chromatius was there in the late fourth and early fifth centuries.

Bouhot countered this argument by suggesting that Chromatius probably taught *competentes* at the end of the week of Easter, much like Ambrose did in Milan, rather than during Lent like Augustine in North Africa.[97] For Bouhot, this would be more consistent with the historical liturgical evidence.

Chromatius' sermons, however, do not conclusively confirm nor deny Puniet's or Bouhot's theses with regard to the LP. What is certain is that the LP played an important part in the instruction of the *competentes* in the fifth century in Northern Italy, probably during Lent, or perhaps during the Easter season.[98]

Chromatius' *Sermons on Matthew* (ca. 400–407[99]) and the sermon known as the *Preface to the Lord's Prayer* (the sermon the Gelasian Sacramentary borrowed[100]) do not indicate in what context the LP was explained in Aquileia during Chromatius' day. Both were probably preached by Chromatius sometime late in his life and only offer some veiled references to a baptismal catechetic context.

Relying heavily upon Tertullian and Cyprian for many of his comments, Chromatius acknowledged when preaching on Matthew 6:9–15 in his *Sermons on Matthew*, that it is through baptism that Christians are adopted and have the right to call God "Father." This raises a problem with works that quote earlier authorities. Is this a reflection of Chromatius' situation or merely a reflection of the fact that he is quoting Tertullian's and Cyprian's views on the LP? Could both hold the same views? Often, it is impossible to know for sure. Likewise, it is often difficult to know whether he was reading Cyprian, which is more likely, or Tertullian, who is used by Cyprian.

Chromatius' initial remarks in his *Preface to the Lord's Prayer* concern the secrecy of prayer; this secrecy as Chromatius notes is grounded in Matthew 6:6 (a verse shortly before the LP appears in Matthew): "But you when you shall pray, enter into your chamber, and having shut the door, pray to your Father in secret, and your Father who sees in secret will repay you." Unlike the secrecy of the *disciplina arcani* of Ambrose and others, Chromatius was not worried about keeping the LP a secret for fear it would fall into the hands of unbelievers; rather, he wanted believers to enter into the "secret place of their hearts" in order to shut out the evils of the world, so that they might be open to Christ alone. Ultimately, this is an appeal to live an upright life. Chromatius noted:

> When [Jesus] says a closet, he does not mean some hidden place, but reminds us that the secret places of our hearts should be open to him alone. And that we should shut the door when we worship God means this, that with a mystic key we should shut our breast to evil thoughts and with closed lips and pure minds speak to God. For God hears our faith, not our voice. Let therefore our breast be shut with the key of faith against the snares of the adversary, and let it be open to God alone whose temple we know it to be, that as he dwells in our hearts so he may be an advocate in our prayers. Therefore the Word of God and the Wisdom of God, Christ our Lord, taught us this prayer that we should pray thus [with the LP].[101]

Chromatius avoids Ambrose's interpretation of this verse, and in so doing may well indicate his context was less secretive about the LP.

Chromatius' sermons indicate that the *disciplina arcani* surrounding the LP probably was not as rigidly followed in Aquileia as it was in Milan under Ambrose. Chromatius' sermons on the LP are an important synthesis of earlier works, but he offers few original insights. This type of explanation became more common after this time and Chromatius' own work influenced many after him in the Middle Ages, particularly because his work is mistaken for other famous authors and because it was included in the Gelasian Sacramentary, where it found a wide audience.

Another Italian, known only later as Peter Chrysologus ("of the golden word"), the bishop of Ravenna (d. 450), preached a number of important sermons on the LP. The actual date of Peter's LP Sermons 67–72 remains uncertain, but they were preached during Lent for pre-baptismal catechetic purposes over a number of years toward the later part of his life.

Modern scholars have debated whether the LP sermons of Peter Chrysologus indicate whether Ravenna used the LP in baptismal catechesis during Peter's day.[102] Bouhot believed that the evidence supports the claim that the LP was a part of post-baptismal catechesis. Others, such as Verbraken and Schnurr, correctly have pointed out that the handing over of the LP occurred during pre-baptismal catechesis in Ravenna during Lent.[103] Puniet concludes that the Northern African baptismal practice of handing over the LP during Lent, which predates the Northern Italian practice, influenced the practice in Ravenna. [104] Peter clearly knew Augustine's writings, and this connection may have been what influenced Northern Italian practices.

Chrysologus mentioned that at least a part of his audience for his LP sermons were catechumens awaiting baptism. Sermon 70 stated that even though the *competentes* have not yet been born again in baptism, they nevertheless live in anticipation of their birth from the womb and in full possession of the gifts that they have yet to receive fully after their births.[105] Chrysologus may have borrowed this basic idea from Augustine, who also used the "womb" language.

Chrysologus, however, made no Augustinian distinction between pre-baptismal "saying" and post-baptismal "praying" of the LP. Rather, he believed that even in the "womb" the catechumen has the right to call God "Father," because catechumens already "are" sons and daughters of God. Chrysologus wrote, "No one should be astonished that one not yet born calls Him Father. With God, beings who will be born are already born; with God future beings have been made. 'The things that shall be,' scripture says, 'have already been.' "[106] Peter thus noted that the uninitiated actually "pray" the LP even before their baptisms.

In fact, the sons and daughters of God in the womb participate fully in the benefits of all adopted sons and daughters who have been born out of the baptismal font.

As a result of this somewhat unusual view, Chrysologus felt the need to defend his innovative theological position; he presented three biblical examples in defense of his ideas that unbaptized catechumens fully participate in their future baptismal adoption. First, Chrysologus compared this pre-baptismal state of catechumens to John the Baptist, who "leaped" in the womb of his mother Elizabeth when she met the pregnant Mary (Luke 1). Though not yet born, John's reaction indicated that he already had the ability to recognize Jesus and dedicate himself to his own salvation. Catechumens similarly in the womb recognize Jesus to be their Savior and have taken the first steps in following him. Therefore, they have the full benefits of such an action, namely, son or daughterhood. First comes the hearing of the faith and then the actual faith, but in both cases it is the same faith, even if it comes before baptism.[107]

Chrysologus pointed at the stories of Jacob and his twin brother Esau in Genesis 25 and the twins of Tamar's in Genesis 38 as representative examples of those who were chosen for salvation even before the foundation of the earth. Jacob contended with Esau (both before and after their births) to win the birthright (Genesis 27) that God desired him to have. Tamar's twins struggled with each other in a like manner while still in the womb; thus, even before their physical births, these two different sets of twins sought to further the kingdom of God and to fulfill God's plan for their lives.[108] In the same way, Peter suggested the *competentes* had already begun to struggle for the kingdom in the womb when they learned and prayed the LP.

We may conclude that there was a recognizable transition in attitudes about the LP in baptismal catechesis at the end of the fourth and into the fifth century. First, authors like Ambrose adhered to a rigid restriction, trying to keep the LP from any but baptized ears and eyes. However, Theodore of Mopsuestia indicates that the practical concern of having catechumens ready to pray the LP immediately after baptism moved him to teach the LP to catechumens during Lent. He, however, did not provide a clear theological justification for such a move. Some contemporary authors did, probably out of necessity. Augustine felt it necessary to justify his actions with an argument that suggested that the LP was like a seed impregnating catechumens so that they might soon be born Christians in baptism and have the right to pray the LP and call God "Father." Peter Chrysologus certainly continues along the lines first laid out by Augustine by finding clever theological justification for giving the LP to catechumens. Peter's justifications demonstrate that attitudes about handing over the LP had developed over a relatively short period of time. Peter is unwavering in his view that even the uninitiated have the right to call God "Father" in prayer. The initial praying of the LP, therefore, literally becomes the point of conception and adoption in the womb, if not the actual spiritual birth, and the point when converts truly can claim God as their Father.

There are other works that mention the LP and baptismal catechesis from this time, but they are all anonymous works whose attribution to author and place are very difficult to make. These writings, as best as can be determined, confirm the idea that the late fourth and early fifth century was a time of transition with regard to the LP and baptismal catechesis.[109]

The Lord's Prayer in Theological Education

Besides teaching the LP to the newly baptized or catechumens, early church authors used the LP as an important text in exegetical and theological training of clergy and mature members of the faith.[110] In this context, the LP was used in a variety of situations and ways to help present Christian truth to mature members of the faith. For example, Gregory of Nyssa, Augustine, Chromatius of Aquileia, and the Arian author of the anonymous *Incomplete Commentary on Matthew*, were not shy about referring to the LP as a central text of theological education. The interpretations of these four authors later on through the Middle Ages became so important that they literally influenced nearly ever other interpretation of the LP that came after them for centuries, and perhaps indirectly even down to the modern age.

Gregory of Nyssa (ca. 335–395), the Cappadocian Father and brother of Saint Macrina, is one of the most famous early Eastern Christian authors to write a commentary on the LP. His five sermons on the topic are remarkable for their literary beauty, timeless metaphors, and freshness of interpretation, which includes an entire theology based on the wisdom of the LP. Gregory is no ordinary preacher, and anyone who reads these homilies will no doubt notice his clever prose, theological sophistication, and at times folksy and even earthy examination of the LP. Up until Gregory's day, only Cyprian and Origen's commentaries on the LP can be said to rival Gregory's comprehensive treatment of the subject, lucidity of language, beauty of imagery, and theological clarity.[111]

As mentioned in the first chapter, one of the most striking features of Gregory's approach to the LP is his remarkable sense of awe for Jesus' words. Although reverence for the LP is clearly a part of all previous commentaries, Gregory's amazement and language transcend earlier shows of respect. Commenting on the wonder of being able to simply call the Almighty God "Father," Gregory states,

> Who will give me those wings that my mind may wing its way up to the heights of these noble words [of the LP]? Then I would leave behind the earth altogether and traverse all the middle air; I would reach the beautiful ether, come to the stars and behold all their orderly array. But not even at these would I stop short, but, passing beyond them, would become a stranger to all that moves and changes and apprehend the stable Nature, the immovable Power which exists in its own right, guiding and keeping in being all things, for all depend on the ineffable will of the Divine Wisdom. So first my mind must become detached from anything subject to flux and change and tranquilly rest in motionless spiritual repose, so as to be rendered akin to Him who is perfectly unchangeable; and then it may address Him by this most familiar name and say, "Father."[112]

These words, and the rest of Gregory's commentary, remind one of the bold spirit of Origen's commentary on the LP, even though the specific content of the two works are at times quite different. In the previous chapter we have shown that Origen approached the LP in a one-of-a-kind way, asking questions of Jesus' prayer that others considered at worst heretical or at best not worthy of the parchment (e.g., the theological question concerning the foreknowledge of God and the LP and the practical issue of to whom prayer should properly be addressed). Gregory's concerns, although different, were no less theologically sophisticated than Origen's: Gregory, for example, was one of the most important theologians writing about the Trinity during his day, and he was unable to resist the opportunity to reflect on God's nature in his commentary.

Also like Origen, Gregory was eager to go into detail when talking about practical issues concerning prayer. Gregory begins his exposition of the LP by developing the entire first sermon around the problem of convincing people that they simply need to pray. He noted that even before he was able to begin working out a theology of prayer, he would have to somehow impress upon his audience, who possessed a remarkable lack of concern for prayer of any type, that they ought to pray regularly. Origen, however, was more concerned with the practical matters, for example, the proper posture for prayer.

It may be said at this point that a characteristic of early Greek or Eastern LP commentaries is that they tend to be similar in tone (i.e., theologically intricate—generally sophisticated in nature) and practical in orientation (i.e., offering specific advice on prayer—generally addressing concrete, everyday concerns), while at the same time tending to be individually unique in content. Generally speaking, there were often some minor points of theological agreement, but overall the works tend to stand alone without much repetition of ideas from commentary to commentary. Gregory also was not shy about holding a position that was contrary to the ideas expressed by Origen (e.g., see their views of the fourth petition, where Gregory interpreted bread as the need for a physical meal, while Origen only saw it as a spiritual feast).[113]

Origen and Gregory's commentaries remain to this day testaments to these great thinkers. And yet, few later commentaries borrow ideas from them in any depth, and therefore, the older works have remained relatively unique in their approach to the LP. The early Eastern works did have some influence on later authors in the East, but Origen's suspect theology limited his ideas about the LP from being picked up by many after him. Manuscripts of Gregory's works were rare in Greek, and didn't make their way into Latin, even though they circulated in Syriac, and so they too had a limited impact.[114]

In the West through the period covered in this book, however, there was a clear tradition of borrowing from earlier interpretations on the LP in both tone and content. Commentaries in the Latin West tended to build upon earlier commentaries like Cyprian's work, which had a tremendous influence on later writers. Some new ideas slowly develop in later works and they also were selectively incorporated further down the line, but the transition appears slow and deliberate. Tertullian's later-in-life Montanist leanings made his orthodoxy suspect, which is similar to Origen's problem. Tertullian's influence continued, however, because the orthodox Cyprian, who wrote one of the most popular early Latin commentaries on the LP, used Tertullian rather extensively. Origen in the East was not so fortunate.

Gregory of Nyssa's uniqueness of interpretation of the LP in particular involves his clear theology and examination of the Christian life in light of the LP. Gregory put forth his thoughts with such a sense of immediacy that even modern readers often feel the force of Gregory's words. His chastisements are as effective on a modern Christian audience as they were on ancient ones of his day.

Since Gregory's commentary remains unique, it is helpful to spell out his theology of the LP, which explains the nature of God and the Christian life. Gregory, in his first sermons on the LP, notes that prayer, generally speaking, is union with God. By contrast, a lack of prayer, or prayer for improper blessings (such as earthly wealth), means disunity with the Divine and attachment to worldly matters, evil, and the Devil. Human passions, such as lust after money, power, and fame, may indeed replace people's desire for God. Greed, pride, and the other vices destroy not only an individual's relationship with the Divine, but they undermine the entire fabric of society. A lack of prayer among Christians, therefore, is at the heart of all of the world's problems.[115]

Gregory's first sermon tackles this issue directly. People covetously long for earthly wealth or pleasure: they trade eternity for comfort in the moment of this present life, spiritual riches for transient goods, and even God for worldly power. Prayer, on the other hand, can cure all that ails the world: people simply need to recognize their need for prayer and pray as if their lives depended upon it, because for Gregory, in fact, they do. The following is a lengthy quote that will not only clarify Gregory's convictions on this point, but will also demonstrate to the reader Gregory's remarkable rhetorical ability at the same time:

> For the person who does not unite himself to God through prayer is separated from God. Therefore we must learn first of all that we ought always to pray and not to faint (Luke 18:1). For the effect of prayer is union with God, and if someone is with God, he is separated from the enemy. Through prayer we guard our chastity, control our temper, and rid ourselves of vanity; it makes us forget injuries, overcomes envy, defeats injustice, and makes amends for sin. Through prayer we obtain physical well-being, a happy home, and a strong, well-ordered society. Prayer will make our nation powerful, will give us victory in war and security in peace; it reconciles enemies and preserves allies. Prayer is the seal of virginity and a pledge of faithfulness in marriage; it shields the wayfarer, protects the sleeper, and gives courage to those who keep vigil. It obtains a good harvest for the farmer and a safe port for the sailor.

Prayer is your advocate in lawsuits. If you are in prison, it will obtain your release; it will refresh you when you are weary and comfort you when you are sorrowful. Prayer is the delight of the joyful as well as solace to the afflicted. It is the wedding crown of the spouses and the festive joy of a birthday no less than the shroud that enwraps us in death.

Prayer is intimacy with God and contemplation of the invisible. It satisfies our yearnings and makes us equal to the angels. Through it good prospers, evil is destroyed, and sinners will be converted. Prayer is the enjoyment of things present and the substance of things to come. Prayer turned the whale into a home for Jonah (Jonah 2:1ff.); it brought Hezekiah back to life from the very gates of death (2 Kings 20:1ff.); it transformed the flames into a moist wind for the Three Children (Daniel 3:19ff.). Through prayer the Israelites triumphed over the Amalecites, and 185,000 Assyrians were slain in one night by the invisible sword (2 Kings 19:35ff.). Past history furnishes thousands of other examples beside these which make it clear that of all the things valued in this life nothing is more precious than prayer.[116]

True prayer, for Gregory, longed for and ran after heavenly matters and even taught Christians what they ought to pray for. Unfortunately, people often dreamed about increasing their earthly wealth and fame, and so they pursued the fantasies of youth. Then, in a typical, but nevertheless remarkable, turn of phrase, Gregory declared that when people prayed for the foolishness of worldly goods, they were literally asking God to share in their own wanton passions. They asked nothing less than that the Divine should succumb to human vice and behave like, and literally become, a beast, which is what people who follow their own passions have become.[117] Such people, who drink from the bitter breast of sin and seek the lowest things from the Highest God, are utterly without hope unless they turn to prayer, where God transforms them into people who share in God's divine nature.[118]

After having established that people require true spiritual prayer in order to overcome evil and seek that which is good in their lives, Gregory turns to the greatest prayer of all: the LP. Prayer, especially the LP, teaches the faithful how to pray, says Gregory. The opening line of Gregory's first sermon on prayer states simply that, "The Divine Word (Logos) teaches us the science of prayer." Instruction in prayer then is nothing less than an introduction into the mystery of God and life. Gregory notes that, like Moses, who handed over the Law to the people of Israel, Jesus, the spiritual lawgiver, offered his people divine grace, leading them not to Mt. Sinai, but to heaven itself. Jesus in the LP presents Christians with a vision of Divine power and the reality of their kinship with God by virtue of the fact that they share in God's Divine nature. Ultimately, Jesus leads believers to God through prayer, of which the highest example is the LP.[119]

Gregory points out that the LP teaches the essence of what can be learned about the great mysteries. The first and greatest mystery of all that the LP teaches is the true nature of God. Gregory notes, when talking about God as revealed in the LP as "Father," that the Divine nature includes absolute goodness, holiness, joy, power, glory, purity, and eternity, while at the same time, God remains the same, or unchangeable.[120]

Later in Sermon 3, Gregory returns to the issue of the nature of God when discussing the third petition. Modern readers are often puzzled when Gregory casually notes that he, at this point, prefers what he calls Luke's version of this petition, which he quotes, "May your Holy Spirit come and purify us," instead of the more familiar version of Matthew: "Your kingdom come on earth as it is in heaven" (for more on this, see Chapter 2). Gregory, in Sermon 4, later takes up the third petition again, but this time he prefers to comment on Matthew's version of this petition. In some ways, Gregory is simply giving the two versions of the third petition equal time. However, Gregory favors the alternate Lucan third petition, in Sermon 3, over the more traditional one, because Luke's version emphasizes the Holy Spirit. Without this alternate Holy Spirit petition, the LP only talks of two persons of the Trinity: with it, however, Gregory feels that he can go into depth explaining all three persons of the Trinity in the context of the discussion of the LP.[121] The three persons of the Trinity, says Gregory, all share the same nature, "For the son of a carpenter is not called a bench, nor would any person in his right mind say that an architect had begot the house; but the names of Son and the Father signify what is joined together in the same nature." At the same time, the Trinity also demonstrates that each person of the Trinity has a "special characteristic" or personality that makes them unique, even though they have a common nature. Gregory explains this by saying, for example, that Christ and the Holy Spirit are like fire because they bear the qualities of light and heat: they illuminate sin and then purge people of their transgressions. So, argues Gregory, even though Christ and the Holy Spirit have distinct characters, they are nevertheless of the same nature, in the same way that one fire can both give off heat and light at the same time; therefore, one nature can indeed have a variety of characteristics, and for Gregory, this is most certainly true of the Trinity.[122]

Gregory goes on to argue that the nature of God in the Trinity is pure and holy. However, once he makes this claim, he is quick to point out that he has a problem: how can people, who are impure, changeable, self-seeking, and evil, claim that God, who is their opposite, is in fact their Father? Gregory feels that the LP teaches that God, who is "Our Father," calls people away from lives that would dishonor their Divine Creator and Parent. Therefore, the faithful ought to follow after "the most sublime life" so they will indeed be God's true children. Those who follow wanton ways, however, are children of the devil. The issue is one of nature. True children of God must have the same nature as their heavenly Father, namely, one of goodness and purity. If they do not, then by nature they are children of evil.[123]

Gregory adds that it is dangerous to pray the LP before one has been purified. To claim to be a child of the Merciful and Pure God, without being merciful and pure oneself, would be to claim that a corrupt nature is related to an incorrupt God, and this would be absurd. Rather, the hidden meaning of the words, "Our Father, who is in heaven" suggests that God honors and lives in relationship with those who lead lives of virtue. Christians are like the Prodigal Son (Luke 15); they have all turned away from the Father and squandered their birthrights. Gregory, in fact, develops the Prodigal Son story as a central theme of his LP commentary. The Prodigal, even though a child of the Father, rejects his familial relationship and wanders off into a far away land to find his own fame and fortune. However, lost in his sin, the Prodigal eventually realized the error of his ways. While living in squalor with pigs, the Prodigal decided to go back to the Father and his home not as a son, but hoping to become the Father's slave. The actual way back for the Prodigal, Gregory argued, was a road of confession. So also for all sinners, says Gregory, repentance is the only way to return to God, who in forgiveness clothes the repentant in the same way the Father dresses the Prodigal upon his return. First, the Father places upon the wayward one the original robe of obedience that he left behind when he first followed after his wanton pleasures. Likewise, the Father now places on his finger a ring, which signifies the regaining of the image of God. Repentant sinners, like the Prodigal Son, are given shoes by the Father, which will protect them from the deadly bite of the serpent, who strikes out at naked heels. In the end, the return of the Prodigal, like the return of any sinner, culminates in the loving embrace of the Father, who renews in the Prodigal a desire to do good works and to be a true and worthy child. By being restored to a virtuous life and by continuing in the way of the same virtue, true sons and daughters of God are restored to their true natures. The image and likeness of the Father is restored in them and they once again are worthy of the title of son or daughter of God, because they share in the same nature of their Father.[124]

Although Gregory does not directly discuss baptism in the previous passage, he does imply that it is in baptism that souls are prepared to speak with bold confidence the words "Our Father." Through baptism, Christians come to bear a resemblance to God in nature, and they shed the evil character traits of envy, hate, slander, conceit, cupidity, lust, and ambition, which is Gregory's concise list of seven vices. To pursue such evil ways of living is to claim the nature of the Devil, and therefore, kinship with wickedness. Rather, Gregory encourages the faithful to clothe themselves in the pure beauty of the Divine, which is free of the blemish of envy and passion.[125] The fact that Gregory is relatively silent on the subject of baptism is a bit unusual, given the content of other commentaries of the time. Cyril of Jerusalem and Ambrose of Milan are very specific in their references connecting baptism to the LP, as have been many authors. Gregory, on the other hand, appears to assume that baptism and the LP are intimately connected, but he is more interest in presenting his sermons on the LP to mature Christians and explaining to them what the LP teaches about life. Therefore, he can assume they will see the connection between baptism and the LP.

Gregory, in Sermon 3, continues to develop the metaphor of being clothed in righteousness, which he began in the explanation of the Prodigal Son story. Gregory here, however, talks about a priest who enters the Holy of Holies robed in beautiful gold, purple, and brilliant-colored clothes. Jesus, the spiritual lawgiver, gives to whoever desires it the grace of priesthood. However, the robes he places upon these new priests are not made of earthly gold and purple, but the gold of a pure conscience and the purple of virtue, that is, Christ's own nature. Their breasts shine with the rays of the commandments, and on their shoulders are the great saints of old. Christ also gives these priests the pants of chastity and fruits, flowers, and bells worthy of their office and paradise. The Holy of Holies is understood not as a building but as the inner part of the hearts of Christians; their heads receive gold wreaths for right reasoning, and they are anointed with holy ointment upon their hair. The priest is thus made ready as an acceptable sacrifice to God. In fact, Jesus himself in the end is clothed with a robe made up of the priests' virtues, with a crown of justice, and he is anointed with heavenly oil, because he dwells in a heavenly Holy of Holies.[126]

At this point in the commentary, Gregory offers some typical explanations of the first two petitions, and these explanations essentially emphasize how God's name is made holy, and how the kingdom comes to those who share in the nature of God through virtuous living. To make this point, he discusses the nature of the Trinity and the third petition, as has been mentioned earlier.[127]

In Chapter 4, Gregory continues his discussion of the third and fourth petitions. Now, however, he shifts to a medical metaphor to explain his views. Gregory, after having consulted a medical expert, concludes that health is the proper proportion of elements—namely, fire, water, earth, and air—which make up the human body. Illness is an imbalance of these elements. For example, too much heat in the body, or fever, is a sign of illness. The remedy is to seek balance, or to cool off the body. Spiritual health, says Gregory, works the same way, except instead of one of the four elements, the person's soul requires the balance of virtue over and against the illness of vice, which threatens to destroy people. Sin is the disease, and the good physician knows that to counter the illness of the poison of disobedience, for example, it must be countered with the medicine of obedience to the will of God. In this case, Jesus is the model, because he was also faced with the temptation to disobey his Father in the garden of Gethsemane, but he remained true by appealing to the petition of the LP, "Your will be done." Since humans are spirit and body and require health in both, they must be attentive to the proper medicines, which involve living the virtuous life. As a result, Gregory's discussion of the fourth petition, on bread, is basically about how Christians are not to be overcome by gluttony, delicacies, and worries about the morrow, for such things consume the rich. Rather, God grants them their daily bread, or all their daily needs, which includes bread, and that is enough. Believers should focus on God's kingdom, not on earthly wealth.[128]

Gregory's last sermon deals with the final three petitions and the key element of the virtue of forgiveness. All who forgive others not only act like God, but they also share in God's true nature. Then, with a remarkable bit of holy audacity, Gregory declares that when people forgive others, they literally become examples to God. God wants Christians to be their own judges, to acquit themselves of being unforgiving, says Gregory, by being gracious to others. Therefore, when the faithful forgive, this bold act is ratified by God, and God literally follows their example, as the LP says, "Forgive us our debts as we forgive our debtors." The King of the Universe imitates the poor beggar, because the charity of the beggar is a true aspect of God's loving nature. Those who forgive others are worthy examples for God, who willingly follows their lead. Says Gregory,

> Adam is, as it were, living in us, we see each other and all these garments of skin around our nature, and also the transitory fig leaves of this material life which we have badly sewn together for ourselves after being stripped of our own resplendent garments. For instead of the Divine garments we have put on luxuries and reputation, transitory honors and the quickly passing satisfactions of the flesh, at least as long as we look at this place of distress in which we have been condemned to sojourn . . . Having been wrapped up in these things (the passions), let us imitate the Prodigal Son after he had endured the long affliction of feeding the swine. When, like him, we return to ourselves and remember the Heavenly Father, we may rightly use these words: *Forgive us our debts*.[129]

Once again, the story of the Prodigal Son comes to the forefront. The LP ultimately, for Gregory, suggests that the way of prayer mirrors that of the life of the Prodigal, namely, it is a way of repentance by which one's true nature is restored. This nature unites believers with God, and thus worldly desires are left behind and prodigal sinners reclaim their true heavenly nature. Once changed, prodigals are able to forgive others in a way that is worthy of God's imitation.

Gregory concludes his final sermon by suggesting that, in the end, God continues to aid the faithful in retaining their divine natures by not leading them into temptation and by delivering them from evil. This is done by separating them from evil and creating in them a desire to be a long way away from any temptation or danger of vice. Says Gregory,

The sea is often dangerous on account of its mighty waves, but not to those who are far removed from it. Fire destroys, but only if flammable matter is near it. War is full of danger, but only to those who take part in battle. As, therefore, a man who wants to escape the terrible calamities of war prays not to become involved in it, and another one who fears fire asks not to find himself in such; as a third one who abhors the sea prays that he may not be obliged to go on a voyage; so also he who fears the assault of the evil one should pray that he may not fall into it.[130]

Gregory's LP commentary stands as a testament to how an entire theology which explains everything from God to the Christian life can be developed from the few words of Jesus' prayer and then be imparted to the faithful in a compelling, enlightening, and educational manner.

Augustine of Hippo is another key example of a theologian who frequently called upon the LP to educate mature members of the faith and to train pastors theologically with regard to matters of doctrine and Christian living. Sometime after the sack of Rome by Alaric of the Ostrogoths in 410, Augustine wrote a letter[131] (perhaps in 412) to a Roman noble widow named Proba, who during her life watched three of her own sons sit as consul in Rome. She fled to Africa in the wake of the Ostrogoth turmoil and established a community of religious women in Carthage. Proba, on one occasion, wrote to Augustine seeking advice on prayer. He responded by sending her a lengthy epistle, a part of which included a full explanation of the LP. The bishop of Hippo instructed Proba not to put her trust in her considerable riches (some believe her husband was one of the wealthiest men in the Roman Empire) but encouraged her to pray instead for true happiness with unceasing and fervent ardor.[132] After cautioning her not to pray with an abundance of words, Augustine noted that words were nevertheless necessary to communicate one's petitions to the Divine. While Jesus was on earth, he, unlike other people, had no need of words in his prayers, to be either informed or influenced by them; still he used them, like the words of the LP, and is a model for humanity. Therefore, reasoned Augustine, a careful use of words in prayer is worthy of anyone longing to catch the ear of God.

Augustine told Proba that the concise words of the LP, in particular, have a twofold function. First, they have the power to make the petitioners aware of what they need to pray for. Second, the words actually create a desire for what is petitioned and encourage those who pray them to lead godly lives. For example, when Christians pray the first three petitions, they long for God's name to be holy, God's kingdom to come, and God's will to be done in all people. The fourth petition is a longing for Christ, the bread of heaven, eternal happiness. The last three petitions move petitioners to long for forgiveness and to forgive earnestly, to escape from temptation, and to seek deliverance from evil. Finally, the words of the LP reveal and encourage what God hopes to impress upon the hearts, minds, and lives of all.[133]

Augustine then offered a brief petition-by-petition analysis of the LP, after which he stated that "all" properly offered prayers seek those truths that are embodied in it. Augustine, like Cyprian,[134] went so far as to say that false prayer is any request that pursues something outside of the parameters of the seven petitions of the LP. Augustine warned, "But, whoever says anything in his prayer which does not accord with this Gospel prayer, even if his prayer is not of the forbidden sort, it is carnal, and I am not sure it ought not to be called forbidden, since those who are born again of the spirit ought to pray only in a spiritual manner."[135]

At this point in the discussion, Augustine made his allusion to baptism in his letter to Proba. To pray in a way that is contrary to the spirit of the LP is sinful, said Augustine: in other words, the way Christians would have prayed before they were baptized. But after being baptized, those who are born again in the spirit need to pray spiritually, or in a way consistent with the LP. Thus, the LP was Augustine's model and rule by which all righteous prayer was to be judged.

Augustine embellished this point rather forcefully by presenting seven brief prayers that reflect the concerns of each of the seven petitions of the LP. However, Augustine readily acknowledged that it is not always easy to tell how some prayers conform to the LP. For example, Hannah's prayer for God to end her barrenness[136] does not appear to be related to any of the seven petitions. Augustine concluded, however, that Hannah's words are to be understood in light of the seventh petition, "Deliver us from evil," because Hannah's barrenness is an evil from which she wishes to be delivered. Therefore, all true prayers always conform to the LP even if they do not necessarily appear to do so at first glance. Augustine concluded this section by boldly declaring, "And if you were to run over all the words of holy prayers, you would find nothing, according to my way of thinking, which is not contained and included in the Lord's Prayer. Hence when we pray, it is allowable to say the same things in different words, but it ought not to be allowable to say different things."[137]

Augustine also briefly developed a theme in his letter to Proba that he discussed more fully in his *Enchiridion*.[138] For Augustine, the three theological virtues of faith, hope, and love work together with the LP to bring Christians into a closer relationship with God. Augustine claimed, "Therefore, 'faith, hope, and love' lead to God those who pray—that is, those people who believe, hope, and desire and who consider what they ask of the Lord in the Lord's Prayer."[139]

Laurentius, a "spiritual son" of Augustine, wrote to the bishop of Hippo ca. 421 asking him to compose an *Enchiridion* (i.e., a "handbook") in order to answer some questions about the essential doctrines of the Christian faith. Augustine responded by saying, "Now, undoubtedly, you will know the answers to all these questions, if you know thoroughly the proper objects of faith, hope, and love. For these must be the chief, nay, the exclusive objects of pursuit in religion. He who speaks against these is either a total stranger to the name of Christ, or is a heretic."[140] Augustine then stated that the basic elements of the Christian faith may be summarized in the two essential prayers of the church: the Apostles' Creed and the LP.[141] These prayers correspond to the three theological virtues. Faith, which believes, is represented by the Creed. Hope and love, which pray, are represented by the LP.[142] The overall structure of the *Enchiridion* emphasizes this connection. Chapters 1–113 explain the Apostles' Creed and faith; chapters 114–116 discuss the LP and hope; and chapters 117–122 deal with love, which is God, the object of prayer and the fulfillment of all that believers seek and desire. Augustine primarily related the LP with the virtue of hope, even though he at times equated it with love as well.[143]

The LP and the Creed complement each other in such a way, for Augustine and many early church authors, that taken together, they encompass the whole of the Christian faith. While the LP is able to be a perfect summary of the faith, the one issue that it does not deal with fully (unless you are Gregory of Nyssa, with an alternative reading of the LP) is the nature of the divine. The Creed fills this gap, and Christians who study it are more readily able to come to know the God in whom they believe. With the LP, they call upon this God with a certain hope that God, who is love, will answer their prayers. For Augustine, it doesn't make sense that believers can call upon a God that they do not know, and so the Creed is essential. Nor can they call upon God without the words of hope in the LP, and so it is possible to have the LP be a complete summary of the faith, but if one has access to the Creed, then all the better. As a result, it made sense for Augustine to start his handbook with a lengthy explanation of the Creed and God, and then to move on to the LP.[144]

In works other than Augustine's *Enchiridion*, the LP and the Creed were often discussed together in early church documents; the earliest documents that included these two prayers side by side come from the turn of the fifth century. Both Ambrose and Augustine often commented on them at the same time. As has already been shown, the two prayers were linked because they were both taught in baptismal catechesis. The *Enchiridion*, which was written toward the end of Augustine's life, is one of the best examples of how the association between the Creed and LP was used to summarize the entirety of the faith for mature members.

For Augustine, the LP gives hope because of the fifth petition, on forgiveness. The brief section on the LP in the *Enchiridion*, chapters 114–116, follows a lengthy and detailed analysis of the Creed. Augustine, in these later chapters, does not discuss the LP in any great detail (nor does he offer a verse-by-verse analysis), because he has already mentioned it six times in chapters 1–113. In each of these instances, Augustine principally discussed what he called "the thunderous warning"[145] of the fifth petition. Christians, all of whom continue to sin after their baptisms, have to be cautious concerning the fifth petition because of its conditional clause, "Forgive us our debts, *as* we forgive our debtors." Sinners must forgive others if they wish to be forgiven themselves. This warning, when heeded, can raise those who are dead in sin to new life in Christ; if it is ignored, eternal condemnation results.[146] Thus, the fifth petition, and by extension the entire LP, offers the very real hope of salvation.

Augustine even went so far as to state in the *Enchiridion* that praying the LP daily makes satisfaction for daily sins or sins of a more venial nature. Augustine wrote, "This [Lord's] prayer certainly takes away the very small sins of daily life. It takes away also those which at one time made the life of the believer very wicked, but which, now that he is changed for the better by repentance, he has given up, provided that as truly as he says, 'Forgive us our debts' (for there is no want of debts to be forgiven), so truly does he say, 'as we forgive our debtors.' "[147] Serious sins, of course, are washed away in baptism, and after baptism, greater sins require not only prayer for forgiveness, but a radical amendment of life together with a willingness to forgive the sins of others. Alms given out of mercy likewise cleanse the soul of sin, but the greatest of all alms, for Augustine, is that of a Christian forgiving the sinful debt of another. Augustine reasoned that alms can only be given by those who have the means to do so, whereas all have the ability to forgive the debt of others, regardless of their financial status, and so these alms are therefore the greatest and most universally available.[148]

Augustine's preoccupation with the fifth petition was also a frequent topic in his sermons, where he emphasized this petition more than any of the others. Sermon 213 (written ca. 410–412) further clarifies why "daily" prayer of the LP, and the fifth petition, is so important. Since Augustine believed that Christians are not allowed to be baptized more than once, Christians need another way of returning to the baptismal font; they need a "daily" baptism in order to deal with daily sins. Sermon 213 makes the stark claim that the LP is a "daily baptism" and an important means by which sinful believers may be reconciled to God regularly. Christians appropriate God's forgiveness not only through amendment of life and alms, but through two baptisms: the first baptism in the waters of the font, and the second baptism in the words of the LP. In particular, the praying of the fifth petition makes this second baptism a reality in the lives of believers. The wonderful gift of this daily baptism, noted Augustine, ought to move the recipients of so great a grace to nothing less than heartfelt, thankful praise.[149]

Augustine, in a few of his sermons on the Gospel of John, presented a similar point. In his discussion about the story concerning Jesus washing the feet of the disciples (John 13), Augustine notes that the water symbolizes both baptism and the LP. Both wash away sins in the same way that Jesus washed the dirt away from the disciples' feet.[150]

The strong emphasis that Augustine placed upon the LP as a means of the forgiveness of sins is something that he returned to frequently. In fact, in the context of his sermons, this is the one theme that Augustine reiterates more often than any other with regard to the LP. Excluding Sermons 56–59, where he deals with all the petitions in a verse-by-verse fashion, the sermons of Augustine that refer to the LP almost invariably focus upon the fifth petition and forgiveness. The following sermons (and their approximate dates) all include discussions of fifth petition: Sermon 9 written ca. 420, Sermon 16A ca. 411, Sermon 17 ca. 425–431(?), Sermon 47 ca. 414, Sermon 49 ca. 420, Sermons 56–59 ca. 410–412, Sermon 114 ca. 424, Sermon 135 ca. 417, Sermon 155 ca. 419, Sermon 163 ca. 417, Sermon 163B ca. 410, Sermon 179 ca. before 409, Sermon 181 ca. 416, Sermon 211 ca. before 410, Sermon 213 ca. 410, Sermon 278 ca. 414, Sermon 315 ca. 416/417, Sermon 352 ca. 398, Sermon 383 uncertain date, and sermon 385 uncertain date.[151] Augustine believed that the LP continues the work of baptism by offering a means of returning to it daily. This emphasis upon the fifth petition is something that can be seen in other authors as well.[152]

Augustine noted in his treatise *On Holy Virginity*[153] that all Christians, even newly baptized converts, are in need of the LP and the fifth petition, on forgiveness. If this were not the case, then the church would teach *competentes* to pray the LP up until their baptism and then stop, but instead, the church teaches those who are baptized to pray the LP, because all sin and fall short of the glory of God (Romans 3:23).[154]

Augustine even mentioned the fifth petition in his rule. He referred to the fifth petition twice in order to urge Christians not to quarrel, but to be forgiving. Similarly, they must also seek forgiveness in order to avoid temptation (the sixth petition).[155]

The preceding evidence indicates that Augustine understood the LP to have a sacramental quality to it. Augustine's understanding of a sacrament is not easily defined.[156] The reason for this is that Augustine himself operated with various definitions of sacrament at the same time. First and foremost, Augustine defined a sacrament as a sign or symbol that pointed beyond itself to a holy reality. Sacraments not only resemble the realities they represent, but they become channels of grace by which the sacred, signified truth becomes a part of the lives of believers and therefore sacraments participate in the reality they reflect.[157] Words, actions, and objects can be sacraments, so long as they point to a sacred reality, such as salvation. Augustine assumed that since this is true, the word "sacrament" may be understood in both a broad and narrow sense.

Broadly speaking, Augustine argued that there are numerous sacraments in the Old and New Testaments, the life of the church, and even in other religions. Some modern scholars refer to these as sacramentals. Sacraments (perhaps the word *sacramentum* in this instance can also be translated "mysteries") of the Old Testament (e.g., the

Sabbath, circumcision, sacrifices, ceremonies, the temple, altars, feasts, the priesthood, anointing, and observations with food) were used by the Jews at one time in order to increase fidelity to God. For Augustine, they existed only temporarily because they became restrictive, a yoke of laws, and a symbol and reality of servitude. In the end, Augustine's allegorical interpretation of scripture allowed nearly every part of the Old Testament to be representative of some New Testament reality: in these instances, Old Testamental mysteries took on a sacramental reality.

Similarly, Augustine's allegorical interpretation of the New Testament allowed nearly every word, event, or object therein to be a representation and reality of some heavenly mystery (e.g., Easter, miracles, anointing, the cross, the laying on of hands, feasts, Amens, and Alleluias). With regard to the life of the church, Augustine called various rites sacraments as well. Such rites included salt on lips, exorcisms, contemplation, the penitential garment, the bowing of one's head, the taking off of one's shoes, the handing over of the *symbolum*, the entry into the catechumenate, the laying on of hands, reconciliation, great feasts and fasts, spiritual songs, and so forth. Other religions, like the ones practiced by some Greeks and Romans, also had sacraments, but for Augustine they served no useful purpose since they did not necessarily lead people to God and often led them astray.[158]

Narrowly speaking, the New Testament, according to Augustine, can at the same time be said to have fewer sacraments than the Old Testament, but New Testament sacraments are nevertheless greater in effectiveness and more useful because they offer freedom. In particular, baptism, the Eucharist, and extreme unction are sacraments of special note, because they are distinguishable from the more broadly conceived sacraments in Augustine's writings. What sets these "visible words" apart is that in them, the word is attached to a physical element in order that God might make absolutely clear the grace bestowed. Likewise, they are greater realities because they point to Christ's death and resurrection specifically.[159] Still, both the broadly and narrowly construed sacraments, for Augustine, bring the believer into a closer relationship with God and the entire Christian community, even if they do so by varying degrees.

Augustine, however, did not define his notion of sacrament as clearly as modern scholars would like. For example, Augustine compared *sacramentum* to a wide range of concepts—figures (*figura*), allegory (*allegoria*), prophecy (*prophetia*), veils (*velamen*), and symbols (*symbolum*)[160]—and so Augustine's works ultimately remain somewhat ambiguous on this subject.

Augustine considered the LP to be a sacrament: at times he talks about the LP as a sacrament in the broad sense of the term and at other times in the narrow sense. The LP is ultimately a sacrament, for Augustine, in that petitioners seek forgiveness through the fifth petition and actually attain forgiveness on account of the fact that they offer up of the words of Jesus in faith. The LP is not only a sign that points to a heavenly reality, namely, forgiveness, but it is also the means by which such forgiveness is accomplished. Clearly, Augustine did not understand the LP as a sacrament only in a narrow sense, because there is no physical element connected with the word. Still, Augustine did not simply understand the LP as a sacrament in the broadest sense, because of the LP's significant role as a daily baptism that aids the believer in attaining not only forgiveness, but salvation as well.

If we compare the LP to the Creed (or the other broad sacraments mentioned earlier), we notice that the Creed is a sacrament for Augustine because it reveals the nature of God to believers and in doing so brings the faithful into a closer relationship with God. However, the LP's intimate connection to baptism through the fifth petition—and the idea that it is a daily baptism—sets it apart as a vehicle by which, at the very least, venial sins may be removed. The Creed mentions the forgiveness of sins, but it does not function in a way that brings about forgiveness directly. The LP does. The LP, therefore, operates somewhere between the broad and narrow definitions Augustine puts forth in that it participates as an extension of baptism in the daily lives of individuals. As a "daily" baptism, it does what baptism does not do: it forgives sins over and over again throughout the life of the faithful. Similarly, as a daily "baptism," it forgives sins in a way that the other broader sacraments do not, namely, even though it is not a removal of original sin, it removes venial transgressions that stand in the way of reconciliation with God. In other words, the LP is a sacrament unlike any other in Augustine's theology. Some modern scholars call the LP a sacramental in Augustine's theological world; however, it seems better to call it a sacrament in order to emphasize its participatory quality of being a daily baptism that brings about that which it seeks, namely, forgiveness and salvation.

Augustine also spent a good deal of time explaining the LP in a scholarly or exegetical fashion. In this context, the LP interprets, and is interpreted by, other parts of the scripture. We have already seen a similar discussion of this in Cyprian. However, Augustine takes this principle to new, creative heights. Augustine, while still a young priest in Hippo, wrote his commentary *On the Sermon on the Mount* (ca. 393–396). His motivation for writing this work had to do in part with his belief that chapters 5–7 of Matthew represented what he called "the perfect manner of Christian living."[161] He wrote this commentary to educate mature Christians, priests, and scholars (who in turn were to educate the laity) in the ways of Christian morality and truth.

The section on the LP includes a sophisticated exegetical comparison of the seven petitions of the LP, the seven beatitudes (Augustine's numbering of what appears to be, on the surface, eight beatitudes) of Matthew 5, and the seven gifts of the Holy Spirit in Isaiah 11. Augustine notes that it was no simple mathematical coincidence that each of these three important scriptural texts had seven parts to them; for him, God must have created the numerical similarities for the purpose of teaching truth. The three groups of seven, Augustine believed, ought to be carefully examined together in order to understand what lessons God intended to teach through them. Augustine combined the three groups of seven in a creative way in order to discover, and ultimately reveal, what he considered to be their spiritual relationship and message.

First of all, Augustine noted that the eight beatitudes of Matthew 5:3–10 are not really eight, but seven. To prove his point, Augustine pointed out that the first beatitude, "Blessed are the poor in spirit, for they shall inherit the kingdom of God," has the same blessing (i.e., the kingdom of heaven) as the eighth beatitude, "Blessed are they that suffer persecution for justice's sake, for theirs is the kingdom of heaven." Augustine concluded that since they share the same reward, the first and last beatitude are therefore, in fact, one and the same. Hence, there are only seven beatitudes.

Augustine called the seven beatitudes maxims (*sententiae*), or degrees (*gradus*).[162] The maxims of the seven beatitudes each correspond to the sevenfold operation of the Holy Spirit of Isaiah 11:2. The seven gifts of the Holy Spirit, said Augustine, are meant to be understood as levels of ascending gradation, moving from the lesser gift (the fear of the Lord, which is the *beginning* of wisdom) to the highest gift (wisdom itself). Isaiah 11 lists these gifts beginning with the greatest gift, wisdom, first; then it descends through the lesser gifts down to the first gift, the fear of God. Augustine reversed the order so that the gifts would line up in a proper manner with the beatitudes. These two groups were then in turn both compared side by side with the seven petitions of the LP.

The following chart illustrates how Augustine made his comparison:

Table 3.2 Augustine's Exegetical Comparison in his Commentary *On the Sermon on the Mount*

Gifts of Spirit	Beatitudes	LP Petitions
Isaiah 11:2–3	Matthew 6:9–13	Matthew 5:3–10
Fear of God: *Timor Dei*	Poor in Spirit: *Pauperes Spiritu*	Holy be your name
Godliness: *Pietas*	The Meek: *Mites*	Your kingdom come
Knowledge: *Scientia*	Those who mourn: *Qui lugent*	Your will be done, on earth as in heaven
Fortitude: *Fortitudo*	Those who hunger and thirst for righteousness: *Qui esuriunt et sitiunt iustitiam*	Give us this day our daily bread
Counsel: *Consilium*	The Merciful: *Misericordes*	Forgive us our debts as we forgive our debtors
Understanding: *Intellectus*	The Pure in Heart: *Mundicordes*	Lead us not into temptation
Wisdom: *Sapientia*	Peacemakers: *Pacifici*	But deliver us from evil.

By lining up the three groups of seven in this way, Augustine believed that he was able to explain the various aspects, or degrees, of the Christian life. For example, about the first level of comparison Augustine wrote:

> It seems to me that this number seven which attaches to these petitions corresponds to the number seven from which this whole sermon began [i.e., the beatitudes].[163] For if it is the fear of the Lord [i.e., gift of the Holy Spirit] through which the poor in spirit are blessed, because theirs is the kingdom of heaven [i.e., the beatitude], let us pray that the name of God may be hallowed [i.e., the petition of the LP] among all through holy fear enduring for ever and ever.[164]

Augustine developed a formula whereby he was able to interpret these scriptures. In this instance, the formula works this way: people who embody a particular beatitude are blessed by the corresponding gift of the Spirit, so that they will possess the accompanying promise of the aforementioned beatitude when they pray the corresponding petition. The preceding thought can be said more simply: Augustine declared that people need to pray the petitions of the LP in order that they might attain the corresponding gifts of the Spirit and embody the beatitudes in their lives. Christians progress from the lowest to the highest level, where finally the peacemakers (the beatitude) are blessed through wisdom (the gift of the Holy Spirit) and are called children of God (the promise of the beatitude). They must pray to be delivered from evil (the seventh petition of the LP) in order to cry out to God as "Abba, Father" in a spirit of adoption. Augustine firmly believed that this was attainable by all Christians while on earth.

This highest level is the one place in all of the seven comparisons where baptism, that is, the adoption, is mentioned. The culmination of the Christian's progress toward a life of faith ends where it begins: in a close relationship with God the Father, who is made the parent of converts through baptism. Indeed, to come to the seventh or highest degree is to acknowledge the reality of the first petition and the first stage of the Christian life, namely, that God is Father and Christians are in a right relationship with God as adoptive children.[165]

The blessings that petitioners seek in the LP pour out upon them in a limited and temporary manner as gifts and beatitudes while they are on earth, but one day they will be perfected eternally in the world to come.[166] In the case of the first level of comparison, those who are poor in spirit (the beatitude) are blessed through their fear of the Lord (the gift of the Holy Spirit) and their reward will be the kingdom of heaven (the gift offered in the beatitude). For this reason, Christians ought to pray "holy be your name" (the first petition) so that God's name will be holy and honored among all here and now, even though it won't truly be holy until the day when the faithful come to their heavenly home.

Why did Augustine compare the seven gifts, beatitudes, and petitions? As previously mentioned, Augustine used the LP most often in works that were baptismal-catechetic in nature. Both the LP and the gifts of the Holy Spirit played an important part within the actual rite of baptism. The baptismal rite that Augustine was familiar with involved both an invocation of the seven gifts of the Spirit of Isaiah 11, and the praying of the LP. After the baptism, unction, and imposition of hands, a blessing was bestowed by the presiding priest, who prayed for the sevenfold gift of the Spirit to come upon those baptized. This was a request for "the spirit of wisdom and understanding, the spirit of counsel and fortitude, the spirit of knowledge and godliness, the spirit of the fear of the Lord" to descend upon those who had recently emerged from the waters of the baptismal font.[167] Therefore, the Isaiah 11 text was a part of the baptismal liturgy. Shortly thereafter in the baptismal rite, the LP was prayed by the initiate for the first time. Since both the LP and Isaiah 11:2 were central in the baptismal liturgy, and since there is what might be called a natural juxtaposition of these texts within the actual liturgy of baptism that Augustine was familiar with, it is not unexpected that the bishop of Hippo would, in a similar manner, place these two groups of seven side by side.

The origin of the comparison between the seven beatitudes and the seven gifts of the Holy Spirit is not as obvious. Very early on in his commentary *On the Sermon on the Mount*, Augustine contrasts the beatitudes and gifts before he compares the three groups together.[168] Did the paralleling of the beatitudes and gifts have any logical connection, like the petitions and the gifts? It appears that the LP itself is the point of contact between both of the other two groups of seven. The LP shares the biblical context of the Sermon on the Mount with the beatitudes, and the baptismal context with the gifts of the Spirit. Since there is no apparent connection between the beatitudes and gifts besides the number seven, the LP is the point of comparison between the other two groups. Thus, Augustine, knowing that he intended to make a threefold comparison between the beatitudes, gifts, and petitions later on in his work, contrasted the gifts and beatitudes early on in order to set up the later comparison. Scripture interprets itself, and since all three groups share the same number, at least in Augustine's numbering system, and similar contexts and concepts, Augustine boldly declared, "Seven in number, therefore, are the things which lead to perfection."[169] Thus, the comparison of the three groups of seven revealed for Augustine how Christians are to live and the way that God brings salvation to them.

Augustine relied on the LP to interpret the gifts and beatitudes, and visa versa, but not until Isidore of Seville (d. 636) and Amalarius of Metz (d. 850) would other scholars return to this same method of comparing sevens. Even Augustine never used it again. After Amalarius, this numerical exegetical approach would not be employed until the twelfth century, but after that time it became more common. A few notable authors who used this type of exegesis later on are Hugh of St. Victor (d. 1142), Peter Lombard (d. 1160), Jordan of Quedlinburg (d. 1340), and Johannes Herolt (d. 1468).[170]

The LP was a sacramental prayer for Augustine, a prayer of hope and forgiveness, grace and salvation, and the very extension of baptism into the everyday lives of believers. Not only was the LP the first prayer out of the baptized believers' mouths, but it was the prayer that moved the faithful to daily return to the hope of their baptism. The mystery, wonder, and power of the LP cannot be understated for Augustine, especially when one looks at it in light of the rest of the Bible. Its seven petitions not only sum up the truth of the scriptures, but they are intimately entwined with other sevenfold realities, such as the beatitudes and gifts of the Spirit, and the LP is able to impart what it calls for, that is, forgiveness.

The LP itself is a sacramental seed that has the ability to help the Christian life to germinate in the hearts of converts even before they have been baptized. Truly, for Augustine, this is a mystery worth contemplating and treasuring. Granted, Augustine did not guard this prayer with a shroud of secrecy as closely as his teacher Ambrose had done, but he nevertheless still held the LP with a mysteriously sacramental respect that he believed the prayer deserved.

Others also taught the LP to the educated pastors and the mature faithful of their congregations. Chromatius of Aquileia's (d. 407) short and remarkably influential sermons on the LP put forth a concise explanation of the LP, which borrowed primarily from Tertullian and Cyprian.[171] Augustine also quoted these authors frequently, and so Chromatius' and Augustine's interpretations often look very similar as well. What we see by the end of the fourth and beginning of the fifth century is a core orthodox interpretation that emerges especially in the writings of Augustine, but also in Chromatius, and that nearly everyone after them throughout the Middle Ages will refer to in some fashion.

Chromatius' *Preface to the Lord's Prayer,* which would later find its way into the late sixth- or early seventh-century Gelasian Sacramentary, became very influential for preachers and authors as the Gelasian Sacramentary became well known, as has been noted earlier.[172] The basic interpretation of the LP in the few short sermons of Chromatius can be summed up rather easily. Their literal approach to the LP is not particularly original, but Chromatius' synthesis was influential in that it was repeated at least in part by numerous later authors.

The concise commentary of Chromatius certainly noted the importance of the first three heavenly petitions over and against the final earthly petitions; nevertheless he spent a majority of his time discussing the fourth and fifth petitions.

For Chromatius, the phrase "Give us this day our daily bread" means that Christians pray daily for spiritual food, that is, Christ, who is the bread of life (John 6:14, 52). The faithful pray for this daily in order that they might attain spiritual healing, be found worthy of Christ, and in the end, not be separated from Jesus, the true bread of life; though not stated specifically, it seems reasonable to imagine that Chromatius implies that this bread is connected with the Eucharist. In his longer sermon on Matthew 6:9–15, Chromatius also added that bread means earthly nourishment (food, clothing, and earthly necessities) and that Christians, in this sense, pray only for their daily needs and not for accumulating riches. In this way, the faithful are also able to not worry about tomorrow.[173]

Chromatius' *Preface to the Lord's Prayer* also has a decidedly eschatological tone. The baptized should keep God's name holy, desire God's kingdom to come to them, and seek to do God's will so that they might persevere (a strong theme in both Cyprian and Augustine) as true daughters and sons of God and come to salvation. The fourth petition says nothing about earthly physical bread, but it does note that Christ is the bread who frees people from sin and brings them to life everlasting. Believers should forgive others so that they may be forgiven and seek God's deliverance from temptation and evil in order that they may attain eternal life on the last day. Therefore, the beloved of God hear and pray the LP so that they may go out into the world, keep this mystery fresh in their hearts, be perfect in Christ, obtain the mercy of Almighty God, and come safely unto the promised kingdom of God. This emphasis is important throughout the history of the interpretation of the LP.[174]

While the previous comments reflect orthodox attitudes toward the LP, we are fortunate to also have one commentary of Arian origins on the LP. An Arian bishop (or priest) wrote a commentary on Matthew during the early to mid-fifth century in the Roman Province of Illyricum, or perhaps in Dacia or Moesia (i.e., in and around the area formerly known as Yugoslavia). Some modern scholars originally thought the work was composed in Greek, but Josef Banning and others have shown that it originated in Latin.[175] Unfortunately, the commentary has only survived in an incomplete form, hence the name *An Incomplete Work on Matthew*. Fortunately for our purposes, the work includes the section on the LP.[176]

The commentary survived—despite the destruction of Arian documents by orthodox authorities—largely because it was at times attributed to John Chrysostom. In the Middle Ages, parts of the commentary became well known; Banning has noted that it "was one of the favorite patristic works of Thomas Aquinas," and this also helped to ensure its popularity. Approximately two hundred manuscripts remain today. Erasmus included it in his edition of Chrysostom's writings (ca. 1530) in order to preserve it, but the erudite reformer denied Chrysostom's connection to the work and speculated that the author was an Arian.[177]

The commentary itself is not polemical in style, but rather, it is a detailed exegetical analysis of the first gospel. Numerous theological and historical references belie the authors' Arian tendencies. The PG 56 divides the commentary into homilies, but this is misleading, because originally this was not the case. The incomplete commentary is significant because it is one of a few early commentaries on Matthew; it provides important evidence for pre-Vulgate Latin translations of the Bible, it is one of the main documents that survives from the later period of Arianism, it reveals much about the development of later classical Latin,[178] and it offers the only detailed extra-Catholic interpretation of the LP during the period covered in this book.

The author either did not know or refused to use Augustine in his commentary.[179] Schnurr has pointed out that some themes from Augustine may be found in this commentary, but most of these ideas may be found elsewhere, for example, in Cyprian or Tertullian. As an opponent of Arian theology, Augustine would no doubt have been a source this author wanted to avoid, even if they overlapped in part on some issues.[180]

The Arian author, however, did not ignore traditional interpretations of the LP as some might suppose. Familiar themes from Cyprian are developed. For example, the anonymous author related to his readers that they pray "Our Father" and not "my Father" because the LP is concerned with all people. Likewise, he noted that God is not made holy by prayer, but in this prayer, Christians ask that God may be made holy in them. When believers pray that God's will be done, they seek that it may be done in their lives. The last two themes are also in Tertullian.

The Arian author in his discussion of the fifth petition mentioned that some avoided praying this petition despite praying the rest of the LP: the concern was of course that people who didn't forgive others were asking God not to forgive them in turn. This is very similar to a concern of Cassian (ca. 360–425), the great monastic author from Gaul, who will be discussed later in this chapter. Cassian noted that some monks refused to pray the words, "... *as we forgive others*," because they did not desire or were unable to forgive those who had sinned against them. There may also be other references here to Ambrose, Chromatius, Origen, and Gregory of Nyssa.[181]

Other commentaries at the turn of the fifth century relied on fairly standard interpretations of the LP and were less original in their exegetical treatments. However, this Arian commentary presents a number of innovative themes and emphases. Whereas earlier commentaries almost always related the words "Our Father" to baptismal themes of adoption, this commentary makes no such comparison. The notion that baptism changes converts into sons and daughters of God and siblings of Christ is not even alluded to. Instead, the emphasis is upon what it takes to remain sons or daughters of God. God prefers to be called Father, rather than Lord, in order to give believers the assurance and hope that they will be heard in their prayers. Servants do not always obtain what they ask for, but good sons and daughters who ask with clear consciences receive God's good gifts. In fact, they deserve to be heard. But those who ask for carnal things do not merit God's ear. Thus, for the Arian community, the connection between the LP and baptism was less relevant in the fifth century. Whether it was ever of concern is impossible to say given the lack of evidence. The importance of the LP for this Arian author, however, was that it supported the Arian theological views concerning the divine and holy living.

The emphasis in the Arian LP interpretation is strongly focused upon God the Father. References to Christ are not made despite the fact that this is Jesus' own prayer that he taught the disciples. The commentary likewise focuses upon God the Father's relationship to believers as sons and daughters. This is the strongest indication that this explanation is Arian, because the Arians emphasized their relationship to the one true God, the Father, and believed that Christ as a son was subordinate to the Father.

In light of the previous comments, the commentary predictably spends most of its time developing the second petition, on the kingdom of God. For the anonymous author, this petition allowed the opportunity to develop views on how good and evil relate in the world. The kingdom of God is either reward (*retributio*) or tribulation (*tribulatio*). The just receive the mercy of justice, while the wicked obtain guilt and the troubles of sin. Thus, the kingdom of God is located in people who are holy (*sancti*); in them the kingdom dwells. The kingdom of God is also justice (another important theme that occurs throughout the commentary), the reward for those who are faithful to God's will. Once again, the emphasis is upon the relationship of the believer to God.

The author also distinguished between "being a ruler" (*regem esse*) and "ruling" (*regnare*). God, by nature, is the ruler of all creation, but the Father does not coerce his subjects, and so he does not necessarily rule all people. Those who do the will of God live in the light and are a part of the kingdom. Those who do not seek God's will are ruled by the Devil, who coerces all under his power; they live in darkness outside of the kingdom of God. Therefore, there are two kingdoms in this world; the kingdom of God and the just, who will one day come to the kingdom of God in heaven (where true justice reigns), and the kingdom of the Devil and sinners, who will pass away in flames.[182]

With regard to the Arian author's view on how Christians cooperate with God in their salvation, two examples are used. In the discussion of the first petition, the commentary mentions that just as well-dressed people seek to keep their clothes clean so that they might remain presentable, so too Christians are to avoid sin in order to keep themselves spotless for God. The discussion surrounding the third petition states that just as a seed needs soil, and soil needs a seed in order to produce a harvest, so God and believers need each other; just as people are not able to do good unless they have the help of God, so God does not work good in people, unless they will it.[183]

The Incomplete Commentary on Matthew demonstrates no variation in the Latin text of the LP per se, probably because, like Origen, it is simply a commentary on a biblical text. However, one unique element presents itself: it does add commentary on the first part of the doxology, "For yours is the kingdom, and the power, and the glory." Since the commentary presents the LP in a verse-by-verse fashion, this probably suggests that these words were a part of the biblical LP text of the Matthew 6:13 verse that the author was reading. The Arian author does not indicate that these words are an addition to the biblical text: however, the author may simply assume his audience knows that. But since other liturgical references to the LP in this commentary are completely lacking, it seems most likely that this was a textual variant in the biblical text of Matthew 6:13 that the Arian author was using.

The Arian author used the doxology as a way to explain the LP a second time. If people ever wonder why they need to pray for God's kingdom to come, asked the author, Christians need to remind them of the words, "Yours is the kingdom." This phrase reveals that the kingdom is not of this world and so believers need to pray for it to come to them. When people question whether God is able to accomplish God's will, Christians are to recall the words, "Yours is the power." This sentence explains that God has the ability to do as God pleases and the third petition is to be understood in this light. Finally, the last four petitions divulge the meaning of the words "Yours is the glory." When God offers bread, forgiveness, and keeps people from temptation and evil, this reveals the glory of God.[184]

The *Incomplete Commentary on Matthew* indicates how Arians understood the LP. Their understanding was neither detached from earlier traditional interpretations of the prayer, nor was it completely dependent upon them. Rather, the anonymous author put forth Arian concerns about the kingdom of God, justice, and the relationship of believers to their heavenly Father in an original commentary, while using what he considered to be the best of the past tradition. There is no sense that the LP itself is sacramental or even instrumental in the process of salvation. Since the work is not polemical, but exegetical in nature, it indicates that for the Arian author, the LP was primarily understood as a prayer that aided their understanding of how God offers salvation to people. The LP reveals a cooperative relationship of God the Father to his sons and daughters in faith, and how they, like seed and soil, together produce a harvest of salvation.

The commentary on the LP as a text of education for mature Christians varied greatly depending upon the author's persuasion. From the soaring, philosophically practical, eloquent heights of Gregory of Nyssa's prose, to the bishop of Hippo's commonsensical and theologically sophisticated views, to Chromatius' succinct but largely unoriginal words, to an anonymous Arian commentary, the LP was a flexible and remarkably adaptable text that inspired awe and wonder as well as rational and sensible attitudes toward God, and faithful thought and action. Each of the representative authors of this section profoundly shaped later views concerning the LP. What is more important is that they were able to do so because of the centrality of the message of the LP that existed among a rich variety of Christian churches concerning God, belief, and the holy life. In some ways, almost every, if not every, medieval Christian commentary on the LP is merely a footnote to these views and interpretations.

The Lord's Prayer in Polemics

Since the LP was a uniquely revered text in the early church, early authors found it helpful to draw upon both its mystery and power in times of need.[185] When a perceived heretical group, like the Arians, used the LP to develop their theological agenda over and against others, so-called orthodox writers often retaliated by placing the LP at the center of their polemical works in order to counter the teaching of their theological opponents. This was particularly true of Optatus of Milevis, Augustine, Jerome, and Cyril of Alexandria.

Very little is known about the mid- to late fourth-century North African bishop Optatus of Milevis. Like Juvencus, Jerome mentions Optatus in his *On Famous Men* (ch. 110), remarking that Optatus wrote an important work entitled *Concerning the Schism of the Donatists*.[186] The first edition of this work was completed in the middle of the 360s, and its final form, an unfinished second edition, was probably written during the mid 380s.

Optatus mentioned the LP three times in the midst of his lengthy attack against the Donatists, each time to make a similar argument. Like Tertullian refuting Marcion, Optatus pointed to the LP in order to challenge what he considered to be the dangerous doctrines of Donatist schismatics. For Optatus, the LP was an important weapon in his apologist's arsenal.

The Donatist movement began in the early fourth century in North Africa after a time of great persecution of Christians. Some lesser clergy and bishops, under the threat of violence from various secular authorities, gave over the scriptures of their churches in order to save their lives. Some clergy, however, refused to do so and became martyrs or confessors. After these days of persecution ended, the church was divided over what was to be done with those clergy who had fallen into apostasy by cooperating with the authorities, rather than suffering faithfully. The Donatists called them traitors and wanted to cast them out of the church, but some churches retained them, if they repented. The Donatists, however, only allowed clergy who had remained faithful during the times of persecution and thereafter. They believed that they themselves were the only true heirs of the faithful pre-persecution church. Donatist clergy were required to be blameless. Clergy who had committed apostasy were outside of the church, even if they repented. As a result, Donatists believed that any sacraments performed by apostate priests were no longer efficacious. Roman Catholics defended a non-Donatist position that argued that it was not the clergy, but God who made the sacraments efficacious, even if imparted to the faithful by means of an imperfect priest. Therefore, appropriately repentant apostate clergy could be reinstated.

Optatus became a significant figure in the Donatist debate, himself anticipating many of Augustine's later theological positions against the very popular movement. Optatus argued that Donatist doctrine contradicted the teaching of the LP concerning the sinfulness of humanity. If, indeed, it is necessary for a Donatist priest to be blameless in order for him to aid his congregation in obtaining forgiveness through the sacraments, why does the priest pray the LP during the worship service? Optatus pointed out that Donatist priests prayed the words, "Our Father who is in heaven, and forgive us our debts and sins."[187] If the priest is in fact holy, then he has no sins that need remittance and this part of the LP does not pertain to him. If the LP does not pertain to the priests, then why do they pray it? If, on the other hand, priests pray the LP, because it does pertain to them, then they are not free from sin, and by their own admission their sacraments are null and void. In any case, the Donatist position is undermined by the very fact that their clergy pray the LP, says Optatus. For the Donatists to say that any, even the clergy, are without sin, is to be deceived by the Devil.[188]

It is important to note that the LP was a place of common ground between the Donatist schismatics and orthodox Catholics. We may assume that both afforded it a central place in their worship, private devotional lives, and in theological education. Therefore, Optatus drew on the LP because it was a text that both sides held as central to their faith. By showing that the Donatists did not adhere to the tenets of the LP, Optatus felt that he proved that the Donatists failed to promote true Christian teachings and practices. In other words, the battle over orthodoxy placed the LP on center stage at times, and thus, the battle over the interpretation of the LP was a battle for orthodoxy itself. If the teachings of the LP could be used to refute schismatic teachings, then the Donatists had indeed gone astray. After all, even Donatist neophytes had been given the LP. Unfortunately for Optatus, they strayed from their roots, the teachings of the LP, and they therefore needed to return to the prayer that had originally brought them into the faith. As the prayer that was specifically identified with the moment of baptismal conversion, the LP also came to be seen as a text of central importance for teaching true Christian doctrine.

The high regard Augustine had for the LP led him, like Optatus, to quote Jesus' prayer frequently in his treatises that attempted to refute "questionable" teachings. These polemical works were not only for the benefit of the "wayward," but they were often meant to be a tool for educated orthodox clergy, who actively had to combat theological heterodoxy. In turn, these clergy used Augustine's ideas in their sermons and writings to teach their congregations about what they considered to be theological truth.

Augustine used the LP in his polemical works in order to defend the faith, in part because the LP had originally been a part of the baptismal ritual. Thus, Augustine sought to direct the "misguided," who in his opinion had strayed from the faith, back to those teachings they learned when they first entered the church.

An example of this comes in Augustine's work *On the Gift of Perseverance* (written late in Augustine's life, ca. 428–429). Augustine set forth the idea that everyone, saint and sinner alike, needed the gift of grace in order to attain eternal life. Those who are initiated receive faith as a gift at the beginning of faith (*initium fidei*). Christians cannot remain faithful, however, without the gift of perseverance. Those who do not persevere in true Christian teachings, said Augustine, are led astray and become heretics who lose salvation unless they return to the faith of their baptisms.[189]

Augustine quoted the LP most often in his polemical works against the Pelagians and the so-called Semi-Pelagians. In his anti-Pelagian writings, Augustine focused his rhetoric primarily on the fifth and sixth petitions. Augustine accused the Pelagians of believing that they were able to lead godly lives free of sin apart from the grace of God, and in so doing, they merited their own salvation. Augustine countered this claim by appealing to the fifth petition, on forgiveness. It was inconceivable, for Augustine, that Christ taught his disciples, and his church, to pray this petition frequently if they were not in need of God's daily grace of forgiveness that is imparted through the LP. Since even the greatest saints prayed this prayer every day, argued Augustine, they admitted that they, and therefore all people, sin throughout their lives. Christ teaches his followers this petition so that they might be humble, acknowledge their sin, and throw themselves upon God's mercy. The Pelagians, argued Augustine, are guilty of pride, because they claim to have no need of God's grace and, ultimately, of God.

Augustine especially stressed the fifth petition in his treatise against the Pelagians entitled *On Nature and Grace* (ca. 413–415), when he commented, "Here, indeed, [in the fifth petition] we have the daily incense, so to speak, of the Spirit which is offered on the altar of the heart, which we are bidden to lift up implying that even if we cannot live here without sin, we may yet die without sin, when in merciful forgiveness the sin is blotted out which is committed in ignorance and infirmity."[190] Sin may be forgiven by God's grace, but it may not be earned by good works, argued Augustine.

The sixth petition teaches that saints need to be kept from temptation because temptation can lead to sin. If Christians are able to keep themselves from sin by their own free wills, as the Pelagians argued, then this petition is unnecessary. But all people are in need of God's grace to avoid temptation. If the fifth petition removes the stain of sin from believers, then the sixth petition prevents believers from further soiling their lives. In *On Nature and Grace*, Augustine expressed this in the following manner:

> Now there are two ways whereby, even in bodily maladies, evil is guarded against, to prevent its occurrence, and, if it happens, to secure a speedy cure. To prevent [sin's] occurrence, we may find precaution in the prayer, "Lead us not into temptation;" to secure the prompt remedy, we have the resource in the prayer, "Forgive us our debts." Whether then the danger only threatens, or be inherent, it may be guarded against.[191]

The emphasis upon the sixth petition in Augustine's polemical works is significant because he ties this petition to perseverance. In another polemical piece against the Pelagians, *On the Perfection of Human Justice* (ca. 415–416), Augustine stated that "...if anyone says that we ought not to use the prayer, 'Lead us not into temptation' (and he says as much who maintains that God's help is unnecessary to a person for the avoidance of sin, and that human will, after accepting only the law, is sufficient for the purpose), then I do not hesitate at once to affirm that such a person ought to be removed from the public ear, and to be anathematized by every mouth."[192] The Pelagians, therefore, stand condemned because of the wisdom of the LP.

Augustine's *On the Gift of Perseverance* (ca. 428–429), which is the second half of Augustine's *On the Predestination of the Saints* (ca. 428–429),[193] was his last in-depth treatment of the LP in his life and his last complete work on grace. Augustine challenged the Pelagian idea that free will, without aid from God, may cooperate in bringing about salvation. Since Christians continue to live in sin after their baptisms, perseverance is not possible without God's grace. Augustine supported his arguments against the Pelagians by appealing to the authority of the LP, the scripture as a whole, the liturgy of the church, and the Early Church Fathers, particularly Cyprian—especially his commentary *On the Lord's Prayer*. Cyprian, "that most lucid and glorious martyr and doctor,"[194] was the first to connect the LP with the concept of perseverance. Cyprian's commentary on the LP anticipated and refuted the doctrines of the Pelagians, said Augustine, almost two centuries before they came into vogue. For Augustine, the LP and its proper interpretation was literally an antidote to "the poison of the Pelagians."[195] Indeed, said Augustine, in the LP, "almost nothing else other than perseverance is understood to be asked for."[196]

The saints of the church pray for perseverance when they pray the LP, says Augustine, and if people were able to persevere without grace, then the LP itself would be unnecessary. Still, Jesus commanded the church to pray it daily. Therefore, Augustine concluded, "Without a doubt the saints are asking to persevere in these goods which they know they have received. If they receive this, obviously they also receive perseverance itself, that great gift of God by which all His other gifts are preserved."[197]

Even the fourth petition, "Give us this day our daily bread," was understood by Cyprian and Augustine to be about perseverance, at least in part. Cyprian declared that the bread refers to the Eucharistic body of Christ, and therefore in praying the fourth petition, "the saints of God ask from the Lord precisely for perseverance . . . that they may not be separated from the Body of Christ, but may remain in that sanctity in which they are not guilty of any sin which would merit their separation from the body."[198]

Six of the seven petitions specifically asked for the grace of perseverance, said Augustine, who also noted, "In [the fifth] petition alone perseverance is not asked for, for past are the sins which we ask to be forgiven us; for although perseverance which gives us salvation for eternity is certainly necessary for the period of this life, yet not for the time already past, but for that which remains even unto the end."[199]

Augustine referred to the sixth petition more frequently than to any other petition in his polemical writings. This petition spelled out most clearly for Augustine how perseverance is a gift of God. Augustine declared, "For no one ceases to persevere in the Christian way of life, unless he is first led into temptation. If, therefore, he be granted what he prays for, namely that he be not led into temptation, he surely by God's help persists—which is a gift of God—in that sanctification which by God's gift he obtained."[200] Therefore, Augustine argued that God demands that all Christians must pray the sixth petition.[201]

Augustine also developed the LP perseverance theme in non-polemical works as well. Augustine began his discussion of the LP in the aforementioned *On the Sermon on the Mount* by first looking at Matthew 6:8 (the verse preceding the LP in Matthew), which states that God knows what the faithful need, even before they pray. People, at times, warned Augustine, falsely believe that this verse means that prayer is not necessary because God knows all things. In prayer, God illumines the intellects and spirits of those who pray so that their hearts might be made calm, clean, and capable of receiving God's divine gifts. This enlightenment enables those who pray to receive and bear the gift of God's divine light so that they might persevere in faith, joy, and blessedness. Augustine boldly concludes his comments on the LP in his *On the Gift of Perseverance* with the following reverence for the LP:

> Therefore, if there were no other proofs, this, the Lord's Prayer alone would suffice for us respecting the cause of grace which we are defending, because it has left us nothing which we might glory as our own, since it shows that our not departing from God must be given only by God when it shows it is from God that we must ask it.[202]

The LP reveals the central theology of the church and therefore stands over and against any who would alter this theology, especially with regard to the necessity of grace, noted Augustine.

Other authors shared Augustine's views on the Pelagians. Prosper of Aquitaine (ca. 390–463) corresponded with and received advice from his friend Augustine, who dedicated the treatises *On the Predestination of the Saints* and *On the Gift of Perseverance* to Prosper, his friend. Prosper also sided with Augustine against the Semi-Pelagians while commenting on the third petition, on God's will, in his *Defense of Augustine* (written ca. 431–432).[203] The Pelagians had used the third petition in order to attack Augustine and Prosper for holding to the belief that Christians necessarily continue to sin after baptism and that they cannot of their own free wills lead godly lives. If this is true, suggested the Pelagians, then God's will, which must be done, must be the cause of sin among Christians. Therefore, Christians who pray the third petition seek their own condemnation, but such an idea was absurd to the Pelagians.

Prosper, on the other hand, retorted that God wills all to be saved and does not cause Christians to sin, but offers them Christ for their salvation. By this grace, God saves Christians, who nonetheless continue to sin due to their corrupted natures. God's will saves the faithful, while others are judged to be imitators of the devil, rather than of God, and they therefore stand condemned.[204]

Jerome also attacked Pelagian doctrines with the aid of the LP at about the same time Augustine wrote his anti-Pelagian works. Jerome's treatise *A Dialogue Against the Pelagians* (ca. 417) is in the form of a dialogue between Atticus, a Catholic, and Critobulus, a Pelagian. Atticus, at a point late in the argument, chides Critobulus for being arrogant enough to suppose that Christians are able to earn salvation by their own abilities to choose, and to lead, sinless lives. Quoting from a letter of Pelagius addressed to a widow named Juliana, Atticus relates that Pelagius told her that she should in good conscience raise her hands to God and pray, "For you know, O Lord, how holy, how innocent, how clean of all fraud, wrong-doing, and rapine are the hands that I stretch out to you; how just, how undefiled, and free of all deceit are the lips, with which I pour out my prayers and supplications to you, to have pity on me."[205] Atticus, however, suggests that these presumptuous words are more reminiscent of the unworthy prayer of the Pharisee in Jesus' parable than the righteous prayer of the tax collector (Luke 18:9ff.). Atticus then turns his attention to the LP, which he believes completely condemns the position of Critobulus and Pelagian theology, as developed in his letter to Juliana.[206]

Atticus explains to Critobulus that the LP needs to be understood within its liturgical context of the Eucharist and baptism. While discussing the fifth petition, Atticus notes that the LP in the worship service is prayed right before the Eucharist: "Thus, did [Jesus] teach his apostles that they who believe should make bold to say daily at the sacrifice of his body: 'Our Father, . . .' "[207] Jerome argued that all Christians are sinners and therefore need the forgiveness offered through the LP before they receive the Lord's Supper. If Pelagius is correct, however, his followers do not need the LP, because they can lead godly lives without God's aid such as is found in the LP. Jerome argued to the contrary, that the positioning of the LP before the Lord's Supper in the liturgy reveals that all Christians need to pray for forgiveness regularly because they are sinful and in need of God's grace.

Jerome also stated that the LP is connected to the liturgical practices surrounding the baptism. Jerome claimed that the praying of the LP immediately following the sacrament of baptism within the baptismal service is even more significant than the liturgical connection between the LP and the Lord's Supper. Atticus rhetorically wonders if there is anyone more perfect or clean than the person who emerges from the waters of baptism. His obvious answer to this question is, "Of course not." And yet, Jerome believed that despite the recent washing away of sins, the newly baptized nevertheless pray the LP and the fifth petition out of necessity. The Pelagians argued that the LP is recited after baptism as a sign of the humility of the believer. Jerome, however, stated:

> They who emerge from the baptismal font and have been reborn in the Lord Savior, having fulfilled what was written of them: "Blessed are they whose iniquities are forgiven, and whose sins are covered," say at the very moment of their first communion of the body of Christ: "And forgive us our debts," debts that had been forgiven them in the confession of Christ. And you [Critobulus], in your arrogance and boastful pride, glory in the purity of your holy hands and the cleanness of your speech. Even though the conversion of man may be as perfect as possible, and his possession of virtues be as complete as possible after faults and sins, can he be as free of fault as they who emerge immediately from the font of Christ? And yet they are commanded to say: "Forgive us our debts, as we also forgive our debtors," not under false pretense of humility, as you interpret it, but rather as a sign of fear of human weakness which dreads its own conscience.[208]

Jerome's appeal to the liturgical context of the LP was an appeal for the Pelagians to return to the teachings they had learned in their baptismal and Eucharistic education. Like Augustine, Jerome was concerned with presenting the LP not only as an authoritative text, but also as a prayer that was an essential part of the lives of believers. Therefore, Jerome made explicit the connection between the LP and the sacraments. However, unlike Augustine, Jerome did not say the LP had a sacramental quality to it per se. The LP was a means by which people received forgiveness, and this was enough for Jerome.

In the remaining parts of his *A Dialogue Against the Pelagians*, Jerome juxtaposed the doctrines of the LP with Pelagian beliefs, and did so in a "You say ... but we say ..." fashion. The first petition teaches that God is holy, but the Pelagians believe that they themselves are holy. The second and third[209] petitions declare that Christians are to place their hopes in God's future kingdom, where the will of God will be fulfilled, whereas the Pelagians trust in their own strength. The fourth petition reveals that the saintly apostles needed to pray for daily bread (i.e., the Eucharistic bread of Christ), but the Pelagians rely on their own holiness. Thus, the Pelagians assume they are able to give themselves those gifts that may only be given by God. The fifth petition has already been mentioned. The sixth and seventh petitions likewise demonstrate that all Christians are in need of God's sustaining grace, but the Pelagians believe that they are able to resist temptation with their own will power. Jerome believed that the Pelagians put themselves at great risk by holding that they do not need God to be delivered from evil. Therefore, Atticus concludes that the prayers of Critobulus, which are best illustrated by the prayer taught by Pelagius to Juliana, are arrogant, and those who pray them stand condemned.[210]

In the end, both Jerome and Augustine connected the LP to baptism in their polemical writings; both sought to recall the Pelagians from their errors by appealing to the LP that they learned in their baptismal catechetic training. Still, Jerome's liturgical theme is strikingly unique. For Jerome, it is the actual position of the LP in the liturgy in relation to the Eucharist and baptism that condemns the Pelagians. No one before him had ever put forth this sort of explanation of the LP, even though the use of the LP before the Eucharist and after baptism was a common practice. Jerome's appeal to the liturgical function of the LP is revealing, because he is primarily known historically as a biblical exegete. This suggests again that part of the appeal of using the LP to counter heretical thought had to do with the fact that it was a central devotional and theological text within the worship life of the church.

Cyril of Alexandria (d. 444) also used the LP in a polemical way. Scholars suggest that Cyril's writings against the Nestorians started in late 428 or 429, or about the time of Nestorius' rise to ecclesiastical power in Constantinople. Again, the reader will note that this is at the same time of some of Augustine's writings against the Pelagians. Cyril's commentary on Luke was written ca. 430, and thus, references in it speak specifically against the Nestorians at times but also against heresy in general.[211] His arguments in his commentary on the LP speak more generally against all heresy. Cyril, like Augustine, believed that the sixth petition of the LP in particular revealed that there were two types of temptations that Christians must avoid. The second type of temptation was that of the passions and lust that plague all people. However, the first type was the universal temptation of all people, and especially Christians, toward heresy. For Cyril, the false teachers and prophets of the world lured the faithful away from the truth by glorifying worldly wisdom, adulterating the language of sacred proclamations, and multiplying blasphemous words. As Cyril suggested, Psalm 74:5 says that heretics set up their horns on high, sounding iniquity against the Creator of the universe. Champions of the truth strive to proclaim the sound doctrines of God, defending God's glory, and praising God's Word. However, heretics persecute these truth seekers and tempt them. Cyril warns that the faithful ought not to be faithless like the soldier in battle who throws his shield aside and flees the war or the athlete who gives up the race. Christians should realize that life is about war, not peace; after all Jesus said, "I came not to bring peace but a sword" (Matthew 10:34). Unfortunately, some heretics also have political power and might, which as a result can cause their persecutions to be terrible. Still, believers ought not to fear them (1 Peter 4:19) nor to flee. Rather, they should always watch so that the thief will not break in and steal their faith (1 Peter 4:15). Finally, all that true followers of Christ can do is to be willing to suffer and die for their faith like the martyrs, who love God (Hebrews 6:10). By fighting the good fight and running the good race, those who resist temptation will find eternal victory (2 Timothy 4:7).[212]

Early authors also made a non-Christian group, namely the Jews, a target of a LP polemic. Like Tertullian and Cyprian, Augustine used the LP in a polemical way against the Jews on a number of occasions. One example will be enough to make this point. In his commentary *On the Sermon on the Mount,* Augustine contrasted the precepts of Jesus' mountain sermon with the Ten Commandments handed over to Moses on the mountain of Sinai. According to Augustine, the precepts of Jesus are superior to those of Moses because Christians become sons and daughters of God, the Father, through Christ in baptism; therefore, they are motivated by kinship and love to obey God. However, the commandments passed on to the Hebrews by Moses suggest that the people of Israel followed God more as slaves and were motivated by fear.[213] The Jews do not have the right to pray to God as Father in the words of the LP, but Christians do. Augustine's supercessionist argument suggested that the Jews, who may have been chosen at one time, no longer deserved the title, and were in fact replaced by Christians, who have come into a familial relationship with God. Those who rejected Christ, by either proper doctrinal ideas or religious practices, therefore turned their backs on Christ's Father and thus forfeited their inheritances. Christians, in turn, became the true heirs of God through baptism. Many, if not all, Christian LP commentaries in the early church made this point, and as a result, it is not farfetched to argue that such early attitudes and polemics against the Jews no doubt led to much of the anti-Semitism that emerged in the early church.

The LP proved to be an important text for early church authors in combating the perceived errors of other groups in the ancient world. Since the LP was one of the first theological and devotional texts taught to the believer, it had the advantage of having authority in both the education and life of believers. The sixth petition of the LP was especially called upon to make arguments against Christian groups who were understood to have gone astray. Nevertheless, in the end, it was probably the prominence and simplicity of the LP in the life of the church that made it so appealing to use in polemical writings. A fight over the right interpretation of the LP was a fight over the very heart of the Christian faith and its teachings. Whoever won this battle over the LP had the upper hand in theological debate, moral behavior, and liturgical rectitude.

The Lord's Prayer in Early Monastic Theology

Another group of early Christians who turned to the LP for inspiration were early monks and nuns. This part of the chapter will focus on one representative author: John Cassian, the renowned early monastic guide (ca. 365–435). Cassian traveled widely in order to learn more about the monastic life. After living in Bethlehem and traveling through Egypt, he went to Rome for awhile, and he eventually settled in southern France in order to form monastic communities there. Two of his works, the *Institutes* (written before 420) and the *Conferences* (ca. 420–429), were composed in order to communicate his ideas about monastic ideals. The *Conferences*, which deals with the interior life of the monk or the nun, brings to completion his thoughts on monastic life and perfection, which he first wrote about in his *Institutes*, discussing the exterior life of monastics.

The *Conferences* recalls conversations Cassian had with fifteen Egyptian fathers: in 24 books, it lays out his ideas about monasticism. His attitudes toward prayer (*Conferences*, chapters 9–10) and perfection (*Conferences*, Chapter 11) are considered by some scholars to be central to this work. Cassian himself says, "The whole purpose of the monk—and indeed the perfection of his heart amounts to this— total and uninterrupted dedication to prayer."[214] Chapters 9–10 of his *Conferences* present his comments on the LP.[215]

Cassian noted that there are as many kinds of prayers as there are numerous conditions and states of the human soul. People pray differently depending upon what it is they are seeking and upon what state their soul is in at the time.[216] Nevertheless, generally speaking, he divided prayer into four basic types, which are discussed in 1 Timothy 2:1: "My advice is that first of all supplication should be offered up for everyone, [then] prayers, pleas, and thanksgiving." The lowest form of prayer, supplication (*obsecratio*), is when the contrite seek pardon for their sins; this type is meant for beginners. The second stage of prayer is what Cassian simply called "prayer" (*oratio*), and this is a vow or promise made to serve God and renounce the world. The third type, called a plea (*postulatio*), is said on behalf of others. And finally, the highest level, thanksgiving (*gratiarum actiones*), occurs when believers are moved to true thankfulness. This happens in one of three ways: through a recollection of God's past kindness, by understanding what God grants in the present, or by a vision of salvation that God will grant in the future.[217] Jesus himself firmly established these four types of prayers by modeling them in his actions and words at various times in his life, says Cassian.[218]

Monks and nuns are able to move through these four stages of prayer to the highest form of prayer, which has no words but is what Cassian called the fiery prayer of the Holy Spirit. Cassian noted:

> Aflame with all [these prayers] their hearts are rapt in the burning prayer which human words can neither grasp nor utter. Sometimes the soul which has come to be rooted in this state of real purity takes on all the forms of prayer at the same time. It flies from one [kind of prayer] to the other, like an uncontrollable grasping fire. It becomes an outpouring of living pure prayer which the Holy Spirit, without our knowing it, lifts up to God in unspeakable groanings.[219]

The four stages of prayer may be prayed separately and at different times or all together at the same time. Either way, these prayers are the means by which petitioners are lifted to the highest level of contemplation, where words are no longer needed.[220]

The goal of prayer, therefore, is to be lifted by the fire of love to a contemplation of God that is above the four basic prayer types. Cassian said about this, "We must be careful to aspire to this state of soul. This is what the beginning of the LP tells us when it says, 'Our Father, . . . '"[221] Cassian's deep respect for the power and mystery of the LP moved him at times to call it the fullness of perfection, an example, or the rule, for all verbal prayer. But ultimately, like the other four prayers that use words, it is a prayer that raises up believers "to that prayer of fire known to so few. It lifts them up, rather, to that ineffable prayer, which rises above all human consciousness, with no voice sounding, no tongue moving, no words uttered."[222]

Cassian understood the LP to be a means to an end, rather than an end in itself as most authors before or after him understood it. The highest type of prayer, the prayer of fire, is even beyond the LP. The LP, in as much as it embodies the four types of prayers, aids petitioners in coming to this highest level of prayer. However, the LP is not the highest kind of prayer itself. All LP commentators before Cassian believed the LP to be an end in itself, the perfect prayer, and the prayer that encompassed all other prayers, but this view was not held by Cassian.

The shortcoming of the LP, for Cassian, is that it includes words. Certainly, as far as wordy prayers go, it is the most important. Nevertheless, it is the prayer of the Holy Spirit which enflames the heart with the greatest ardor, lifts the soul beyond earthly prayer, and attains the highest form of prayer, which is uttered in groans too deep for words. Jesus himself, Cassian pointed out, withdrew to the Mount of Olives alone and with silent petitions offered a prayer with so great a fervor that his sweat became blood (Luke 22:44); thus, Jesus gave monks and nuns an example of how he himself in his own deepest prayers ascended beyond the words of the LP.[223]

Beside this uniqueness, Cassian's explanation of the individual petitions of the LP is, for the most part, like earlier commentaries, but he added his own unique thoughts as well. For example, Cassian noted that the words, "Our Father" indicate that all who pray the LP proclaim that God is Lord of the universe and Father, and they are no longer servants, but adopted sons and daughters of God.[224] But even though this echoes Tertullian and Cyprian, there is also an important difference. While the notion of adoption has in the past always implied baptism, Cassian interpreted adoption to mean the state that monks and nuns find themselves in when they pray the LP. In other words, the LP declares the reality of their intimate relationship with God. This is a striking difference from earlier works. Outside the mere mention of the word "adoption," there is no reference in Cassian's LP commentary to baptism.

Cassian also noted that since God is their adoptive Father, the monks and nuns ask in the LP that they might do nothing that would make them degenerate sons and daughters. The LP encourages them as children to hallow God's name (the first petition) in their deeds, and in so doing, to glorify God. In this way, God is made holy, that is, honored, by their perfection and good works. For Cassian, the kingdom of God (the second petition) comes to the most pure souls, or the holy ones over whom Christ reigns. This happens when fornication is vanquished and chastity rules, anger is overcome and peace is king, and pride is trampled and humility is sovereign. Cassian believes that chastity, peace, and humility are essential virtues for monks and nuns, and therefore, his interpretation of the LP continues to promote monastic virtues and perfection. In the end, the devil's power is driven out of monastic hearts through the expulsion of sin's foulness, and God's rule begins amid the good odor of virtuous deeds.[225]

Promoting other monastic virtues, Cassian interpreted the fourth petition in a traditional manner, namely, that bread means spiritual needs. But when he discussed the notion of praying this petition "daily," he said that his audience's "daily poverty," another important monastic virtue, should encourage them not to eat anything more than is needed for the strengthening of their hearts. Also, those who do not partake of this spiritual bread in this life will not be able to eat of it in the next.[226]

Likewise, Cassian had a unique view of the fifth petition. After pointing out how monks and nuns need to forgive others in order to be forgiven (as earlier authors had argued concerning all Christians), Cassian cautioned that forgiving others too easily can be a problem as well. To indulge people in their weaknesses by being too gentle on their sins brings both sides to condemnation.[227] This concern reflects Cassian's interest in dealing with the vices that threaten the perfection of the lives of monks and nuns.

Cassian also noted that there was another problem related to the fifth petition, which we have already alluded to in the discussion about the Arian *Incomplete Commentary on Matthew*. Again, some monks had apparently gotten into the habit of not praying the forgiveness petition, or at least not the last part of it, or they merely fell silent during its recitation in worship. They did not pray "Forgive us . . . *as* we forgive . . . ," because they feared that God would not forgive them due to their own unwillingness to forgive others. Therefore, they did not say it. However, Cassian warned that skipping this part of the prayer would do these deceivers no good; God knows their hearts and will judge them accordingly.[228]

Cassian's interpretation of the LP, therefore, was the first directed at a strictly monastic audience. While his explanations clearly borrowed from earlier commentaries, Cassian adapted the prayer and made it relevant for his monastic audience. All the same, it is rather remarkable to note that Cassian definitely broke with tradition when he did not finally regard the LP as the greatest of all prayers per se. Certainly he believed it to be the highest form of prayer that employed words, but its function was to move people to that greater wordless and fiery prayer of the Holy Spirit. This is perhaps one of the clearest indications of how the interpretation and use of the LP adapted and diversified in an increasingly complex Christian world during the fifth century.[229]

Conclusions: The Flourishing Lord's Prayer

By the end of the fourth century, a widespread concern for keeping the LP as a cherished, and even hidden, part of orthodox Christian teaching and practice had clearly blossomed in some locales. In many ways, this attitude reached its zenith in Ambrose. His stern, respect-ful attitude toward the LP slowly gave way to a slightly more relaxed, but no less respectful, attitude during the early decades of the fifth century, thanks especially to Augustine's views on this subject. What-ever *disciplina arcani* that existed around the LP slowly drifted into the past. For now, however, the fourth century can be categorized as a time when the LP continued to grow in importance in the life of the church despite the fact that there were relatively few commentaries written on it during the fourth century. This fact, no doubt, is consistent with a cautious attitude that at times desired to not even write down the Creed or the LP, even for educational purposes. As a result, much of the instruction on the LP during this century probably occurred in a verbal manner.

At the beginning of the fourth century, however, Juvencus was will-ing to include his paraphrase version of the LP in his larger work as a tool to persuade non-Christians of the enlightened teachings of Jesus of Nazareth. However, such an attitude of public exposure with regard to the LP was a minority opinion in that time. Nonetheless, Juvencus inspired others, like Coelius Sedulius, and as a result, one of the most popular forms of interpretation of the LP that developed in this period was poetry.

Optatus of Milevus, Didymus the Blind, Jerome, Augustine, Cyril of Alexandria, and other polemical writers felt that the LP was a prayer not only worth defending against the heterodox, but a tool by which suspect teachings could be exposed, undermined, and effec-tively refuted. The use of the LP with what was considered problematic Christian groups was not an issue, because they already knew the LP and were using it in their worship, private devotions, and theology. The issue was not one of guarding the LP from these groups, but rather, guarding of the proper interpretation of the LP from what was considered to be false and dangerous theological explanations of the beloved words of Jesus.

Gregory of Nyssa, on the other hand, saw in the LP as an entire theology of Christian practice and belief, a prayer of beauty and unpar-alleled wonder. For bishops like Ambrose of Milan, Cyril of Jerusalem, and Augustine of Hippo, the LP was an object of mystery and awe which communicated the essence of Christian teaching and life, and therefore it was essential for baptismal catechesis, either before or after baptism.

The fourth and fifth centuries were times when the LP intensified in importance in the lives of Christians as a pearl of great price, a treasure of the faithful. Among monastic communities, like the one surrounding Cassian, the LP became a key element of monastic life. While not necessarily the pinnacle of prayer for Cassian, the LP represented the peak of prayer that employed words. The LP, all the same, held tremendous sway over the lives of the faithful, regardless of whether they were wet-behind-the-ears neophytes, who had just been baptized, or the most advanced monks and nuns of some remote community. Either way, the LP fell from their lips more often and more belovedly than any other words they would ever utter. In the end, the LP flowered in every part of the Christian landscape. At times, the LP beautified thought and life in a way that brought a fresh scent of fragrant virtue to the church; at other times, the flower felt prickly, and the thorns of polemic and of marginalizing others poked into the conversation. Nevertheless, the LP blossomed in every corner of Christianity, helping it to organize Christian thought and life around its seven simple petitions.

Conclusion: A Jewel of Unsurpassed Worth

There is something very satisfying about sorting through dusty books and ancient manuscripts, which transport readers back into the very hearts, lives, and minds of great writers and, by extension, their audiences. Shadowy glimpses of the past pour forth from the vellum to reveal not just complex beliefs, but flesh and blood people who often passionately attempted to live faithful lives of service dedicated to their God. Sadly, the illuminating light was at times accompanied by smoky images that are all too often incomplete, clouded by partial evidence and only wispy visions of the past. The scholar's task is to attempt to make as much sense of the disparate sources as is feasible. Frequently, the distance of time, place, and cultures makes this task very difficult. As scholars attempt to peer beyond the centuries into the lives and mindsets of both the folks in the pews and the erudite thinkers in their studies, they discover, in this case, a people of honest, heartfelt, and pious convictions that show a remarkable reverence for the words "Our Father." At times, their passions got the better of them, and vigorous arguments ensued or prejudices developed. When they were at their best, however, early Christians infused the LP into every aspect of their Christian lives and thought in a way that made the prayer a beloved treasure, a pearl of great price.

As early authors sought to understand the LP and its wisdom, they were in some ways seeking to peak into the mind of God, so to speak. To understand more fully what they believed God's will to be for their communities, a clear, concise overview of the major aspects of the interpretation of the LP as a whole is needed. By way of conclusion, then, it will be helpful to put forth a brief general survey of the theological interpretations of the LP in the early church in order to complete our historical examination of the LP.

Generally speaking, the two major parts of the LP, that is, its heavenly (petitions 1–3) and earthly (petitions 4–7) sections, demonstrated conclusively for early scholars that the LP covered every conceivable aspect of Christian life and thought, and that it even had much to suggest about the very nature of the cosmos. First and foremost, scholars noted that the prayer was primarily a communal prayer, because of its regular use of words like "our" or "us."[1] Therefore, even though early Christians were encouraged to pray the LP in their own devotional practices, the prayer was understood primarily to be concerned with the needs of community. This fact alone made the LP especially suitable for communal worship.

The interpretation of the opening address, "Our Father, who is in heaven," and the heavenly petitions was profoundly affected by the baptismal catechetic use of the LP, as has been suggested in earlier chapters. God, the Father, who was once seen as the formidable Judge[2] or Lord,[3] through the waters of baptism changed the sinful lives of its dripping recipients into a children of God, that is, into the sons or daughters of the most high God.[4] God's name changed in the LP, suggesting that the distant Creator[5] had become an intimate loving parent for these newly adopted baptismal children. Before baptism, they were slaves to sin and children of the devil,[6] but in baptism they were reborn to new life as heirs of God, their Father.[7] This meant then that they were royal children, inheritors of the Kingdom of God,[8] and people who should be bold in prayer.[9] In baptism, God becomes a Father, Christ a brother,[10] the church a mother,[11] and the baptismal font a womb from which the faithful are born to new life.[12]

Despite the fact that the first three petitions revealed a heavenly reality, they were nonetheless troublesome. The sticky issue that appeared in nearly every commentary was the concern about whether praying to make God's name holy, for God's kingdom to come, and for God's will to be done, somehow suggested a lack of these realities; i.e., do the faithful pray these petitions because God's name is not holy,[13] the kingdom has not or will not come,[14] and God's will is not done?[15] In each instance, the commentators noted that such logic was foolish. Rather, these petitions revealed that God's name is already, and always will be, holy,[16] God's kingdom comes in and of itself,[17] and God's will is always done.[18] These petitions instead encouraged the faithful to keep God's name holy,[19] to seek the kingdom of God,[20] and to do God's will in their lives.[21] Indeed, people are not able to offer to God anything that God either needs or does not already possess.[22] Early authors argued that the first three petitions are accomplished primarily through baptism; people are made holy in baptism, and in this way, God's name is sanctified,[23] God's kingdom comes,[24] and God's will is done.[25] Likewise, if Christians wish to persevere in their baptisms, then these petitions can help bring them to eternal life.[26] The goal of Christian living is to honor God with prayer,[27] worship,[28] and holy living in order to avoid blaspheming or dishonoring the familial relationship of sons and daughters with their Father, God.[29] Early church scholars generally understood the words "on earth as in heaven" to apply to all of the first three petitions (despite the fact that it was attached to the third).[30]

The basic interpretations of the heavenly petitions were established by the time of Augustine, and they were repeated in various forms throughout the Middle Ages, the Reformation, and down to the modern era. However, the context of the use of these interpretations changed, and therefore, the explanations took on different nuances over time. Still, the context of baptismal catechesis in particular was the most important factor shaping the interpretation of the heavenly petitions during the period of the early church.

With regard to the earthly petitions, many early writers called attention to a shift of emphasis in the fourth petition away from the heavenly focus of the first petitions. Tertullian stated simply that the fourth petition is the first earthly directed part of the prayer. In it, there is a move away from praying that God's eternal will may be done, toward a discussion directed at earthly or human issues.[31]

The main concern in the fourth petition, in particular, was how to define "bread." Cyril of Alexandria, for example, believed that this petition was about both physical bread for the body and spiritual bread for the soul.[32] Pseudo-Quodvultdeus noted that if there is a famine without bread, the body dies, and if there is a famine of the word (Amos 8:11), then the soul dies. Only the ignorant think that the body is more important than the soul, notes Pseudo-Quodvultdeus; therefore, the foolish strive only to satisfy their bellies, while the wise hope to fill their souls with the true spiritual nourishment of heavenly bread. Theodore of Mopsuestia noted that believers should be content with everyday bread-like needs, such as food, clothing, and other necessities, but that they also ought to avoid seeking more than what is desired of earthly life, namely, luxury. For Theodore of Mopsuestia, the first three petitions lay out the principles required of the perfect life, and the fourth petition, although more physically oriented, is still directed at promoting the goals of the first three petitions.[33] Chromatius of Aquileia agreed and connected the spiritual bread of the LP to the eating of the bread and drinking of the wine in the Eucharist. In particular, he was concerned with partaking of the Eucharist improperly. He quoted 1 Corinthians 11:29, which says, "For he that eats the bread of the Lord unworthily, and drinks from the chalice, eats the body and drinks the blood of the Lord to judgment." Christians ought to pray this petition and partake of the Eucharist with a contrite heart so that they will not be separated from the bread of life by the act of impious eating.[34] Therefore, the fourth petition was an appropriate middle petition, or bridge petition, between praying for the heavenly concerns of the first three petitions (i.e., the bread as heavenly Eucharist and spiritual needs) and the earthly concerns of the last petitions (i.e., bread as daily physical needs, including food, clothing, and shelter).

Early commentators, almost universally, held the fifth petition to be the most important and primary petition of the LP. It was a means by which Christians attained forgiveness for their sins and returned to a right relationship with God when they sinned after their baptisms. As a result, this was the petition that commentators discussed more than any other. Tertullian and Cyprian had declared that the fourth petition (and its concern for bodily necessities) avails very little unless forgiveness, the most basic spiritual need, is also granted.[35] Some made a similar observation, noting that there is a logical progression from the fourth to the fifth petition: first the bread petition nourishes the body, and then the debt petition nourishes the soul.[36] Theodore of Mopsuestia noted that the fifth petition is perfectly placed within the context of the LP, because if Christians fail to live up to the first four petitions, the fifth offers them amendment of life, so they may return to pursuing the virtues encouraged previously in the LP.[37]

The focus of the fifth petition upon sin, and especially upon the need for regular confession and forgiveness and the necessity of forgiving others, was echoed by all. Scholars often solved the problem of the difference in wording (namely, "debts," which is Matthew's word in the fifth petition and the word in liturgical versions of the LP, and "sins," which is Luke's word in the fifth petition in the LP) without much comment. They simply noted that the variation was merely two ways of saying the same thing.[38]

Augustine noted that Jesus was always willing to forgive the debts of anyone who truly prayed the fifth petition, because it acted as a true confession of their sins.[39] Indeed, Augustine emphasized this point more forcefully than any other writer of this period. Put simply, Augustine believed that those who earnestly prayed the fifth petition were, at the very least, cleansed of sins committed after baptism, particularly venial ones. The fifth petition continued the work of forgiveness that was begun in baptism, and therefore he even referred to the LP as a "daily baptism."[40] Augustine used two images to further stress the previous point. First, he referred to John 13 and noted that just as Jesus desired to wash his disciples' feet, so also he wished daily to cleanse believers of their sins through the LP.[41] Second, he argued that after baptism, Christians continue to sin in the same way that a leaky boat takes on water. Unless the water is pumped out daily, the boat will sink. Praying the fifth petition is like pumping the bilge water of sin out of the hole-riddled lives of the faithful.[42]

Many commentators were quick to point out that one particularly unique aspect of the fifth petition was its conditional clause, "Forgive us our debts, *as we forgive our debtors*." The necessity of forgiving others in order to be forgiven was of paramount importance for early writers. The conditional phrase is in both Matthew and Luke and is a part of the earliest LP tradition. Clement of Rome (ca. 96), Tertullian, Clement of Alexandria, Cyprian, Cyril of Jerusalem, Ambrose,[43] and almost all authors of this period echoed the firm conviction that God will not forgive those who do not forgive others. Cyril of Jerusalem cautions that it would be foolish to risk God's anger simply in order to hold onto a grudge on some trivial matter.[44] Theodore of Mopsuestia took a slightly different approach to this part of the petition, saying that people were to forgive others, so that they might then truly have "confidence" that God will do the same with their sins. In turn, Christ commanded believers to forgive others, and in doing so they led virtuous lives and were imbued with a confidence that God forgives them in return.[45] Cyprian and Augustine concluded that Christians will either be imitators of Christ and forgive others, or they will be imitators of Judas, who was unwilling to seek repentance and therefore brought about discord. A willingness to forgive others, however, brings peace and unity to the church.[46]

Generally speaking, once commentators reached this point in their LP commentaries, they often hurried through the last two petitions, many times discussing them together and with very brief expositions.[47] For example, Augustine lumps the final two petitions together into one discussion because, as he says, they are connected with the conjunction "but." For Augustine, this indicates that they both have the same focus and should be taken together.[48] Augustine, like Tertullian before him, pointed out that the sixth petition follows logically from the fifth. Tertullian had argued that the LP has a powerful logic behind it; namely, after people are forgiven of their sins, they only need two things: first of all, to be kept from falling into temptation again, and finally, not to be overcome by sin and evil.[49] Augustine stated that the concerns of the sixth and seventh petitions, which are directed at things that will happen in the future, appropriately follow after the fifth petition, which deals with sins of the past.[50] Most scholars, however, didn't spend much time discussing either petition. They even sometimes ended their commentaries after the fifth petition, as if that was all that needed to be said.

When authors did examine the sixth petition,[51] they noted a problem with the words "And lead us not into temptation." None denied that temptation is a part of life, but many wondered if it was possible for God to tempt people to evil. The very idea seemed oxymoronic. Peter Chrysologus simply says, "In the world life itself is temptation."[52] But if this is true, does this petition then suggest that God actually leads people into temptation? Tertullian answered this question with an emphatic "God forbid such a thought!" Tertullian and Cyprian countered such obvious, but for them, ultimately misguided, queries by referring to James 1:13–14: "No one, when tempted, should say 'I am being tempted by God'; for God cannot be tempted by evil and he himself tempts no one. But one is tempted by one's own desire, being lured and enticed by it."[53]

For Gregory of Nyssa, temptation mainly meant the opportunity to sin. The solution to the problem of falling into temptation was simply to avoid being in a situation where temptation presented itself. Temptation is like bait on the hook of evil, says Gregory, and therefore, the best way to avoid it is to steer clear of any dangerous desire that might lure people away from God. Gregory notes that the sea is dangerous, but if people go inland, they have nothing to fear of the mighty winds on the ocean. Fire can destroy only if flammable matter is nearby. War can kill many, but only if people are in the battle. Therefore, to avoid falling into temptation, people must basically stay far away from those vices that have the power to destroy.[54]

Augustine also considered daily deliverance from temptation to be the gracious gift of perseverance in the faith.[55] Augustine believed that the goal of both the sixth and seventh petitions was ultimately perseverance, which is only given as a gift by the grace by God. The saints need this grace in order to endure, and the Pelagians are therefore in error when they argue that they are able to persevere by means of their own abilities. Thus, Augustine frequently quoted the sixth petition in his writings against the Pelagians, and he saw it as one of his main theological weapons against heretics in general. For him, the LP revealed that there is nothing in which anyone might glory in, save God. Believers need to seek forgiveness daily, and likewise, they need the perseverance that God grants through the sixth petition.[56]

Early scholars also argued that the value of the seventh petition was that taken by itself, it was a potent statement of faith. Whoever prayed it declared that God had the power to deliver humanity from evil.[57] Once freed from evil, believers were free to fulfill God's will by overcoming temptation[58] and doing what is good.[59]

This summary helps to provide an overall sense of how early Christians typically interpreted the LP. Early writers believed that the power and mystery of the earthly petitions of the LP were able to aid Christians in godly living by meeting all present needs, overcoming past sins, and giving hope to the faithful with regard to future trials. In the end, the earthly petitions, when prayed and made manifest in the lives of the faithful, helped believers to pursue the goals of the heavenly petitions (namely, to honor God's name as holy, to seek God's kingdom, and to do God's will on earth). As a result, the pearl of great price, the real treasure of the church and a central focus of private and public faith, was not only the most important prayer of the early church, it was also the most useful; it not only sought, but delivered heaven into the ordinary earthly lives of believers and made Christ's words a reality in their hearts, bodies, minds, and souls.

The perceived mystery and power of the LP created an awe-filled attitude concerning the LP for the people of the early church; such wonder proved an essential dimension of the LP's widespread popularity and remarkable adaptability. Wherever the LP appeared, local congregations adapted it to regional theological and practical concerns by using alternative variations on the actual wording of the LP. Despite the fact that no single, standard liturgical version of the LP emerges with any regularity until the end of the fourth century, no one seemed to have minded in the least. The words of the LP were the wondrous spoken prayer of Christ, authoritative in and of themselves, no matter what version was being used. The fact that two accounts of the LP existed in the Bible simply reinforced this idea, and as a result, Christian churches even to this day still live fairly comfortably with a variety of LP texts that float around in various congregations and denominations. Oddly enough, even traditions that claim to focus on literal interpretations of the bible almost never pray the precise words of Matthew or Luke in their worship services or private devotions. The primary debate over which wording of the LP is more accurate has only occurred recently in scholarly circles that have been concerned with questions about the historical Jesus. However, for the early church, the LP was a pearl of great price, a spoken mysterious jewel that was daily revered, dusted off, and piously polished in regular communal worship and private devotional practices.

Throughout the time of the early church, the LP was clearly the most widely known and used prayer in Christianity. Various bishops and local churches, however, responded differently to how this gem should be handled. Some, like Ambrose, cradled it cautiously within the confines of the church as a means to inspire the believers to lead godly lives. At the same time, Ambrose guarded his treasure jealously from outsiders. This Bishop of Milan sought to protect and even hide its beauty, along with the other mysteries of the church, from unsuspecting eyes that might see and unknowingly covet the reality of the words, that those who spoke out "Our Father" were indeed children of the Most High Creator and Judge of the universe.

Others, like Augustine, while still embracing the LP with tremendous reverence, slowly allowed the prayer to be taught to those who were outside the fold but who, nonetheless, sought membership in the body of Christ. However, against those who were Christian but were perceived to misinterpret the LP, Augustine passionately defended its interpretation, as did others. These so-called heretics deserved this title, according to some early authors, in part because they did not understand the obvious and magnificent teachings of the LP. Hence, the jewel was transformed into a weapon of orthodox argument that was wielded against any perceived enemy. Or to put it in another way, the prayer in some ways was also the very battleground upon which the war of words was waged. The battles with and over the LP became a fight to define the "true" faith of the early church. The strife over the LP spilled over from being a strictly Christian affair to engaging those outside the walls of church, that is, Jews and "pagans." Sadly, the aforementioned rhetoric often ended in attitudes of intolerance, and with regard to the Jews, it even developed into anti-Semitic tendencies at times.

Within the confines of Christianity, some mused over the sheer beauty of the LP, considering it to be a precious jewel that inspired rapturous poetry and remarkable lyrical prose. Juvencus and Sedulius placed the prayer at the center of their epic works, and generations throughout the Middle Ages came to appreciate and memorize their imaginative reworkings of the LP in their poetry. Gregory of Nyssa and Peter Chrysologus even pondered with noteworthy beauty whether any prose could rise to the lofty heights of the prayer's pulchritude. In his monastery, Cassian likewise loved the LP above all other prayers with words, but he also acknowledged that prayers inspired by God, especially those without words, were able to go beyond the LP in importance. Nevertheless, for Cassian, God's intervention was required for such wordless prayers of spiritual groaning, and since it was the same God who offered the LP, and the summit of prayer outside of the auditory world, there was no contradiction in making such a claim. Even what might be considered mundane and ordinary biblical exegesis or catechesis often waxed with remarkably polished prose when focused on the pearly LP.

It does not seem far-fetched to argue that the early church in part took shape around its simplest and most wondrous expression of the faith: the LP. Indeed, the LP became so vital to the life of the early church that it is impossible to imagine Christianity as we know it without its pearl of great price at the core of Christian ritual and theology. Helmut Theilicke once wrote, "The Lord's Prayer is truly the prayer that spans the world: the world of everyday trifles and universal history, the world with its hours of joy and bottomless anguish, the world of citizens and soldiers, the world of monotonous routine and sudden terrible catastrophe, the world of carefree children and at the same time problems that can shatter grown men [and women]."[60] Early Christians would have agreed with this statement wholeheartedly. For them, the LP defined the world in a way that ordered their chaos, cleansed them of wretchedness, and provided hope for their future. The LP was like a holy of holies for early Christians, the heart of the temple of scripture and the central courtyard of Christian living. Anyone could enter into its wordy sanctuary and find mystery. It was simple enough for the weakest of minds to memorize and wondrous enough for the most learned scholars to contemplate for a lifetime. And so it was treasured, loved, and cherished as a jewel of unsurpassed worth, a pearl of great price.

Notes

Chapter 1

1. Bible verses are taken from the New Revised Standard Version of the Bible unless noted otherwise.
2. Ambrose, *De Sacramentis.*
3. Ambrose, *De Sacramentis* 5.18; cf. both SC 25, pp. 93ff. and CSEL 73, pars 7, pp. 65–66 for two variant readings of this section.
4. Peter Chrysologus, Sermon 67:1–2; CCL 14A, p. 402, English translation in Saint Peter Chrysologus, *Selected Sermons* (New York: Fathers of the Church Inc., 1953), p. 115. A similar passage may be found in Peter Chrysologus, Sermon 70; CCSL 24A, p. 420; the following translation, cf. *Selected Sermons*, pp. 119ff., of this passage is slightly altered by Roy Hammerling, "However, at nothing does heaven stand so much astonished, or earth tremble, or all creation fear exceedingly, as at that which you are going to hear from us today [through the reciting of the LP]. The servant dares to call his Lord Father, the guilty name their judge parent, people in their earthly state bring to themselves by their own voices adoption as God's children. Those who have lost earthly goods deem themselves the heirs of Divinity."
5. Gregory of Nyssa, *The Lord's Prayer, The Beattitudes*, Ancient Christian Writers Series (ACW), Vol. 18 (Westminster, MD: Newman Press, 1954), pp. 37–38; Johannes F. Callahan, ed., *Gregorii Nysseni: De Oratione Dominica, De Beatitudinibus* (Leiden: E.J. Brill, 1992), pp. 21–22.
6. One who has expressed this idea is Karlfried Froehlich, "The LP in Patristic Literature," *Princeton Seminary Bulletin*, Supplemental Vol. 2 (1992), pp. 71–87.
7. Tertullian, *De Oratione* 1; Evans, *Tertullian's Tract on The Prayer*, p. 5; CCL 1, p. 258. Chromatius of Aquileia quoted this statement by Tertullian in his *Tractatus in Matthaeum*; CCSL 9, p. 430.
8. Tertullian, *De Oratione* 1; Evans, *Tertullian's Tract on The Prayer*, p. 15; CCSL 1, p. 262, translation by Sister Emily Joseph Daly in *Tertullian: Disciplinary, Moral and Ascetical Works* (New York: Fathers of the Church Inc., 1959), p. 167.

9. Ambrose similarly declares, "Behold, how brief the (Lord's) Prayer is and how full of all power." Ambrose, *De Sacramentiis,* 5.4.18; SC 29, "Uides quam breuis oratio et omnium plena uirtutum."

10. Cyprian, *De Dominica Oratione* 9; CCL 3 A, p. 94, translation in FC 36, p. 133.

11. Paschasius Radbertus, *Expositio in Mattheo Libri XII*, CCSL 56, pp. 380, 387, 408–409.

12. Theodore of Mopsuestia speaks of the perfection that Jesus conveniently taught in a few brief words. Theodore of Mopsuestia, *Liber ad Baptizandos*, Part 2, Chapter 1, in Theodore of Mopsuestia, *Commentary of Theodore of Mopsuestia on the LP and on the Sacraments of Baptism and the Eucharist* (*Liber ad Baptizandos*), trans. and ed. A. Mingana, Woodbrooke Studies, Vol. 6 (Cambridge: W. Heffer & Sons. Limited, 1933), pp. 1–8. Theodore notes that the perfection of the words is important because anyone praying to God ought to be careful about what they ask God, and the LP is the perfect example of what believers ought to seek in their lives, if there be any doubt as to what people should petition.

13. Cassian, *Conlationes* 9.25; SC 54, p. 61 translation in John Cassian, *Conferences*, trans. Colm Luibheid, (New York: Paulist Press, 1985), p. 116. For another example of one who honors the mystery and power of the LP see Rabanus Maurus, ca. 784–856, in the PL 107:332–333 and his *De institutione clericorum* 2.16. As an aside this sentiment may be found even in modern day commentaries. For example, Joachim Jeremias in his *The Lord's Prayer* (Philadelphia: Fortress Press, 1964), v–vi states, "The Lord's Prayer commands perennial interest—because we know it so little and because we know it so well . . . the prayer is terse in its phraseology but universal in the aspiration of its petitions . . . For all Christians the Lord's Prayer is holy ground."

14. In particular, look at Gregoryii Nysseni, *De Oratione Dominica*, Sermon 3, pp. 31–44; ACW 18, pp. 45–56.

15. Cyprian, *De Dominica Oratione* 28; CCSL 3 A, p. 107, translation in FC 36, p. 151.

16. Cyprian, *De Dominica Oratione* 28; CCSL III A, p. 107, which quotes Isaiah as, "Verbum consummans, inquit, et breuians in iustitia, quoniam sermonem breuiatum faciet Deus in toto orbe terrae." Translation from FC 36, p. 15. The Vulgate version of Isaiah 10:22–23 differs from this version, but clearly is the verse Cyprian referred to. Chromatius of Aquileia in his *Tractatus in Matthaeum* in CCSL 9:430 uses Cyprian's analysis of this passage.

17. Paschasius Radbertus quoted Cyprian on this matter and made the same point in Radbertus, *Expositio in Mattheo Libri XII*; CCSL 56, pp. 408–409.

18. Origen, *On Prayer*, 21.

19. Tertullian, *De Oratione* 1; CCSL 1, p. 258, translation in Evans, *Tertullian's Tract on The Prayer*, p. 5.

20. Gregoryii Nysseni, *De Oratione Dominica*, pp. 17–19; ACW 18, pp. 32–33. Later on, Benedict in his Rule Chapter 20 sets a tone for prayer that involves brevity. Benedict notes that individual prayers, unless "prolonged

by the inspiration of divine grace," should be short. Benedict qualifies this further when he states, "In community, however, prayer should always be brief..." Cf. Benedict, *RB 1980* (Collegeville, MN: Liturgical Press, 1981), p. 65.

21. Tertullian, *De Oratione* 1; CCSL 1, p. 257.
22. Tertullian, *De Oratione* 9; CCSL 1, p. 263.
23. Ulrch Luz, *Matthew 1–7: A Commentary* (Minneapolis, MN: Augsburg, 1985), p. 375.
24. Cyril of Jerusalem, *Catechesis* 23 (*Mystagogica* 5), PG 23:117ff., "De sacra liturgia et communione." Cf. Raymond Brown, "The Pater Noster as an Eschatological Prayer," *Theological Studies* 22 (1961), p. 179.
25. Brown, "The Pater Noster as an Eschatological Prayer," p. 180. For more on this see Lohmeyer, *Our Father,* pp. 11ff.
26. Pseudo-Boniface, Sermon 5; PL 189:853.

Chapter 2

1. This is the traditional numbering of the petitions, which will be used throughout this book to refer to various petitions. This English translation includes in parentheses some ambiguities of the text that exist in either translation or manuscript variance.
2. The Greek reads:

> Πάτερ ἡμῶν ὁ ἐν τοῖς οὐρανοῖς,
>   ἁγιασθήτω τὸ ὄνομά σου,
>   ἐλθέτω ἡ βασιλεία σου,
>   γενηθήτω τὸ θέλημά σου,
>   ὡς ἐν οὐρανῷ καὶ ἐπὶ γῆς.
> Τὸν ἄρτον ἡμῶν τὸν ἐπιούσιον δὸς ἡμῖν σήμερον:
>   καὶ ἄφες ἡμῖν τὰ ὀφειλήματα ἡμῶν,
>   ὡς καὶ ἡμεῖς ἀφήκαμεν τοῖς ὀφειλέταις ἡμῶν:
>   καὶ μὴ εἰσενέγκῃς ἡμᾶς εἰς πειρασμόν,
>   ἀλλὰ ῥῦσαι ἡμᾶς ἀπὸ τοῦ πονηροῦ.

The Latin reads:

> Pater noster, qui es in caelis:
>   sanctificetur nomen tuum.
>   Adveniat regnum tuum.
>   Fiat voluntas tua,
>   sicut in caelo, et in terra.
> Panem nostrum supersubstantialem da nobis hodie.
> Et dimitte nobis debita nostra, sicut et nos
>   dimittibus debitoribus nostris.
> Et ne nos inducas in tentationem.
> Sed libera nos a malo. Amen.

3. The Greek reads:

Πάτερ,
ἁγιασθήτω τὸ ὄνομά σου:
ἐλθέτω ἡ βασιλεία σου:
τὸν ἄρτον ἡμῶν τὸν ἐπιούσιον δίδου ἡμῖν τὸ καθ' ἡμέραν:
καὶ ἄφες ἡμῖν τὰς ἁμαρτίας ἡμῶν,
καὶ γὰρ αὐτοὶ ἀφίομεν παντὶ ὀφείλοντι ἡμιν:
καὶ μὴ εἰσενέγκῃς ἡμᾶς εἰς πειρασμόν.

The Latin reads:

Pater, sanctificetur nomen tuum.
Adveniat regnum tuum.
Panem nostrum cotidianum (or quotidianum) da nobis cotidie.
Et dimitte nobis peccata nostra, siquidem et ipsi dimittimus
omni debenti nobis.
Et ne nos inducas in temptationem.

For another brief survey on this topic see Kenneth W. Stevenson, *The Lord's Prayer: A Text in Tradition* (Minneapolis: Fortress, 2004), p. 19.

4. Ernst Lohmeyer, *Our Father* (New York: Harper and Row, 1965), pp. 291–296.
5. Joachim Jeremias, *The Prayers of Jesus* (London: Alec R. Allenson, Inc., 1967), pp. 88ff.
6. Hans Dieter Betz, *The Sermon on the Mount* (Minneapolis, MN: Fortress Press, 1995), pp. 372ff. The question of Jesus' authorship of the prayer is hotly disputed, and to summarize all the arguments would take this book away from its focus and duplicate Betz, who has an excellent discussion of this.
7. Jeremias, *Prayers of Jesus*, p. 90.
8. Betz, *Sermon on the Mount*, p. 372.
9. James H. Charlesworth, "A Caveat on Textual Transmission and the Meaning of Abba: A Study of the Lord's Prayer," in *The Lord's Prayer and Other Prayer Texts from the Greco-Roman Era* (Valley Forge, PA: Trinity Press International, 1994), pp. 1ff.
10. Jeremias, *Prayers of Jesus*, p. 93.
11. Ulrich Luz, *Matthew 1–7: A Commentary* (Minneapolis, Minnesota: Augsburg Publishing House, 1985), pp. 369ff.
12. Willy Rordorf, "The Lord's Prayer in the Light of its Liturgical Use in the Early Church," *Studia Liturgica* 14 (1980/81), pp. 2–3.
13. Luz, *Matthew*, pp. 369ff.
14. Betz, *Sermon on the Mount*, p. 373.
15. Origen, *On Prayer* 18.3; trans. Rowan Greer, p. 118. Cf. Origen, *Prayer and Exhortation to Martyrdom*, trans. by John J. O'Meara (New York: Newman Press, 1954), p. 66 and Froehlich, Karlfried, "The Lord's Prayer in Patristic Literature," *The Princeton Seminary Bulletin*, Supplemental vol. 2 (1992), p. 76.

16. Origen, *On Prayer* 30.1; Origen, *Prayer and Exhortation to Martyrdom*, p. 162.

17. Augustine, *Enchiridion* 116; CCSL 46, p. 111. Cf. James Moffatt, "Augustine on the Lord's Prayer," *The Expositor* 106 (1919), p. 260. Augustine dealt with the problem of various versions at times. For one example of this see Augustine's discussion of the sixth petition in his *De dono perseverantiae* 6.12 in *The De Dono Perseverantiae of Saint Augustine*, Dissertation by Sister Mary Alphonsine Lesousky (Washington, D.C.: Catholic University of America Press, 1956), pp. 120–121.

18. Froehlich, "The LP in Patristic Literature," pp. 79, 87.

19. Tertullian, *De Oratione* 6; Cassian, *Conlationes* 9.21; Augustine, *De Sermone Domini in Monte* 2.7; Augustine, Sermons 56–59; Chromatius of Aquileia, *Tractatus in Matthaeum* 5.1; Caesarius of Arles, Sermon 147. SC 42, pp. 58–59.

20. Clement of Rome, *First Epistle to the Corinthians* 13.2.

21. Irenaeus, *Adversus Haereses* 5.17.1. Irenaeus also referred to the Father while discussing Romans 8:15 and Galatians 4:6 in *Adversus Haereses* 3.16; 4.9; and 4.8.

22. Clement of Alexandria, *Stromatesis* 7.13.1. Clement of Alexandria refers to the LP more than any other early extra-biblical author during the first and second centuries. For other references see Clement of Alexandria, *Paedagogus* 1.8.73; *Stromatesis* 4.8.66; *Adumbrationes in Judam II*.

23. Mark Kiley, "The Lord's Prayer and Matthean Theology," in *The Lord's Prayer and Other Prayer Texts from the Greco-Roman Era* (Valley Forge, PA: Trinity Press International, 1994), pp. 15ff. Günter Bornkamm has argued that the material of Matthew 6:19–7:12 was intended to serve as a kind of sayings commentary on the LP. Matthew 6:9–13; cf. Günter Bornkamm, "Der Aufbau der Bergpredigt," *New Testament Studies* 24 (1978), pp. 419–432. Asher Finkel has suggested that the LP was the ordering principle of the woes in Matthew 23; cf. Asher Finkel, "The Prayer of Jesus in Matthew," in *Standing before God: Studies on Prayer in Scriptures and in tradition with Essays in Honor of John M. Oesterreicher* (New York: KTAV, 1981), pp. 131–170.

24. *Martyrium Polycarpi* 7.1.

25. Clement of Alexandria, *Stromatesis* 4.8.66.

26. Cf. Burton Scott Easton's translation and notes in Hippolytus, *The Apostolic Tradition of Hippolytus* (Cambridge: Archon Books, 1962), pp. 95–96, which discussed these biblical verses in light of later materials.

27. Rordorf, "LP in the Light of its Liturgical Use," p. 4. Note that by "infant," Rordorf means infant in the faith, and not the age of the one baptized.

28. Clement of Alexandria, *Paedagogus* 1.8.73, also makes brief mention of the words "Our Father, who is in heaven."

29. One other reference in early writings may come from Justin Martyr (ca. 100–165), who offers a veiled comment regarding the LP when he says that catechumens are taught to pray as soon as they are baptized (1 *Apology* 61.2; cf. 65:1–2). Willy Rordorf believes that this refers to the LP. He

justified his remarks by observing that both the *Didache*, which specifically refers to the LP, and Justin talk about prayer and fasting in the same way, and therefore Justin probably means the LP. Rordorf, "LP in the Light of its Liturgical Use," p. 15 n. 11.

30. Cf. Adalbert Hamman, *Early Christian Prayers* (London: 1961) and his *Le Pater expliqué par les Pères* (Paris: Éditions franciscaines, 1952); F. E. Vokes, "The Lord's Prayer in the First Three Centuries," *Studia Patristica* 10 (1970), p. 255.

31. For more on this see Vokes, "The Lord's Prayer in the First Three Centuries," pp. 253–260; Gordon J. Bahr, "The Use of the Lord's Prayer in the Primitive Church," *Journal of Biblical Literature* 84 (1965), pp. 153–159; and Adalbert Hamman, *Le Pater expliqué par les Pères* (Paris: Éditions franciscaines, 1952).

32. J.-P. Audet, *La Didaché. Instructions des apôstles* (Paris: 1958), dates it as early as 60; Betz, *Sermon on the Mount*, p. 8, dates it to 90; For more see Froehlich, "The LP in Patristic Literature," p. 73, and A. Tuilier, "Didache," in *Theologische Realenzyklapädie*, vol. 8 (Berlin and New York: Walther de Gruyter, 1981), pp. 733ff. Many notable scholars argue for the first century date, such as Willy Rordorf: cf. *The Encyclopedia of the Early Church*, vol. 1, p. 234. Discovered in the late nineteenth century, the only Greek manuscript dates to 1056. Two Latin fragments, which may date to the third century, were in manuscripts that date as far back as the ninth or tenth century: cf. Quasten, *Patrology* 1, pp. 29ff. The date of the *Didache* is certainly debatable, but many scholars do place it in the late first century.

33. *Didache* 8. Many modern scholars treat the no-longer-extant source that both Matthew and Luke use, known simply as Q, to be a separate source. Q also may have included a section on the LP, and therefore could be considered a fourth first-century version of the LP. For more on this interesting topic, see Stanley Anderson, Sterling Bjorndahl, Shawn Carruth, and Christoph Heil, *Q 11:2-4*, in the series *Documenta Q: Reconstructions of Q through Two Centuries of Gospel Research Excerpted, Sorted and Evaluated* (Leuven: Peeters, 1996). For more on this, see note 37.

34. Paul Bradshaw, *Daily Prayer in the Early Church: A Study of the Origin and Early Development of the Divine Office* (New York: Oxford University Press, 1982), p. 26. For an extensive study on prayer three times a day in the early church, see *The Apostolic Tradition*, Paul F. Bradshaw, Maxwell E. Johnson, and L. Edward Phillips eds (Minneapolis: Fortress Press, 2002), pp. 194–215.

35. Cf. Siegfried Heinimann, *Oratio Dominica Romance* (Tübingen: Max Niemeyer Verlag, 1988), p. 73.

36. Froelich, "The LP in Patristic Literature," pp. 73–74. The bibliography on this topic is considerable. See in particular: Donald Atkinson, "The Origin and Date of the 'Sator' Word Square," *Journal of Ecclesiastical History* 2 (1951), pp. 1–8; Hugh Last, "The Rotas-Sator Squre: Present Positions and Future Prospects," *Journal of Theological Studies*, 3 (1952), pp. 92–97; S. Euringer, "Das Sator-Arepo-Quadrat," *Historiches Jahrbuch*

71 (1952), pp. 334ff.; Duncan Fishwick, "On the Origin of the Rotas-Sator Square," *Harvard Theological Review* 57 (1964), pp. 39–53; H. Fuchs, "Die Herkunft der Sator-Arepo-Formel," *Heimat un Humanitaet*. Festschrift für K. Meuli (Basel: Krebs, 1951); W.O. Moeller, *The Mithric Origin and Meanings of the Rotas-Sator Square*, "Études préliminaires aux religions orientales," 38 (Leiden: Brill, 1973), esp. pp. 44–52 for a more extensive bibliography. For citations on how some connect the LP to the magical material of Greek Magical Papyri, see Hans Dieter Betz, *The Sermon on the Mount*, p. 300, which mentions Robert Daniel and Franco Maltomini, *Supplementum Magicum* I (Papyrologica Coloniensia 16.1 (Opladen: Westdeutcher Verlag, 1990) no. 29, pp. 79–82, and Horsley, New Documents, 3.103–5; 4.191; 5.144. Brian French from the University of Western Sydney, Australia, plans on publishing a work on the numerous medieval examples of the Sator Rotas square. Dr. French at present believes that the Sator Rotas square may be a secret sign of the LP, but has not found evidence that the medieval church used the square in this way.

37. Some modern biblical scholars have argued that Matthew and Luke used a common source besides the Gospel of Mark when composing their gospels. Some suggest that this document, known simply as Q (short for the German word *Quelle,* meaning the "Source"), included a text of the LP. Others feel that the LP was not in Q. This is a very complicated issue, and it will not be discussed here in detail. Suffice it to say that there is strong evidence for the document Q's existence, even though no such document is extant today. A helpful work that summarizes some scholarly opinions on Q is John S. Kloppenborg, *Q Parallels: Synopsis, Critical Notes, and Concordance* (Sonoma, CA: Polebridge Press, 1988). A more comprehensive survey of the literature on the LP in Q is available in Stanley Anderson, Sterling Bjorndahl, Shawn Carruth, and Christoph Heil, *Q 11:2–4* in the series *Documenta Q: Reconstructions of Q through Two Centuries of Gospel Research Excerpted, Sorted and Evaluated* (Leuven: Peeters, 1996). I am indebted to Dr. Shawn Carruth, who allowed me to read this study before it was published.

38. For more on this, see Frederic Henry Chase, "The Lord's Prayer in the Early Church" in J. Armitage Robinson, ed., *Texts and Studies: Contributions to Biblical and Patristic Literature*, Vol. 1 (Cambridge: Cambridge University Press, 1891), pp. 50–51.

39. Carmel McCarthy, *Saint Ephrem's Commentary on Tatian's Diatessaron* (Oxford: Oxford University Press, 1993), pp. 1ff.

40. Carmel McCarthy, *Saint Ephrem's Commentary on Tatian's Diatessaron*, p. 14.

41. Latin text CCSL 1, pp. 257–263; English translations in FC 40 (1959), pp. 157–168 and Ernest Evans, *Tertullian's Tract on The Prayer* (London: SPCK, 1953). Unless otherwise noted, Tertullian translations are by Evans.

42. Tertullian, *Adversus Praxean* 5 and *De monogamia* 2.

43. It should be noted here that although Tertullian in the formal commentary starts with the prayer as reading, "Father, in heaven . . . ," at times, he

discusses the words "Our Father." He may well have used a version that began with a more Matthean emphasis, but this is how it appears in the commentary.

44. The Latin from Tertullian's *On Prayer* reads,

> Pater, qui in caelis es . . . ,
> sanctificetur nomen tuum . . .
> Fiat voluntas tua in caelis et in terra . . .
> Veniat . . . regnum tuum . . .
> Panem nostrum quotidianum da nobis hodie . . .
> . . . (petamus) dimitti nobis debita nostra, . . . quod remittere nos
>   quoque debitoribus nostris . . .
> Ne nos inducas in temptationem,
> sed devehe nos a malo.

Cf. Moffatt, *Tertullian*, p. 25. The Latin version, though never quoted in and of itself by Tertullian, is taken from the petition by petition commentary of Tertullian's exposition as found in CCSL 1, pp. 258ff. Cf. Siegfried Heinimann, *Oratio Dominica Romanice*, p. 74. The ellipses simply show how and where Tertullian divided up the text in his commentary.

45. Ernest Evans, *Tertullian's Tract on The Prayer* (London: SPCK, 1953), p. 11. Tertullian's tone and verse-by-verse explanation of parts of Matthew 6 reflect a homiletic style. Phrases "O blessed ones" in the first part of the sermon and "to him be honor and power forever and ever" in the concluding lines were both common sermonic devices. *On Prayer*, however, probably represents a detailed collection of sermon notes, rather than a finely crafted homily. Ernest Evans has pointed out that the work has an "unkemptness" in places that supports such an idea. A comparison of *On Prayer* with Tertullian's earlier work *On the Dress of Women* (which Tertullian refers to in *On Prayer* 20), reinforces such a claim. Indeed, some of the theological concepts set forth in *On Prayer* are handled in such an abbreviated fashion that "it is doubtful whether most congregations could have grasped Tertullian's meaning without further explanation." Therefore, he probably offered clarifying comments orally at the time when the sermon was preached in order to make the sermon more comprehensible to his congregation. It is also possible that the text was written down by a scribe and then added to by Tertullian after he preached it. Ernest Evans, *Tertullian's Tract on The Prayer* (London: SPCK, 1953), p. 11; also Klaus Bernhard Schnurr, *Hören und handeln* (Freiburg: Herder, 1985), pp. 23ff.; Quasten, *Patrology* II, pp. 296ff.; and Angelo Di Berardino, ed., *Encyclopedia of the Early Church* II (New York: Oxford University Press, 1992), pp. 818ff.

46. Timothy David Barnes, *Tertullian: A Historical and Literary Study* (Oxford: Clarendon Press, 1971), p. 117.

47. William Harmless, *Augustine and the Catechumenate* (Collegeville, Minnesota: Liturgical Press, 1995), pp. 50ff.

48. Alistair Stewart-Sykes, "Maumission and Baptism in Tertullian's Africa: A Search for the Origin of Confirmation," *Studia Patristica* (2001), pp. 129–149.

49. Tertullian advocated praying at the third hour of the day (the hour when the Holy Spirit came at Pentecost in Acts 2:15), the sixth hour (when Peter saw the vision of all creatures in Acts 10:9), and the ninth hour (when John healed the paralytic in the Temple in Acts 3:1–7); *De oratione* 25; CCSL 1, pp. 272–273; Evans, *Tertullian's Tract on The Prayer*, p. 35. *Didache* 8 noted that the LP should be prayed three times a day, but specific times are not mentioned. Cyprian suggested prayer three times a day at the third, sixth, and ninth hours, but does not mention the LP specifically, though the context of the work might imply it; *De dominica oratione* 34. Tertullian mentioned the specific times of prayer, but did not directly refer to the LP to be prayed at these times. However, given the similarity between the *Didache* and Tertullian, these references may indicate not only when, but that the LP was meant to be prayed three times a day in the early church at the third, sixth, and ninth hours.

50. Tertullian, *De Oratione* 1; CCSL 1, p. 257; Evans, *Tertullian's Tract on The Prayer*, pp. 2–3.

51. Tertullian, *De Oratione* 2; CCSL 1, p. 258; Evans, *Tertullian's Tract on The Prayer*, pp. 4–5.

52. Tertullian, *De Oratione* 3; CCSL 1, p. 259; Evans, *Tertullian's Tract on The Prayer*, p. 7.

53. Tertullian, *De Oratione* 29; CCSL 1, p. 274, "Oratio murus est fidei, arma et tela nostra aduersus hostem . . . ."

54. Tertullian, *De Oratione* 1, 2, 14, and 28.

55. Tertullian, *Adversus Marcionem* IV.26; SC 365 (Book 1), SC 368 (Book 2), and SC 399 (Book 3); E. P. Meijering, *Tertullian Contra Marcion: Gotteslehre in der Polemik: Adversus Marcionem I-II* (Leiden: E.J. Brill, 1977); Latin and English in Ernest Evans, *Adversus Marcionem*, 2 vols. (Oxford: Oxford University Press, 1972); and ANF 3, pp. 288ff.

56. Cf. Evans, *Adversus Marcionem*, pp. 480–481. Jeremias, *The Lord's Prayer*, p. 2.

57. Jeremias, *The Lord's Prayer*, p. 3.

58. T. Zahn, *Das Evangelium des Lucas 3. und 4. durchgeshene Aufl.*, (Leipzig: A. Deichert, 1920), p. 769; J. C. O'Neill, "The Lord's Prayer," *Journal for the Study of the New Testament* 51 (1993), pp. 8–10, says that the original Lucan opening read, "Father, let your Spirit come and cleanse us."

59. The Luke connection makes sense for some scholars because Luke has an emphasis upon the Holy Spirit. Therefore, they argue this petition might be consistent with an earlier version of the gospel and the LP in it. Cf. A. R. C. Leaney, "The Lucan Text of the Lord's Prayer (Lk xi 1–4)," *Novum Testamentum* 1 (1956), pp. 104–105, and A.R.C. Leaney, *A Commentary on the Gospel According to Luke*, (London: Adam & Charles Black, 1958), pp. 60–61; O'Neill, "The Lord's Prayer," pp. 8–10; John Meier, *A Marginal Jew. Rethinking the Historical Jesus*, Vol. 2, *Mentor, Message,*

and Miracles. The Anchor Bible Reference Library (New York: Doubleday, 1994), p. 356, mentions that the Lucan variations come in the eleventh-century manuscript entitled simply MS 700 and a twelfth-century MS 162. It also says that Maximus of Turin (d. 430), who was probably relying on Gregory of Nyssa, also referred to this. In the end, Joachim Jeremias, *The Lord's Prayer* (Philadelphia: Fortress Press, 1964), p. 3, concluded that this text tradition remains weak, and the original version should be considered to be what was in Luke as the earlier versions record it. For more on Maximus Confessor see Maximus Confessor, *Selected Writings* (New York: Paulist Press, 1985), pp. 107ff.

60. Cf. Gregoryii Nysseni, *De Oratione Dominica*, pp. 40–44; ACW 18, pp. 53–56.

61. Cf. M. J. Lagrange, *Évangile selon Saint Luc* (Paris: Libraire Lecoffre, 1921), p. 323; Burnett H. Streeter *The Four Gospels* (London: Macmillan Co., 1925); Gordon W. Lampe, *Studies in the Gospels, Essays in Memory of R.H. Lightfoot,* (Oxford: Basil Blackwell, 1955), p. 170; T. W. Manson, "The Lord's Prayer," *Bulletin of the John Rylands University Library of Manchester* 38 (1956), pp. 105–106; and Meier, *A Marginal Jew*, p. 356.

62. F. C. Burkitt in a review of B.H. Streeter's, "Four Gospels," *Journal of Theological Studies* 26 (1925), pp. 288–290.

63. A. Plummer, *A Critical Study and Exegetical Commentary on the Gospel According to St. Luke* (Edinburgh: T&T Clark, 1896), p. 295; J. M. Creed, *The Gospel According to St. Luke* (London: Macmillan, 1930), p. 156; F. Hauck, *Das Evangelium des Lukas* (Leipzig: Hinrichs'sche Buchhandlung: 1934), p. 134; Lampe, "The Holy Spirit . . . ," p. 170; Manson, "The Lord's Prayer," (1956), pp. 105–106; I.H. Marshall, *The Gospel of Luke: A Commentary on the Greek Text,* (Grand Rapids, Michigan: Eerdmans, 1978), p. 458; Meier, *The Marginal Jew*, p. 356.

64. Jeremias, *The Lord's Prayer*, p. 3. Also cf. Jeremias, *New Testament Theology,* (New York: Charles Scribner's Sons, 1971), p. 194, states that the logical place to connect the LP and the Holy Spirit is in the ceremony of baptism.

65. F.E. Vokes, "The Lord's Prayer in the First Three Centuries," p. 257. Cf. Shawn Carruth's analysis of this discussion and the detailed work on Marcion in *Q 11:2–4* in the series *Documenta Q: Reconstructions of Q through Two Centuries of Gospel Research Excerpted, Sorted and Evaluated* (Leuven: Peeters, 1996).

66. Jeremias, *New Testament Theology*, p. 194.

67. Ernest Evans, *Adversus Marcionem* (Oxford: Oxford University Press, 1972) and SC 365, 368, 399 are only books 1–3. Translation in ANF 3, p. 369, slightly altered by this author.

68. Some have said that the request for the Holy Spirit was in place of the name petition, while others feel that it was in place of the kingdom petition. The latter suggestion does not seem possible since Tertullian referred to this petition in his analysis. Cf. Evans, *Adversus Marcionem*, pp. 480–481.

69. Liturgical scholars looking at the works of Tertullian for the shape and content of the baptismal and catechetical ceremonies surrounding baptism will be disappointed. Tertullian alluded to a catechumenate practice, but just how the North African church carried out its baptismal preparation program remains largely unknown. Even Tertullian's *De Baptismo*, CCSL 1 is not much help. Roy Defferari has claimed that Tertullian's work mentioned the ceremonies for baptism; FC 36, p. 125. However, such a claim cannot be sustained. For more on this, cf. Michel Jujarier, *A History of the Catechumenate: The First Six Centuries* (New York: William H. Sadlier, 1979), pp. 41–63; Michel Dujarier, *Le Parrianage des adultes aux trois premiers siècles de l'Egliese. Recherche historique sur l'évolution des garanties et des étapes catéchuménales avant 313* (Paris, 1962); Joseph Lynch, *Godparents and Kinship in Early Medieval Europe* (Princeton, NJ: Princeton University Press, 1986), pp. 93ff.

  With regard to infant and adult baptism, Tertullian believed that baptizing infants was not necessary, and he even disapproved of the practice, questioning, "Why should innocent infancy be in such a hurry to come to the forgiveness of sins? Let them come while they are maturing, while they are learning, while they are being taught what it is they are coming to. Let them be made Christians when they have become able to know Christ." Tertullian, *De Baptismo*, 18.5; CCSL 1, p. 293; translation in Jaroslav Pelikan, *The Emergence of the Catholic Tradition (100–600)* (Chicago: University of Chicago Press, 1971), p. 290.

70. Some debate over the date of *De dominica oratione* exists. Some, like Defferari (FC 36, p. 125), believe Cyprian wrote it after his work *De unitate ecclesiae,* while others, like Saxer, *Encyclopedia of the Early Church*, p. 211, hold to the date of 250 or before *De unitate*. Some key themes of *De dominica oratione* do not anticipate, but rather flow out of, the concerns expressed in *De unitate ecclesiae* and therefore 252 is more likely accurate, that is, some time shortly after *De unitate* was written.

71. Cyprian, *De Dominica Oratione* 7; CCSL 3A, p. 93; FC 36, p. 132.

72. . . . *et ne patiaris induci nos in temptationem.* Ambrose's (d. 397) LP is almost identical to Cyprian's, except for the word order of the sixth petition, which reads, *et ne nos patiaris induci in temptationem.*

73. Ambrose, *De sacramentis*, 5.5.29.

74. Cyprian had a few practical suggestions about prayer in this treatise. For example, Cyprian stated that God quickly lends an ear to those who add good works, such as fasting and almsgiving, to prayers (*De Dominica Oratione*, 32–33). For a comparison with Augustine on this point see Sermon 206 where Augustine noted that it is through humility, love, fasting and almsgiving that prayer flies supported on the wings of virtue straight and swiftly to heaven.

75. Cf. Roy Defferari; FC 36, p. 125.

76. Cyprian, *De Dominica Oratione* 8; CCSL 3 A, pp. 93–94, "Ante omnia pacis doctor atque unitatis magister singillatim noluit et priuatim precem fieri, ut quis cum precatur pro se tantum precetur. Non dicimus: *pater meus,*

qui es in caelis... Publica est nobis et communis oratio, et quando ora-
mus, non pro uno sed pro populo toto rogamus, quia totus populus unum
sumus... Perseuerabant in oratione unanimes orationis suae et instantia
simul et concordiam declarantes, quia Deus qui inhabitare facit unanimes
in domo non admittit in diuinam et aeternam domum nisi apud quos est
unanimis oratio." Translation in FC 36, pp. 131–132. For more on the
theme of "unity," cf. Cyprian, *De Dominica Oratione* 23 and 30.

77. Cyprian, *De Dominica Oratione* 23, 30; FC 36, pp. 147, 153; CCSL 3 A,
pp. 104, 108.

78. Cyprian, *De Dominica Oratione* 23; CCSL 3 A, p. 104; FC 36, p. 147.
Note that Tertullian had argued the same point.

79. Cyprian, *De Dominica Oratione* 9; CCSL 3 A, p. 94; FC 36, pp. 133–134.

80. Cyprian, *De Dominica Oratione* 2.

81. Cyprian, *De Dominica Oratione* 9; CCSL 3 A, p. 94, here quoted John
1:11–12, "He came unto his own and his own received him not. But as
many as received him, he gave the power to become sons of God, to those
who believe his name." Translation in FC 36, p. 134.

82. Cyprian, *De Dominica Oratione* 10; FC 36, pp. 134–135; CCSL 3 A, p. 95;
Cf. Froehlich, "The Lord's Prayer in Patristic Literature," pp. 74–75; *Apostolic Constitutions* 7:45; and Willy Rordorf, "The Lord's Prayer in the Light
of Its Liturgical Use in the Early church," *Studia Liturgica* 14 (1980/81),
pp. 1–19.

83. Cyprian, *De Dominica Oratione* 12; CCSL 3 A, pp. 96–97, "... id petimus
et rogamus, ut qui in baptismo sanctificati sumus in eo quod esse coepimus
perseueremus. Et hoc cottidie deprecamur. Opus est enim nobis cotidi-
ana sanctificatio, ut qui cotidie delinquimus delicta nostra sanctificatione
assidua repurgemus." Translation in FC 36, p. 136.

84. For more on the theme of perseverance, see Cyprian, *De Dominica Oratione*
12–13, 36, CCSL 3 A, pp. 95–96, 113; FC 36, pp. 134ff., 159. Later on
Augustine will develop this theme further.

85. Cyprian, *De Dominica Oratione* 22; CCSL 3 A, p. 104, "Ideo et fidelem
dixit Dominum ad dimittenda peccata fidem pollicitationis suae reseruan-
tem, quia qui orare nos pro debitis et peccatis docuit paternam misericor-
diam promisit et ueniam secuturam." Translation FC 36, p. 147.

86. Cyprian, *De Dominica Oratione* 9–10; CCSL 3 A, pp. 94ff.; FC 36,
pp. 133ff.

87. Cyprian's work *On the Lord's Prayer* proved to be enormously popular.
Hilary of Poitiers (ca. 315–367) in his commentary on Matthew found
no reason to comment on Matthew 6:9–13, because, as he put it, Cyprian
had already said all that needed to be said (PL 9:913). Augustine, in a letter to Valentinus, explained that he used Cyprian's commentary on the LP
because Cyprian had anticipated the "poison of Pelagius." Augustine, Sermon 215; FC 32, p. 64. Even modern scholars have gone so far as to call
Cyprian's commentary "the best work on the (LP) in the long history of
Christianity." FC 36, p. 125.

88. A. F. J. Klijn, *The Acts of Thomas* (Leiden: E. J. Brill, 1962), p. 142.

89. Edgar Hennecke, ed., *New Testament Apocrypha*, vol. 2 (Cambridge: James Clarke & Co, 1992), p. 396. The section on the *Acts of Thomas* is done by Han J.W. Drijvers. For more on the complicated history of this particular version of the LP, see Drikjver's discussion in the aforementioned work.

90. *New Testament Apocrypha*, vol. 2, pp. 427ff.

91. *New Testament Apocrypha*, vol. 2, p. 426.

92. New Testament Apocrypha, vol. 2, pp. 428ff.

93. Origen, *On Prayer* XXIV.5; Origen, *An Exhortation to Martyrdom, Prayer and Selected Works*, Classics of Western Spirituality (New York: Paulist Press, 1979), pp. 130–131.

94. Origen, *On Prayer* XIII.2; Origen, Classics, p. 118.

95. Origen, *On Prayer* V.1-VII; Origen, Classics, pp. 90–97. Gregory of Nyssa and Augustine are examples of other authors who at times express some similar concerns.

96. Origen, *On Prayer* XVI; Origen, Classics, pp. 112–114.

97. Origen, *On Prayer*, P. Koetschau, ed., *Die Griechischen Christlichen Schriftsteller der ersten drei Jahrhunderte* (Berlin: Akademi Verlag, 1899); *Origen*, Classics of Western Spirituality (New York: Paulist Press, 1979); LCC 19.

98. Origen, *On Prayer*, P. Koetschau ed., *Die Griechischen Christlichen Schriftsteller der ersten drei Jahrhunderte* (Berlin: Akademi Verlag, 1899); *Origen*, Classics of Western Spirituality (New York: Paulist Press, 1979); LCC 19.

99. Origen, *On Prayer* II.1-II.6, XXV.1-2, XXVII.2, XXVII.10–11, XXVIII.2–3; Origen, Classics, pp. 82–86, 131–133, 138, 142, 147–148.

100. Tertullian, *De Oratione* 6; translation by Evans, p. 11; CCSL 1, p. 260. For another example of this, see Theodore of Mopsuestia (ca. 350–428), *On the Lord's Prayer*, p. 8.

101. Augustine, *Enchiridion* 11; CCSL 46, pp. 110–111; translation from St. Augustine, *The Enchiridion on Faith, Hope and Love*, ed. Henry Paulucci (South Bend, Indiana: Regnery/Gateway, Inc. 1961), pp. 132–133. Also see the discussion of the third and fourth petitions of Cassian, *Conlationes* 9.20–21; SC 42, pp. 57ff.; Cassian, *Conferences*, Luibheid, pp. 113–114.

102. *Sermon on the Mount* II.10; CCL 35, p. 127; translation from ACW 5, p. 124.

103. Augustine, Sermon 58.12; PL 38, p. 399; translation from Augustine, *Sermons: The Works of Saint Augustine*, trans. and ed. Edmund Hill, Augustine's *Sermons*, Vol. III/3 (Brooklyn: New City Press, 1990), p. 124.

104. For more on early Latin versions of the LP see Bonifatus Fischer, *Die Lateinischern Evangelien bis zum 10. Jahrhundert* (Freiburg: Verlag Herder, 1990), pp. 5–48, 309–317.

105. For more on this, see Ingemar Furberg, *Das Pater Noster in der Messe* (Lund: CWK Gleerups Förlag, 1968); Siegfried Heinimann, *Oratio Dominica Romanice* (Tübingen: Max Niemeyer Verlag, 1988); Willy Rordorf, "The LP in the Light of its Liturgical Use in the Early Church," *Studia Liturgica* 14 (1980), pp. 1–19; and for more see Monica Dorneich, *The Lord's Prayer: A Bibliography* (Freiburg in Breisgau: Herder, 1982).

106. Willy Rordorf, *Der Sonntag* (Zurich: Zwingli Verlag, 1962), pp. 263ff., 284ff., in the English Translation *Sunday*, pp. 267–271, 289–293, mentions that the LP formed an integral part of the *Missa fidelium* and that congregation prayed it like other prayers standing with hands extended facing East.
107. The *Didache* 8 implies that people prayed the LP three times a day. Cf. Paul F. Bradshaw, "Prayer, Morning, Noon, Evening, and Midnight—an Apostolic Custom?" *Studia Liturgica* 13 (1979), pp. 57–62. Rordorf, "The LP in Light of its Liturgical Use," p. 15, warns that scholars have often over-emphasized the LP in private practice; an example of this is Noele-Maurice Denis-Bôulet, *La Maison-Dieu* (1966).
108. Betz, *Sermon on the Mount*, p. 371.

Chapter 3

1. Klaus Schnurr has quite appropriately called this the *Initiatorisch-katechetische Auslegung*; Schnurr, *Hören und Handeln*, p. 277.
2. For more on all of these and other such terms see Cheslyn Jones, Geoffrey Wainright, Edward Yarnold, eds., *The Study of the Liturgy* (New York: Oxford University Press, 1978), pp. 97ff.
3. Works where Augustine has sizeable or important commentary on the LP are his *Against Two Letters of the Pelagians, Enchiridion,* Letter 130 to Proba, *On Correction and Grace, On Grace and Free Will, On the Works of Pelagius, On the Gift of Perseverance, On Marriage and Concupiscence, On the Merits of Sinners, Forgiveness,* and *On the Baptism of Infants Against Marcellinus, On Nature and Grace, On the Perfection of Human Justice, On the Sermon on the Mount, On Holy Virginity, The Rule of St. Augustine,* and Sermons 56–59, just to name a few of the most important works.
4. Jerome, *De Viris Illustribus*, Chapter 84, "Juvencus, nobilissimi generis, Hispanus presbyter, quatuor Evangelia hexametris versibus paene ad verbum transferens, quatuor libros composuit, et nonnulla eodem transferens, quatuor libros composuit, et nonnulla eodem metro ad sacramentorum ordinem pertinentia. Floruit sub Constantino principe." The literature on Juvencus is limited but for more see Otto J. Kuhnmuench, *Early Christian Latin Poets from the Fourth to the Sixth Century* (Chicago: Loyola Univ. Press, 1929); R. Herzog, *Die Bibelepik der lateinischen Spätantike*, vol. 1 (Munich: 1975); J. Fontaine, *Naissance de la poésie dans l'occident chrétien. IIIe-VIe siècles* (Paris: Etudes augustiniennes, 1981); M. A. Norton, "Prosopography of Juvencus" in J. M. F. Maricq (ed.), *Leaders of Iberian Christianity* (Boston: 1962); I. Opelt, "Die Szenerie bei Iuvencus," *Vigiliae Christianae* 19 (1975), pp. 191–207. For editions of the *Evangeliorum Libri IV* see PL 19:53–546 and CSEL 24; CPL 1385.
5. F. J. E. Raby, *A History of Christian Latin Poetry from the Beginnings to the Close of the Middle Ages* (Oxford: Clarendon Press, 1953), pp. 17ff.; Otto J. Kuhnmuench, *Early Christian Latin Poets from the Fourth to the Sixth Centuries* (Chicago: Loyola University Press, 1929), pp. 13ff.

6. Juvencus, *Evangeliorum Libri IV* 1.590–600; CSEL 24, p. 32; PL 19:131ff.
7. Juvencus, *Evangeliorum Libri IV* 1.580–589; CSEL 24, pp. 31–32.
8. Various other first names such as Caelius, Cellius, Caecilius, C. Caecilius, and Circilius have also been applied to Sedulius. The early manuscripts, however, only use Sedulius. Carl P. E. Springer, *The Gospel as Epic in Late Antiquity: The* Paschale Carmen *of Sedulius* (Leiden: E.J. Brill, 1988), p. 29.
9. Springer, *The Gospel as Epic*, pp. 55ff.; A. J. O. J. Kuhnmuench, *Early Christian Latin Poets* (Chicago: Loyola University Press, 1929), p. 13, also notes that there are 40 manuscripts of the *Evangeliorum* that are extant, with the oldest of them dating to the seventh or eighth century. Also, between 1490 and 1700, there were 28 printed editions of this work.
10. Springer has suggested that Sedulius taught philosophy and poetry in Italy, but wrote his works in Greece. His *Paschale carmen* neither confirms nor denies this. A. D. McDonald suggests that Sedulius was from southern France, northern Spain, or northern Italy, because Sedulius' description of the slaughter of the innocents is similar to the iconographic tradition in those areas, namely, that the children were not killed by the sword, but dashed upon rocks. A. D. McDonald, "The Iconographic Tradition of Sedulius," *Speculum* 8 (1933), pp. 150–156, also argued that there are parallels with the women at the tomb story. But Carl Springer has noted that Sedulius also may have been following Prudentius' description of the infants of Bethlehem. Prudentius used the image of dashing upon rocks as well. Paschasius Radbertus claimed Sedulius was a *rhetor Romanae ecclesiae* (*De partu virgine* 2, PL 120:1385), but there is no firm evidence for this.
11. *Paschale carmen* 1.23–26; Springer, *Gospel as Epic*, pp. 28ff., 60ff.; *Encyclopedia of the Early Church* (EEC) 2, p. 766; Isidore of Seville called him presbyter (*De viris illustribus* 10; PL 83:1094); Alcuin referred to him as a bishop (PL 101:609) and Sigibert of Gembloux (PL 160:549) dated him to the time of Constantine's sons; he also said he was a bishop, but these sources are so late that they are not reliable. For more cf. Quasten 4, p. 322.
12. In the introduction, Sedulius admitted this title comes from a phrase in 1 Corinthians 5:5, "*pascha nostrum immolatus est Christus*" or "Christ our pasch (paschal lamb) has been sacrificed." The focus is clearly on Christ the miracle worker, the one who has come as the lamb to perform the greatest miracle of all, to save the world. Critical editions of the *Paschale carmen* may be found in PL 19:433–752, which has a convenient side-by-side edition of the *Paschale carmen* and *Paschale opus*; CSEL 10; for partial English translations, see George Sigerson, *The Easter Song* (Dublin: Talbot Press Ltd., 1922), R. A. Swanson, "Carmen Paschale I," *Classics Journal* 52 (1957), pp. 289–298, and Kuhnmuench, *Early Christian Latin Poets*; and for Italian and Dutch translations, see F. Coraro, *Sedulio poeta*, (Catina, 1956) and N. Schefs, *Sedulius Paschale Carmen*, Boek I en II (Delft: 1938).
13. Cf. J. P. Lewis, *A Study of the Interpretation of Noah and the Flood in Jewish and Christian Literature* (Leiden: E.J. Brill, 1968), pp. 101–120.
14. Coelius Sedulius, *Paschale carmen* 1.38–44.

15. Coelius Sedulius, *Paschale carmen* 1:49–59. Certain Christian writings, for example, the *Confessions* of Augustine, clearly demonstrate how Christianity had an appeal among the educated elite of the late fourth and fifth century world, and how brilliant philosophers at times converted to Christianity. Augustine's *Confessions* mention how Ambrose, Augustine, Victorinus, and numerous other noted philosophers converted to Christianity.
16. This group was mentioned in the prefatory letter at the beginning of the *Paschale carmen*. For more cf. Springer, *Gospel as Epic*, pp. 30ff.
17. Sedulius, *Paschale carmen* 2.234–236; CSEL 10, p. 58.
18. Sedulius, *Paschale carmen*, Preface 15–16; Cf. Springer, *Gospel as Epic*, p. 83.
19. Springer, *Gospel as Epic*, pp. 83ff.
20. Juvencus, *Evangeliorum Libri IV* 1.591–592.
21. Sedulius, *Paschale carmen* 2.244–248; CSEL 10, pp. 60–61.
22. Sedulius, *Paschale carmen* 2.249–254; CSEL 10, pp. 60–61,

> Now may "Your Kingdom Come," namely, that
> (kingdom where there is neither) resting
> in death nor being cut off in the end,
> where in eternity no time follows,
> because there time does not have night,
> but only continuous day: where with Christ the Prince,
> his head being encircled with a noble eternal crown,
> the victor like a soldier will rejoice carrying away rich reward.

23. Springer, *Gospel as Epic*, pp. 100–109.
24. Sedulius, *Paschale carmen* 2:298–300; CSEL 10, p. 64.
25. Cf. Springer, *Gospel as Epic*, pp. 87ff.
26. Sedulius, *Paschale carmen*, 2.285–287; CSEL 10, p. 63:

> Therefore on account of this let us take a step back
> and in the heart may we seek the narrow way,
> the narrow path which leads by the narrow gate to the celestial kingdom.

27. Sedulius, *Paschale carmen* 2.263–268; CSEL 10, pp. 61–62:

> We hope for the loaves of faith along with daily bread,
> Lest our fasting minds ever feel the hunger of doctrine
> from Christ, who by himself with his body and from his mouth
> feeds us, just as he himself abides in the word and food.
> How sweet are the words of our Lord upon our palates,
> they are more than all the honey and honeycombs (to my mouth)
> (Psalm 118/119:103).

28. Springer, *Gospel as Epic*, p. 68.
29. Pierre de Labriolle, *History and Literature of Christianity* (New York: Barnes & Noble, 1968), p. 475 notes that Macedonius wanted him to rewrite the *Paschale carmen* in order to "repair (as he explains in the preface) the omissions which the *angustia metricae necessitatis* had imposed upon him." The actual letter (*Paschale opus*, 171.29) reads in a translation by Michael

Robbers, *Biblical Epic and Rhetorical Paraphrase in Late Antiquity* (Liverpool: Francis Cairns, 1985), p. 79, "You have instructed me, reverent sir, to rewrite in rhetorical prose the text of my *Paschale carmen* which in humble performance of my duty of perfect devotion I presented to you to read. I feel myself wavering, uncertain in my judgment, whether you wanted the work duplicated because it pleased you or, as I am inclined to believe, you thought it should be written in a more unhampered style, because as it was, it displeased you. Nevertheless I have not resisted your holy commands but have undertaken the task enjoined on me . . . " Roberts believed, p. 80, that this text is not to be taken too seriously and that it is merely a rhetorical device for providing a justification for the *opus*. Roberts continued by arguing that Macedonius was not displeased and that Sedulius merely wanted to write his work again, this time without the constraints of meter.

30. Quasten 4, p. 324.
31. Springer, *Gospel as Epic*, p. 20.
32. This may be an indication that Sedulius is relying upon Augustine, who makes similar statements, see especially Augustine's *De Sermone Domini in Monte* on the introduction to the LP.
33. Sedulius, *Paschale opus* 2.17; CSEL 10, pp. 220–221.
34. Sedulius, *Paschale opus* 2.17; CSEL 10, p. 222.
35. Sedulius, *Paschale opus* 2.17; CSEL 10, p. 222.
36. Sedulius, *Paschale opus* 2.17; CSEL 10, pp. 224–226. John Cassian (d. 435), a close contemporary of Sedulius, said that there were four levels of interpretation, namely, 1. the literal, 2. the tropological or moral, 3. the anagogical or those things dealing with salvation and the end times, and 4. the allegorical or spiritual meaning.
37. Quasten 4, 322.
38. For more, see Springer, *Gospel as Epic*, p. 82; E. R. Curtius, *European Literature and the Latin Middle Ages*. Trans. Willard Trask, (London: Routledge and Kegan Paul, 1953), p. 148; Roberts, *Biblical Epic and Rhetorical Paraphrase in Late Antiquity*, pp. 78–79.
39. Springer, *Gospel as Epic*, pp. 128ff.
40. For the critical edition of Remigius' commentary on the *Paschale carmen*, see CSEL 10, pp. 316–59, with the section on the LP being on pp. 336–338.
41. Springer, *Gospel as Epic*, p. 1.
42. Quasten 4, 324. Sigerson pointed out that during the years 1501–1588, no less than 75 editions of the *carmen* found their way to print. Sigerson, *The Easter Song*, pp. 69–70.
43. Edward Sievers, *Heliand* (1935 reprint of his 1878 edition); *The Heliand: The Saxon Gospel*, G. Ronald Murphy trans. and commentary (New York: Oxford University Press, 1992); John Knight Bostock, *A Handbook on Old High German Literature* (1976), pp. 168–186.
44. Francis and Clare, *The Complete Works* (New York: Paulist Press, 1982), p. 104; Kajetan Esser, "Die dem hl. Franziskus von Assisi

zugeschriebene 'Expositio in Pater Noster,'" *Collectanea Franciscana* 40 (1970), pp. 241–271.

45. Francis Mary Schwab, *David of Augsburg's 'Pater Noster' and the Authenticity of His German Works* (München: C.H. Beck'sche Verlagsbuchhandlung, 1971).

46. Dante, *Purgatorio*, Canto 11.

47. Siegried Heinimann, *Oratio Dominica Romanice* (Tübingen: Max Niemeyer Verlag, 1988), pp. 80ff.

48. Kuhnmuench, *Early Christian Latin Poets*, p. 13, notes that Juvencus used the Vetus Itala Latin version of the Bible and that Juvencus was later on widely quoted and was even used in early church school textbooks. The *Evangeliorum Libri IV* survives in 40 MSS, the oldest of which dates to the seventh or eighth century; likewise, it was printed in 28 editions between 1490 and 1700. For various versions of paraphrased and poetic Pater Noster's cf. Siegried Heinimann, *Oratio Dominica Romanice* and H. Walther, "Versifizierte Paternoster und Credo," Revue du Moyen Age Latin 20 (1964), pp. 45–64. Also, for an interesting comical later parody of the Lord's Prayer cf. Paul Lehmann, *Die Parodie im Mittelalter* (Stuttgart: Anton Hiersemann, 1963), pp. 195ff.

49. An earlier version of this section of the chapter previously appeared in a slightly different form in Roy Hammerling, ed., *A History of Prayer: The First to the Fifteenth Century* (Leiden: Brill, 2008), pp. 167–182, where it is entitled "The Lord's Prayer: The Cornerstone of Early Baptismal Catechesis."

50. Ambrose, *De Sacramentis* 5.18; SC 25, p. 93.

51. Fr. Petit, "Sur les catéchèses post-baptismales de saint Ambroise. A propos de *De sacramentis* IV, 29," *Revue Bénédictine* 68 (1958), pp. 156–265. Later on we will see that Ildephonsus of Toledo (d. 669) also taught the LP after baptism, but in his case, after baptism and before the Eucharist was celebrated; cf. Whitaker, *Documents of the Baptismal Liturgy*, p. 115.

52. Cyril of Jerusalem, *Mystagogic Catechesis* 5; Edward Yarnold, *Cyril of Jerusalem*, (London: Routledge, 2000), pp. 34–55, 182–187; SC 126, pp. 156–175.

53. Alexis James Doval, *Cyril of Jerusalem, Mystagogue: The Authorship the Mystagogia Catechesis* (Washington DC: Catholic University of America Press: 2001), 160 who also points to Gregory Dix, *The Shape of the Liturgy* (London: Dacre Press, 1964), pp. 108–109, 130–131. Doval also points out that the Apostolic Constitutions, which date from the same period, state that the Our Father was prayed by recently baptized converts as a part of the baptismal rite after the chrismation (*Apostolic Constitutions* 3:18). Doval concludes that the LP became a part of the Eucharistic Liturgy in the early fourth century. He points also to Josef Andrewas Jungmann, *The Mass of the Roman rite: Its Origins and Development* (Missarum Sollemnia), trans. Francis A Brunner, 2 vols. (New York: Benziger, 1951–1955), 2:280.

54. Originally intended to be the text that was recited by converts at their baptism, the Apostles' Creed was handed over by Ambrose on Palm Sunday.

Those wading in the water, awaiting baptism were asked, "Do you believe in God the Father?" and they responded by reciting the first article of the Creed. In turn, the questions, "Do you believe in God the Son?" and "God the Holy Spirit?" were asked and they in turn responded with the second and third articles. For more on this in Ambrose, see *Epistolae* 20.4; PL 16:1037. Also, for an analysis of the Milanese situation with regard to the baptismal rite down through the Carolingian Era, see F. D. C. Fisher, *Christian Initiation*, pp. 30ff. and Leonel L. Mitchell, "Ambrosian Baptismal Rites," *Studia Liturgica* 1 (1962), pp. 241–253.

55. Cyril of Jerusalem, *Catechesis* 5.12; Yarnold, Cyril of Jerusalem, pp. 112–114; SC 126, pp. 160–161. Cf. Sozomen (early fifth century), *Historia Ecclesiastica* 1.20, which also does not write down the Nicene Creed, suggesting that it is for the initiated alone and not to be written.

56. Peter Chrysologus, Sermons 60 and 61; CCSL 24, pp. 335ff.

57. Cf. Peter Chrysologus, Sermons 57; FC 17, pp. 103ff.; CCSL 24, p. 318.

58. Didymus, *De Trinitate* 3.39; PG 39:978ff.

59. Cf. Yarnold, *The Awe-Inspiring Rites*, p. 56.

60. CSEL 32, p. 369, "Est etiam illa commendandae orationis et uoti disciplina, ut non diuulgemus orationem, sed abscondita teneamus mysteria, sicut tenuit Abraham, qui subcinericias fecit." Translation in FC 42:391–392. Cf. Bouhot, *Une ancienne homélie catéchétique*, p. 71; Fr. Petit, "Sur les catéchèses post-baptismales de saint Ambroise. A propos de De sacramentis IV, 29," *Revue Bénédictine* 68 (1958), pp. 156–265.

61. CSEL 32, p. 370, "Caue ne incaute symboli uel dominicae orationis diuulges mysteria." For more on this, see the discussion of the Lord's Prayer in Ulrich Luz's, *Matthew 1–7: A Commentary* (Minneapolis: Augsburg, 1989).

62. Ambrose, *De Sacramentis* 5.18; cf. both SC 25, pp. 93ff. and CSEL 73, pars 7, pp. 65–66. for two variant readings of this section.

63. Cf. St. Ambrose, *On the Sacraments and On the Mysteries*, trans. T. Thompson, ed. and notes J.H. Srawley (London: SPCK, 1950), p. 4; FC 44, p. 266; Ambrosius, *De Sacramentis, De Mysteriis*, ed. Josef Schmitz (Freiburg: Herder, 1990), pp. 9ff.

64. Cf. O. Faller's introduction who edited *Sancti Ambrosii Opera, pars vii*, CSEL 73, (Vienna: Hoelder-Pichler-Tempsky, 1955).

65. Ambrose, *On the Sacraments and On the Mysteries*, trans. T. Thompson, ed. and notes J. H. Srawley, pp. 4ff. Others have offered alternate interpretations that are not completely satisfactory in light of this evidence. For example, L. L. Mitchell, "Ambrosian Baptismal Rites," *Studia Liturgica* 1 (1962), p. 241.

66. The authorship of these two works has long been debated. More recent scholarship has tended to hold that these two works are authentic and that some of the problems with attributing them to Ambrose can be explained. For more on this, see Ambrose de Milan, *Des Sacrements, Des Mysterères*, SC 25 (Paris: Tour-Maubourg, 1949), pp. 7ff.; St. Ambrose, *On the Sacraments and On the Mysteries* (London: S.P.C.K., 1950), pp. 3ff.

67. Ambrose of Milan, *Traité sur l'Évangile de S. Luc*, SC 45, pp. 9ff., cf. also SC 52.
68. Yarnold, *Cyril of Jerusalem*, pp. 53–54.
69. Egeria, *Pilgrimage* 47.2.
70. John Chrysostom, *Baptismal Instructions* (New York: Newman Press, 1963), p. 167; cf. Yarnold, *The Awe-Inspiring Rite*, p. 57.
71. Leonel L. Mitchell, *A Faithful Church*, pp. 57ff.
72. This is certainly true in Ambrose and Cyril of Jerusalem, but numerous examples abound later on as well. For another example of this see Peter Chrysologus, Sermons 57 and 61; CCSL 24, pp. 318ff. and 341ff.; FC 17, pp. 103ff. For more on the *disciplina arcani*, see *The Study of Liturgy*, pp. 109–110; Edward Yarnold, *The Awe-Inspiring Rites of Initiation* (London: St. Paul Publications, 1971), pp. 11f, 50ff., 99ff. Henry G. J. Beck, *The Pastoral Care of Souls in South-East France During the Sixth Century* (Rome: Apud Aedes Universitatis Gregorianae, 1950), notes how by the time of Caesarius of Arles (d. 543), this practice had completely disappeared in French lands, p. 182.
73. More will be said about this later, especially in the discussion concerning Augustine.
74. I'm thankful to Dr. Ralph Quere for introducing me many years ago to John Chrysostom, who died in 407, and giving me a passion for these texts.
75. The whole collection of sermons was also translated into Latin at the end of the twelfth century by Burgundius Pisanus, d. 1194. Quasten 3, pp. 436ff.
76. Chrysostom, *Homilies on Matthew* 19.9–11.
77. The manuscript tradition regarding the baptismal homilies of Chrysostom is complicated. For a good discussion of the three main manuscript traditions, aka the Montfaucon, Papadopoulos-Kerameus, and Stavronikita Series, see Paul W. Harkins, trans., St. John Chrysostom: *Baptismal Instructions*, ACW Series Vol. 31, (New York: Newman Press, 1963).
78. Chrysostom, *Baptismal Instructions*, p. 222, n. 39, has a summary of the scholarly debate over the issue of a *redditio symboli* in Chrysostom.
79. Chrysostom, *In epistolam ad Colossenses homiliae 1–12*; PG 62:299–392; translation in Thomas M. Finn, *The Liturgy of Baptism in the Baptismal Instructions of St. John Chrysostom* (Washington D.C.: Catholic University of America Press, 1967), p. 187.
80. Theodore of Mopsuestia, *Commentary of Theodore of Mopsuestia on the LP and on the Sacraments of Baptism and the Eucharist (Liber ad Baptizandos)*, trans. and ed. A. Mingana, Woodbrooke Studies, vol. 6 (Cambridge: W. Heffer & Sons Limited, 1933), ix–xv. For the Syriac text with a French translation, see *Les homélies catéchétiques de Théodore de Mopsueste*, Studi e Testi 145, ed. Raymond Tonneau and Robert Devreesse (Vatican: Biblioteca Apostilica Vaticano, 1949). Theodore said that the Creed explains the mysteries and the LP teaches good works; Theodore, Catechetical Homily 11.1 Tonneau & Devreesse; Mingana 6:1.
81. Theodore of Mopsuestia, *Liber ad Baptizandos*, Part 2, Chapter 1, in Mingana, pp. 1–8.

82. Augustine, Sermons 56–59; PL 38:377ff.; Edmund Hill, Augustine's *Sermons*, Vol. III/3, pp. 95ff., especially see p. 125 n. 3; Pierre Patrick Verbraken, "Les Sermons CCXV et LVI de Saint Augustin *De Symbolo* et *De Oratione Dominica*," *Revue Bénédictine*, 68 (1958), pp. 5–40. Also cf. Froehlich, "The LP in Patristic Literature," pp. 74ff.; Schnurr, *Hören und Handeln*, pp. 111–112.

83. Perhaps the earliest sermon by Augustine to *competentes* is Sermon 216, dated by some scholars to 391, or soon after Augustine's ordination as a presbyter. This sermon offers Augustine's explanation of who the *competentes* are, namely, those who seek and ask about salvation. Cf. Edmund Hill, Augustine's *Sermons*, Vol. III/6, pp. 167ff.

84. The history of scrutinies is long and complicated. Early on, scrutiny simply meant the time when candidates for membership in the church were in the last stages of preparation for baptism; candidates underwent exorcisms and rigorous character analysis before they were allowed to enter the font. Later on, during the time of Augustine, scrutinies were used to determine whether adult candidates had learned the Creed and other central tenets of the Christian faith. Augustine did not use the term "scrutiny" (*scrutinium*), but the concept was certainly a part of the thinking and practice in his church. Whitaker, *Documents of the Baptismal Liturgy*, p. 256, also offers a broader definition, namely, that scrutinies later on were simply "any assembly in preparation for baptism." For more on the history of catechesis and scrutinies, see Michel Dujarier, *A History of the Catechumenate: The First Six Centuries* (New York: William H. Sadlier, 1979); John H. Westerhoff III and O. C. Edwards, Jr. eds., *A Faithful Church: Issues in the History of Catechesis* (Wilton, Connecticut: Morehouse-Barlow Co., Inc., 1981); *Made, Not Born* (Notre Dame, IN: Univ. of Notre Dame Press, 1976); Aidan Kavanaugh, *The Shape of Baptism: The Rite of Christian Initiation* (New York: Pueblo Pub. Co., 1978); J. D. C. Fisher, *Christian Initiation: Baptism in the Medieval West* (London: S.P.C.K., 1965); Josef Andreas Jungmann, *Handing on the Faith* (New York: Herder and Herder, 1959); Lawrence D. Folkemer, "A Study of the Catechumenate," *Church History* 15 (1946), pp. 286–307; *Adult Baptism and the Catechumenate*, Vol. 22 in Concilium: Theology in the Age of Renewal (New York: Paulist Press, 1967).

85. Cf. Edmund Hill's comments on this in, Augustine's *Sermons*, Vol. III/3, p. 106 n. 1.

86. Cf. Edmund Hill, Augustine's *Sermons*, Vol. III/3, p. 125, n. 3.

87. Sermon 58:1; PL 38:393; partially altered translation from Edmund Hill, Augustine's *Sermons*, Vol. III/3, p. 118.

88. Sermon 58:12–13; PL 38:299; translation in Edmund Hill, Augustine's *Sermons*, Vol. III/3, pp. 124–125.

89. Here Augustine borrowed from Cyprian. Indeed, for the rest of his life, Augustine argued that not only *competentes* but also all Christians ought to first learn the Apostles' Creed and then the LP.

90. Lynch, *Godparents and Kinship*, p. 115, has noted that Clement of Alexandria, *Stromata*, 4.25 is the first known reference to the baptismal font as

a womb; cf. Walter Bedard, *The Symbolism of the Baptismal Font in Early Christian Thought* (Washington, D.C.: Catholic University Press, 1951), pp. 17–36; and Joseph C. Plumpe, *Mater Ecclesia: An Inquiry into the Concept of the Church as Mother in Early Christianity* (Washington, D.C.: Catholic University Press, 1943); Karl Delahaye, *Ecclesia Mater: Chez les Péres des Trois Premieres siécles* (Paris: Latour-Maubourg, 1964).

91. Sermon 56:5; PL 38:379; translation Hill, Augustine's *Sermons*, Vol. III/3, p. 97.

92. Augustine, Letter to Proba; *Enchiridion* 7, 114–116.

93. Nathan Mitchell, "The Dissolution of the Rite of Christian Initiation," in *Made, Not Born* (Notre Dame, Indiana: University of Notre Dame Press, 1976), p. 52.

94. Jean-Paul Bouhot, "Une ancienne homélie catéchétique pour la tradition de l'oraison dominicale," *Augustinianum* 20 (1980), pp. 71–72.

95. For the works of Chromatius on the LP, see his Sermon 40 the *Praefatio Orationis Dominicae* in CCSL 9, p. 445 and also in CCSL 9A, pp. 171ff. and in SC 164, pp. 225ff.; and Chromatius' *Tractatus* 28 on Matthew 6:9–15 in CCSL 9A, pp. 328ff. The work of Chromatius on the LP, though short, deserves our attention for a number of reasons, not the least of which is that Chromatius was ordained by Ambrose, he was a friend of Jerome and Rufinius, and he was one of the few bishops Chrysostom appealed to after his deposition in 404.

96. Puniet, "Les trois homélies catéchétiques," *RHV* 6 (1905), p. 313, "L'*Expositio Orationis Dominicae* du sacramentaire Gélasian serait donc l'oeuvre de S. Chromatius, évéque d' Aquilée de 388 à 408. Ce n'est évidemment qu'une hupothése, mais elle a pour elle bien des vraisemblances." Since this sacramentary was very influential, Chromatius had a significant impact upon this later important baptismal rite. More will be said about Chromatius and the Gelasian Sacramentary later on.

97. Cf. Chromatius of Aquileia, Sermon 40 in SC 164, pp. 7ff., does not offer any clear indication of when it was preached. Also see the relevant works of Chromatius in CCSL 9, pp. 429ff., Tractatus XIV on Matthew 6:9–15 and in the same volume, pp. 445ff., and Chromatius' *Praefatio Orationis Domincae*; CCSL 9A, pp. 329ff. and Tractatus 28 on Matthew 6:9–15. For more on the liturgical context of Chromatius. see SC 164, pp. 91ff.

98. Cf. Bouhot, Une ancienne homélie catéchétique, p. 72; Pierre de Puniet, Les trois homélies catéchétiques, *RHV* 4 (1904), pp. 505–521, 755–786; *RHV* 6 (1905): pp. 170–179, 304–318.

99. Chromatius of Aquileia, Sermon 14 CCSL 9, pp. 429ff., and Sermon 28 CCSL 9A, p. 328, are the same sermon, both of which deal with Matthew 6:9–15, which is the section on the LP. The sermons may also be found in SC 154 & 164; PL 20:357ff.

100. CCSL 9, pp. 445; PL 74;1091ff.

101. Chromatius of Aquileia, *Praefatio orationis dominicae*, CCSL 9, p. 445; cf. Gelasian Sacramentary 36, *Liber Sacramentorum Romanae Aeclesiae Ordinis Anni Circuli*, pp. 51–52.; translation in Whitaker, *Documents of*

the Baptismal Liturgy, pp. 177ff.; and the *Ordo XI* Chapter 69 in Andrieu, *Les Ordines Romani* 2, p. 437.

102. Peter Chrysologus, Sermons 67–72; CCSL 24A, pp. 402ff.; PL 52:390–406; Sermons 67 and 70 in FC 17, pp. 115ff. Thanks to the groundbreaking work of Alexandri Olivar, most scholars identify 168 authentic sermons with Peter Chrysologus, but the actual number is still a matter of debate.

103. Bouhot, *Une ancienne homélie catéchétique*, p. 73; Pierre Patrick Verbraken, "Les sermons CCXV et LVI de saint Augustin 'De symbolo' et 'De oratione domica'," *Revue Bénédictine* 68 (1958), pp. 5–40; Schnurr, *Hören und Handeln*, p. 250.

104. Puniet, *Les trois homélies catéchétiques*, RHV 6 (1905), pp. 315ff.

105. Peter Chrysologus, CCSL 24A, pp. 431; FC 17, p. 120.

106. Peter Chrysologus, Sermon 70; CCSL 24A, p. 421; translation in FC 17, p. 119.

107. Peter Chrysologus, Sermon 67; CCSL 24A, p. 402; cf. FC 17, p. 115.

108. Peter Chrysologus discussed John and Jacob in Sermon 69 in CCSL 24 A, p. 418 and Sermon 70 in CCSL 24A, p. 421; and John, Jacob, and Tamar's twins in Sermon 72, CCSL 24A, pp. 431–432.

109. A list of the anonymous fifth-century LP commentaries are as follows: First, a sermon commonly attributed to Pseudo-Quodvultdeus on the LP has had some scholarly work done on it. G. Morin thought that the sermons of Quodvultdeus and a LP homily in Wolfenbüttel Codex 4096 (which is a collection of sermons attributed to Augustine) were similar, so he attributed this sermon to Quodvultdeus, who became bishop of Carthage ca. 437. Cf. G. Morin, *Augustini tractatus* (Kempten: 1917), p. 181, also Ps.-Quodvultdeus, *De dominica oratione* in PLS 3:299–303. For more on Quodvultdeus, see Augustine's *epistulae* 221 and 223 and Augustine's *On Heresies* (PL 42:21–50), and Quodvultdeus *De promissionibus Dei*; SC 101; CCSL 60; and V. Saxer, *Saints anciens d' Afrique du Nord* (Vatican City, 1979), pp. 184ff. Many modern scholars, however, have considered Morin's attribution impossible to confirm (cf. Schnurr, *Hören und Handeln*, p. 235). The sermon is probably from fifth-century North Africa or Italy, and it most likely concerns the handing over of the LP to catechumens during Lent. The sermon may draw on Peter Chrysologus' LP writings. For example, the style and content of the Pseudo-Quodvultdeus introduction echoes Chrysologus. The anonymous author boldly states, "Prayer pierces heaven, strikes the ears of God, obtains the key of indulgence, cleanses the vessel of our bodies, and adorns the temple of the spirit with holiness" (Ps-Quodvultdeus, *De dominica oratione*; PLS 3: 299). This evidence suggests that this sermon was preached no earlier than the 450's (Schnurr, *Hören und Handeln*, pp. 235, 248, n. 42).

Second, an anonymous work entitled simply *A Homily on the Lord's Prayer*, was falsely attributed to Chrysostom, but Jean-Paul Bouhot has suggested that it is from Northern Africa, dating to the time of Augustine. Cf. Bouhot, "Une ancienne homélie catéchétique," pp. 69–78. Klaus Schnurr remains uncertain about authorship, date, or place; however, he feels that this sermon and Pseudo-Quodvultdeus may share similar origins. Schnurr, *Hören und Handeln*, pp. 250, 259, n. 31. The sermon reflects no themes from later than the turn of the fifth century and certainly was written before the time of Caesarius of Arles (d. 542). Pseudo-Chrysostom was familiar with the interpretative tradition of the LP, at least up through the time of Augustine. A few references may even be allusions to Peter Chrysologus and Chromatius of Aquileia. The commentary itself has no unique insights or historically distinguishing remarks beyond the fact that it is a sermon for adult catechumens, which would also help to place it no earlier than the time of Augustine. Cf. Schnurr, *Hören und Handeln*, pp. 250ff.

Third, another anonymous homily, known as Pseudo-Augustine Sermon 65 (PL 39) has drawn little scholarly interest. Klaus Schnurr and P. Vallin have written about it, but both admit that there is little to say concerning its historical context other than the fact that it is a typical LP catechetical sermon presented for catechumens probably from the fifth century; Schnurr, *Hören und Handeln*, pp. 135ff. and P. Vallin, "'Prex Legitima': Pseudo-Augustine, Sermon 65.1," *Revue des études Augustiniennes* 26 (1980), pp. 303ff.

Fourth, a work entitled *An Explanation of the Lord's Prayer*, which has been falsely attributed to Fortunatus in some manuscripts, has gone virtually undiscussed by scholars. For a list of early printed editions of the Fortunatus' LP Commentary, see D. Tardi, *Fortunat. Etude sur un dernier représentant de la poésie latine dans la Gaule mérovingienne* (Paris, 1927), p. ix. For editions of these works, see PL 88:59–592 (PL 88:313–322 the *Expositio orationis dominicae* section), with the PL 88 being a reproduction of the edition of the Benedictine A. Lucchi (Rome, 1786–87). The critical edition is MGH, AA 4:1–2. The commentary appears in Book 10 of a collection entitled *The Songs* (the *Carmina*, aka the *Miscellanea*, Book 10). Significantly, it appears alongside *An Explanation of the Apostles' Creed* (*Expositio Symboli*). For more on the manuscript tradition, see MGH *Auctorum antiquissimorum* 4/1, pp. v–xxv. Some believe that this LP sermon was written late in Fortunatus' life (ca. 590–600, when he was a bishop). Judith W. George, *Venantius Fortunatus: A Latin Poet in Merovingian Gaul* (Oxford: Clarendon Press, 1992), pp. 208ff., talks about the differing views of Koebner and Meyer, who suggests that the later collection was made by friends of Venantius. A few scholars have accepted Venantius as the author of the LP homily simply because it appears in the critical edition, while others have remained skeptical. Some authors who have considered Fortunatus to be the author of the *Expositio orationis dominicae* are Joseph Vives, Morton W. Bloomfield, and P. G. Walsh. In the most detailed argument on this work, Walsh in a brief article, "Venantius Fortunatus," *The Month* 120 (1960), pp. 292–302, discusses the importance of this work in regard to the Fortunatus' corpus. A thorough study of Fortunatus, by Judith W. George's *Venantius Fortunatus: A Latin Poet in Merovingian Gaul* offers (in appendix 2, p. 210) a passing reference to the LP commentary: "Of the two final books (of the *Carmina*), the first poem in Book 10 is a prose dissertation on the Lord's Prayer, which appears to be incomplete." In the critical edition itself, MGH AA 4/1, p. 24, Fridericus Leo has noted that there has been some dispute over various works of Fortunatus, but earlier editors included the *Expositio orationis dominicae* as being a part of the manuscript tradition, and therefore he included it in his critical edition. *Teuffel's History of Roman Literature* by George C. W. Warr, vol. 2 (New York: Burt Franklin, 1967), p. 555 (paragraph 491.5) simply accepts Fortunatus' authorship without any explanation why.

Paul Antin, however, in his comments on the *Dictionnaire de Spiritualité*, noted in vol. 5, p. 725, "On peut négliger son Expositio symboli d'apres Rufin (11,1; MGH, pp. 253–258, et PL 88:345–351), et son Expositio orationis dominicae (10,1; MGH, pp. 21–119, et PL 88:313–322), encore que ce dernier texte puisse donner lieu des remarques intéressantes." Many standard reference works do not mention the *Expositio orationis dominicae* in their discussions of Fortunatus. In this regard, see especially the *Lexicon für Theologie und Kircke*, Max Manitius, *Geschichte der lateinischen Literatur des Mittelalters*, vol. 1 (München: C.H. Beck'sche Verlagsbuchhandlung: 1911), Michael Grant, *Greek and Latin Authors: 800 B.C.-A.D. 1000* (New York: The H. W. Wilson Company, 1980), F. J. E. Raby, *A History of Secular Latin Poetry in the Middle Ages* (Oxford: Clarendon Press, 1957), vol. 1, and Franz Brunhölzl, *Geschichte der Lateinischen Literatur des Mittelalters*. Internal evidence, however, suggests the probability that this work was written during the fifth century and therefore excludes the authorship of Fortunatus. One historic reference in particular points to this conclusion. The author argued that converts have the right to call God "Father" after baptism. However, after baptism, believers still may reject their heavenly Father if they stray from the faith by either doctrinal error or moral conduct. The notion that baptism can be undone is reminiscent of Caesarius of Arles' writing on the LP, but does not suggest this author necessarily knew Caesarius, because the opposite may also be true, namely, that Caesarius knew this author and was borrowing from him/her. The author declared that God is not for "Arius, the Jews, Photinus, Manichaeus, and Sabellius," and therefore whoever follows them has Satan as their Father. MGH AA 4.1:13, p. 223 states, "Also, it is well that [the words] 'Our Father' are added [to this prayer], because unless one believes rightly in Christ, he is not able to have a Father in heaven. For the Father himself is not for Arius, a Jew, Photinus [Bishop of Sirmium, d. 376], Manichaeus, Sabellius [third century] and the remaining pestilence, or those who have been cut down with a perversely poisonous scythe of an infected heart and of the worst kind of confession. These have been unjustly counted as being from the Son as much as from God our Father; [the heretic] sins against the Father [being of] the devil's own fruit. Therefore the Father in heaven is for us, who rightly confess the Son on earth." The Jews were often condemned by Christians for not recognizing Christ as the Messiah, and numerous LP commentaries reflect this sentiment; Photinus appears to be the bishop of Sirmium in Galatia (d. 376) who was condemned by both Eastern and Western churches during the fourth century for his Monarchian tendencies; Manichaeus and his followers challenged the Catholic church during the third to the fifth centuries; Sabellianism, for the most part, was of little concern by the fifth century, but Arianism troubled orthodox Christianity during the fourth to the sixth centuries and was considered a problem in parts of Europe (including France) until the seventh century. Henry G. J. Beck, *The Pastoral Care of Souls in South-East France During the Sixth Century* (Rome: Universitatis Gergorianae, 1950), pp. 43, 184. A similar list of heretics comes from the fifth century *Paschal Song* of Sedulius, which attacked Sabellius, Arius, and the Jews. However, he made no mention of the Manichaeans or Photinus. For more on the context of Sedulius in these matters, see Carl P. E. Springer, *The Gospel as Epic*, pp. 36ff. The inclusion of Arius and the Jews might reflect the concerns of the late sixth and early seventh centuries, i.e., concerns from around the time of Fortunatus. However, the earlier heresies were not of particular concern during Fortunatus' day. The practice of referring to earlier heresies by later authors is not uncommon; nevertheless, an earlier fifth century date would make more sense in light of the complete list. The baptismal catechetic context reflected in this work also points to a fifth century date. The author does not mention a Lenten handing over of the LP to converts and mentioned that it was only after baptism that the believer had a right to pray the words "Our Father." Therefore, the work reflects Augustine's theology on the LP, but not the later fifth-century ideas of Peter Chrysologus or Pseudo-Quodvultdeus. The sixth-century concerns of Caesarius of Arles to educate parents, godparents, and children with the LP in baptismal catechesis is completely absent from the *Explanation of the Lord's Prayer*, which if it was written by Fortunatus, would have postdated Caesarius by half a century. Once again, a fifth-century date seems most probable.

110. The part of this chapter that deals with Augustine appears in a slightly different and earlier form in Roy Hammerling, ed., *A History of Prayer: The First to the Fifteenth Century* (Leiden: Brill, 2008), pp. 183–200, where it is entitled "St. Augustine of Hippo: Prayer as Sacrament."

111. Roy Hammerling, "Gregory of Nyssa's Sermons on the Lord's Prayer: Lessons from the Classics," *Word and World* 22 (Winter 2002), 64–70.

112. Gregory of Nyssa, *The Lord's Prayer, The Beattitudes*, ACW, Vol. 18 (Westminster, Maryland: Newman Press, 1954), pp. 37–38; Johannes F. Callahan, ed., *Gregorii Nysseni: De Oratione Dominica, De Beatitudinibus* (Leiden: E.J. Brill, 1992), pp. 21–22.

113. Cf. Hilda Graef's introduction in ACW 18, p. 16. Another important Eastern author that Gregory is drawing upon is Cyril of Jerusalem, who is Gregory's contemporary and for purposes of theme has been placed after

Gregory in this chapter. Cyril also held Origen's idea that in the fourth petition, bread means spiritual bread.

114. Johannes F. Callahan, ed., *Gregorii Nysseni: De Oratione Dominica, De Beatitudinibus* (Leiden: E.J. Brill, 1992), pp. ix-xxx.

115. For two excellent studies on Gregory of Nyssa and the Lord's Prayer in the context of the Greco-Roman, world please read Michael Joseph Brown, "Piety and Proclamation: Gregory of Nyssa's Sermons on the Lord's Prayer" in Roy Hammerling, ed., *A History of Prayer: The First to the Fifteenth Century* (Leiden: Brill, 2008) and also Brown's *The Lord's Prayer through North African Eyes: A Window Early Christianity* (New York: T & T Clark, 2005).

116. Gregoryii Nysseni, *De Oratione Dominica*, pp. 5–8; ACW 18, pp. 23–25.

117. Gregoryii Nysseni, *De Oratione Dominica*, pp. 15–16; ACW 18, p. 29.

118. Gregoryii Nysseni, *De Oratione Dominica*, pp. 18–19; ACW 18, pp. 33–34.

119. Gregoryii Nysseni, *De Oratione Dominica*, pp. 5–6; ACW 18, pp. 21–22.

120. Gregoryii Nysseni, *De Oratione Dominica*, pp. 21–22; ACW 18, p. 38.

121. We cannot say for certain whether Gregory preferred the Holy Spirit version of the petition over the Kingdom of God petition. This petition clearly had a tradition in his area biblically, and maybe even liturgically and in private prayer. Later on, Maximus Confessor, another famous author, will also refer to this petition. Cf. Maximus Confessor, *Selected Writings* (New York: Paulist Press, 1985), pp. 107ff.

122. Gregoryii Nysseni, *De Oratione Dominica*, pp. 41–42; ACW 18, p. 54.

123. Gregoryii Nysseni, *De Oratione Dominica*, pp. 21–23; ACW 18, pp. 38–40.

124. Gregoryii Nysseni, *De Oratione Dominica*, pp. 23–25; ACW 18, pp. 41–43.

125. Gregoryii Nysseni, *De Oratione Dominica*, pp. 28–30; ACW 18, pp. 43–44.

126. Gregoryii Nysseni, *De Oratione Dominica*, pp. 31–33; ACW 18, pp. 45–47.

127. Gregoryii Nysseni, *De Oratione Dominica*, pp. 33–44; ACW 18, pp. 47–56.

128. Gregoryii Nysseni, *De Oratione Dominica*, pp. 44–58; ACW 18, pp. 57–70.

129. Gregoryii Nysseni, *De Oratione Dominica*, pp. 70–72; ACW 18, pp. 76–77.

130. Gregoryii Nysseni, *De Oratione Dominica*, pp. 72–74; ACW 18, pp. 83–84. For more on Gregory and other early Eastern writers on the LP see Kenneth W. Stevenson, The Lord's Prayer: A Text in Tradition, pp. 43–70.

131. CSEL 44, pp. 40–77; translation in FC 18, pp. 376–401.

132. John Leinenweber ed., *Letters of Saint Augustine* (Liguoiri, Missouri: Triumph Books, 1992), p. 160.

133. CSEL 44, pp. 65ff.; FC 18, pp. 392–393.

134. Cyprian, *De Dominica Oratione* 9; CCSL 3 A, p. 94.

135. Augustine's Letter 130; CSEL 44, p. 65; translation in FC 18, p. 393.

136. 1 Kings 2 in Latin or Vulgate translation bibles; 1 Samuel 2 in modern bibles.

137. Augustine, Letter 130; CSEL 44, p. 66; translation in FC 18, p. 394.

138. A.k.a. *The Enchiridion of Faith, Hope, and Love* or *Enchiridion de fide, spe, et caritate.*

139. Augustine, Letter 130; CSEL 44, p. 68. For an alternate translation see FC 18, p. 395.

140. Augustine, *Enchiridion* 4; CCSL 46, p. 50; translation in Augustine, *The Enchiridion on Faith, Hope, and Love*, Henry Paolucci trans. (Washington D.C.: Gateway Books, 1961), p. 4.
141. Cf. Augustine's Sermons 56–59.
142. Augustine, *Enchiridion* 7; CCSL 46, p. 51. Later scholars connected the LP to the three theological virtues and even connected the seven heavenly virtues to the seven petitions. For example, see Hugh of St. Victor, Peter Lombard, Jordan of Quedlinburg, and Johannes Herholt.
143. Augustine, *Enchiridion* 7; CCSL 46, p. 51.
144. Augustine, *Enchiridion* 7; CCSL 46, p. 51.
145. Augustine, *Enchiridion* 74; CCSL 46, p. 89.
146. Cf. Augustine, *Enchiridion* 22, 71, 73, 74, 78, 81.
147. Augustine, *Enchiridion* 71; CCSL 46, p. 88; translation in Augustine, *The Enchiridion*, Henry Paolucci, p. 84.
148. Augustine, *Enchiridion* 70–80; CCSL 46, pp. 87ff. For a similar idea, see Augustine *In Johannis Evangelium Tractatus CXXIV* 124.5.
149. Augustine, Sermon 213:9; Miscellanea Agostiniana, Vol. 1, *Sancti Augustini Sermones Post Maurinos Reperti* (Rome: Tipografia Poliglotta Vaticana, 1930), p. 449; translation in Edmund Hill, Augustine's *Sermons*, Vol. III/6, p. 146, "But since we are going to go on living in this world, where nobody can live without sin, for that reason the forgiveness of sins is not confined only to the washing clean of sacred baptism, but is also to be had in the LP which is also a daily prayer, and which you are going to receive in eight days' time. In it you will find, as it were, your daily baptism. So you must thank God for having granted his Church this gift, which we confess in the Creed; so that when we say *in the holy Church*, we join unto it *in the forgiveness of sins.*" Note that this emphasis upon two baptisms is similar to an idea in Cyprian, namely, that the praying of the LP, because it seeks forgiveness of sins, is a type of baptism, which washes away sin. Cyprian, *De Dominica Oratione* 12; CCSL 3 A, pp. 96–97; translation in FC 36, p. 136.
150. Augustine, *In Johannis Evangelium Tractatus CXXIV* 57.4, 58.1, 58.6, 59.5.
151. Dates have been taken from Edmund Hill's analysis of the sermons in Augustine, *Sermons*, 10 volumes. Certainly there are many varying opinions on the dating of these sermons. When speaking about this particular petition, however, Augustine emphasizes how this petition spells out the way by which a person may be forgiven, and that is to forgive in order to be forgiven. This petition, nevertheless, though a part of the LP, also demonstrates one of the key functions of the whole prayer, which is to seek forgiveness.
152. Prosper of Aquitaine (ca. 390-463) quoted the fifth petition on at least five occasions in his commentary on the Psalms (*Expositio Psalmorum*). In each case, Prosper encouraged his learned audience to give glory to God in all things. Prosper noted that Christians must pray the fifth petition and seek God's forgiveness if they wish to walk in the way of the Lord. Indeed, this petition, which Jesus taught, heals the sinner and acknowledges that God alone is worthy of praise. (Prosper of Aquitaine, *Expositio Psalmorum* 118:3,

129:4, 140:5, 142, 144:12; CCSL 67A; pp. 85ff., 142ff., 177ff., 184ff., 192ff.). Thus, Prosper turned to the fifth petition frequently in much the same way Augustine did.

Pope Leo I, Sermons and Letters in CCSL 138, 138A; PLS 3:329–500; PL 54–56; SC 22, 49, 74, 200; English translation of select sermons and letters in LNPF 12, series 2 and FC 34. Leo I referred to the LP in at least five sermons (46, 49, 50, 90, 93). Leo used the LP in two ways. First, he quoted it almost exclusively in his sermons during Lent, or when talking about fasting. Second, like Prosper and Augustine, the primary reason for referring to the LP is to emphasize the fifth petition and forgiveness.

Pope Gregory the Great (ca. 540–604) briefly mentioned the LP on four occasions. Twice he referred to the fifth petition, stressing the theme that Christians must forgive others if they wish to be forgiven. (Gregory the Great, *Moralia in Iob*, Book 10, ch. 15; PL 75:937; CCSL 143, p. 558; *Homilae in Evangelium* Book 2, Homily 27 on John 15:12–16; PL 76:1204). Gregory also mentioned the third petition and how Christians on earth should seek God's will as the angels of heavens do (Gregory, *Moralia*, Book 27, ch. 39; PL 76:438; CCSL 143B, pp. 1382ff.). Lastly, he spoke of the fourth petition on bread, suggesting that the bread is "ours," only in the sense that it is a gift from God. Just like "our" righteousness is from God, so also everything believers require in life is a gift of God (Gregory, *Moralia*, Book 24, ch. 7; PL 76:293; CCSL 143, pp. 1196ff.). The preceding references have nothing to do with a baptismal catechetic context. In this context, the LP holds no particular importance for Gregory: it is simply one text among all the other texts to be used—in this case rather infrequently—to explain other biblical passages. Gregory the Great, Prosper of Aquitaine, and Pope Leo I do not so much focus on the LP, as they use it to illuminate other works.

Vokes, "The Lord's Prayer in the First Three Centuries," p. 259, has also added about Gregory, "Whatever may have been the action of Gregory the Great, whether he introduced the Lord's Prayer into the Roman Mass or merely changed its position, we should not interpret his statement in *Letters* IX 12 to mean that the Apostles used the Lord's Prayer as a prayer of consecration. In the words 'Quia mos apostolorum fuit ut ad ipsam solummodo orationem oblationis hostiam consecrarent,' 'oblationis' is to be construed with *orationem* to mean that the Apostles only used a prayer of oblation, not the Lord's Prayer, which he, Gregory, thinks on the contrary ought not to be omitted . . . Even if Gregory really meant that the Apostles used the Lord's Prayer for consecration, it is again unlikely that he had any true knowledge of the history of the apostolic liturgy."

153. Augustine, *De sancta uirginitate*, written ca. 401.

154. Augustine, *De sancte uirginitate* 48; CSEL 41; FC 26. Augustine makes a similar point in Sermon 181.

155. Augustine, *Regula Sancta Augustina* 6.2 and 8.2; L. Verheijen, *Le Règle de Saint Augustin* (Paris, 1967), pp. 417–437; George Lawless, *Augustine of Hippo and His Monastic Rule* (Oxford: Clarendon, 1987), pp. 99 and 103.

156. When researching Augustine's view of the sacraments, one notices immediately that a recent comprehensive work on the subject is lacking. Secondary literature on this topic from the 1970's is scarce. Most secondary sources tend to repeat the opinions stated by Frederic van der Meer in *Augustinus der Seelsorger: Leben und Wirken des eines Kirchenvaters* (Köln: J. P. Bachem, 1951), in English G. Battershaw and G. R. Lamb translators, *Augustine the Bishop* (London: Sheed & Ward, 1961).

157. Augustine, *De Doctrina Christiana* 2.1.1; *Epistola* 138.7; *De Civitate Dei* 10.5.

158. Meer, *Augustine the Bishop*, pp. 280ff.; William A. Van Roo, *The Christian Sacrament* (Rome: Pontificia Universita Gregoriana, 1992), pp. 38ff.

159. Augustine, *In Evangelium Joannis Tractatus Centum Viginti Quatuor* 80.3 and *Contra Faustum Manichaeum Libri Triginta Tres* 19.13–16; *De Doctrina Christiana* 3.9.13 says, "The Lord and likewise the commands of the Apostles have, instead of handing over many, handed over only a few—the sacrament of baptism, the feast of the body and blood of the Lord; they are easy to make use of, most wonderful for those that understand them, and they are administered with great decency [*observatione castissima*]." Meer, *Augustine the Bishop*, p. 280.

160. In a text where Augustine talked about Jacob's struggle with an angel (Genesis 32), he said, "What comparison can there be of the power of an angel and that of a man? Therefore it is a mystery; therefore it is a sacrament; therefore it is a prophecy; therefore it is a figure; therefore let us understand." Sermon 122.3.3; PL 38:682.

161. Augustine, *De Sermone Domini in Monte* 1.1; CCSL 35, p. 1; ACW 5, p. 11; cf. Augustine's *Retractiones* 1.19. In contrast to Augustine's commentary, his contemporary Jerome (ca. 347–419) has a brief literal commentary simply called *On Matthew* (*In Mattheum*; SC 242 and 259; CCSL 77). Though brief, grounded in past interpretations of the LP, and literal in its approach to explaining the LP, Jerome's comments on the LP are frequently quoted in the future.

162. Augustine, *De Sermone Domini in Monte* 1.3.11.

163. Augustine, at the beginning of this work, compared the seven beatitudes and gifts of the Spirit separately. Then after proceeding straight through the Sermon on the Mount, he came to the discussion of the LP, and then he related his earlier comparison (found in *De Sermone Domini in Monte* 1.4.11) to the LP petitions.

164. Augustine, *De Sermone Domini in Monte* 2.11.38; CCSL 35, p. 128; translation in ACW 5, pp. 125–126.

165. *De Sermone Domini in Monte* 2.10.38.

166. *De Sermone Domini in Monte* 2.10.36.

167. This evoking of the sevenfold Spirit, or gifts of the Spirit, was also a practice with Ambrose. See Ambrose, *De sacramentiis* 3.8; *De mysteriis* 42.

168. *De Sermone Domini in Monte* 1.2–4.

169. *De Sermone Domini in Monte* 1.3.10; CCSL 35, p. 128, "Septem sunt ergo quae perficiunt."

170. The sermons of Pope Leo I (d. 461) also connected the beatitudes with the petitions of the LP. However, his comparisons are brief and not nearly as thorough as Augustine's comparisons. Leo, in Sermon 49, directly linked the fifth petition with the same beatitude Augustine did, namely, "Blessed are the merciful for they shall receive mercy." Sermon 50 also related the beatitudes: "Blessed are the pure in heart for they shall see God," and "Blessed are those who hunger and thirst for righteousness sake, for they will be satisfied," with the fifth petition in a way that Augustine did not.

171. Chromatius' Sermon 14 CC 9, pp. 429ff. and Sermon 28 CC 9A, p. 328 are the same sermon, both of which deal with Matthew 6:9–15, or the section on the Lord's Prayer. The sermons may also be found in SC 154 & 164; PL 20:357ff. Also, *Preface to the Lord's Prayer* or *Praefatio Orationis Dominicae*; CC 9, p. 445; PL 74:1091ff.

172. *Preface to the Lord's Prayer* or *Praefatio Orationis Dominicae*; CC 9, p. 445; PL 74:1091ff.

173. Chromatius' Sermon 14 CC 9, pp. 429ff.; Sermon 28 CC 9A, p. 328; SC 154 & 164; PL 20:357ff. Also, *Preface to the Lord's Prayer* or *Praefatio Orationis Dominicae*; CC 9, p. 445; PL 74:1091ff.

174. Such an eschatological understanding of the LP was always a part of LP interpretations from the beginning, as has been noted. Again, cf. Raymond Brown, "The Pater Noster as an Eschatological Prayer," *Theological Studies* 22 (1961), pp. 175–208 and Willy Rordorf, "The LP in the Light of its Liturgical Use in the Early Church," *Studia Liturgica* 14 (1980/81), pp. 1–19.

175. Zahn, Hort, Stiglmayr, and Nautin argued that the Greek was the original text; Banning believed that J. Zeiller, *Les origines chrétiennes dans les provinces danubiennes de l'Empire Romain* (Paris:1918) was correct in suggesting that the first edition was in Latin. Josef van Banning, "The Critical Edition of the *Opus Imperfectum in Matthaeum*: An Arian Source" *Studia Patristica* (17/1), p. 383.

176. Cf. Josef van Banning's detailed introduction to the work in both the CCSL 87B and his "The Critical Edition of the *Opus Imperfectum in Matthaeum*: An Arian Source" *Studia Patristica* (17/1), pp. 382–387. Both works include helpful bibliographical references to this work.

177. Banning, *Studia Patristica* (17/1), p. 382 and CCSL 87B, p. v.

178. Banning, *Studia Patristica* (17/1), p. 384.

179. Banning, *Studia Patristica* (17/1), p. 386.

180. Schnurr, *Hören und Handeln*, pp. 203ff.

181. Schnurr, *Hören und Handeln*, pp. 200ff. is helpful in pointing out some of these sources.

182. PG 56:712–713.

183. PG 56:711–712.

184. PG 56:714–715.

185. A version of this section of the chapter appears in a slightly different form in Roy Hammerling, ed., *A History of Prayer: The First to the Fifteenth Century*

(Leiden: Brill, 2008), pp. 223–244, where it is entitled "The Lord's Prayer in Early Christian Polemics to the Eighth Century."
186. *De schismate Donatistarum*, aka *Adversus Parmenianum Donatistam.*
187. Optatus, *De schismate Donatistarum* 2:20, CSEL 26, p. 56.
188. Optatus, *De schismate Donatistarum* 2:20–21, 3:9–10; and 7:1–2 in CSEL 26, pp. 53ff., 92ff., and 158ff.
189. Augustine, *De dono perseverantiae* 3.6; PL 45:997; translation in Mary Alphonsine Lesousky, *The Dono Perseverantiae of St. Augustine: A Translation with an Introduction and a Commentary*, A Dissertation (Washington D.C.: Catholic University of America, 1956), pp. 112–113, "By this (Cyprian) clearly shows that the beginning of faith is also a gift of God, since the Holy Church prays not only for the faithful, that faith may be increased or persevere in them, but also for unbelievers, that they may begin to have it when they did not have it at all, and when indeed they entertained hostile feelings against it."
190. Augustine, *De Natura et Gratia* 1.35.41; PL 44:267; translation in *Nicene and Post-Nicene Fathers*, Philip Schaff, ed., vol. 5 (Grand Rapids, MI: Wm. B. Eerdmans Pub. Co., 1956), p. 135. Also, for other references concerning the fifth petition in works dealing with the Pelagian heresy, see Augustine's comments in *De Natura et Gratia* 1.35.41, 1.60.70, 1.67.80–81; *De Peccatorum meritis et remissione* 2.4, 2.21, 2.25, and 3.25 along with his comments on the same work in his *Retractiones*, 2.23; *De spiritu et littera* 65; *De perfectione iustitae hominis* 6, 11, 15, 21: *De Gestis Pelagii* 27, 55: *De Nuptiis et Concupiscentia* 1.38; *Contra Duas Epistolas Pelagianorum* 1.27, 2.5, 3.23, 4.17; *De Gratia et Libero Arbitrio* 26; *De correptione et Gratia* 35; and *De Dono Perseverantiae* 5.
191. Augustine, *De Natura et Gratia* 80; PL 44:287; translation in *Nicene and Post-Nicene Fathers*, vol. 5, p. 149. For a similar passage in Augustine, see *De Gratia et Libero Arbitrio* 26.
192. Augustine, *De perfectione iustitae hominis*, 21.44; PL 44:317–318; translation in *Nicene and Post-Nicene Fathers*, vol. 5, p. 176. For other works that deal with Augustine's discussion of the sixth petition in light of the Pelagian heresy, see *De perfectione iustitae hominis* 10, 19, 20, 21; *De Peccatorum meritis et remissione* 2.2 and 2.4; *De Natura et Gratia* 1.53.62, 1.59.69, 1.67.80; *De Gestis Pelagii* 20; *Contra Duas Epistolas Pelagianorum* 1.27; *De Gratia et Libero Arbitrio* 26; and *De Dono Perseverantiae* 5.9, 6.11, 6.12, 7.15, 17.46, 21.56, 22.62, and 23.63. For a work that uses the sixth petition against the Manichean heresy, see *De Sermone Domini in Monte* 2.9.30–35.
193. Besides these two works against the Semi-Pelagians, Augustine wrote *On Grace and Free Will* (*De Gratia et Libero Arbitrio*) and *On Correction and Grace* (*De Correptione et Gratia*).
194. "*Gloriosus martyrus et doctor lucidissimus*," Augustine, *De dono perseverantiae* 19.49; PL 45:1029; Lesousky, *The Dono Perseverantiae*, pp. 186–187.

195. Augustine, *De dono perseverantiae* 2.4; PL 45:996; cf. Lesousky, *The Dono Perseverantiae*, pp. 108–109; cf. another English translation in *The Nicene and Post-Nicene Fathers*, First Series, vol. 5, pp. 527ff.
196. Augustine, *De dono perseverantiae* 2.3; PL 45:996; translation in Lesousky, *The Dono Perseverantiae*, pp. 108–109.
197. Augustine, *De dono perseverantiae* 2.4; PL 45:996-997; translation in Lesousky, *The Dono Perseverantiae*, pp. 110–111.
198. Augustine, *De dono perseverantiae* 4.7; PL 45:998; translation in Lesousky, *The Dono Perseverantiae*, pp. 114–115.
199. Augustine, *De dono perseverantiae* 5.8; PL 45:998; translation in Lesousky, *The Dono Perseverantiae*, pp. 114–115.
200. Augustine, *De dono perseverantiae* 5.9; PL 45:999; translation in Lesousky, *The Dono Perseverantiae*, pp. 116–117.
201. See Augustine's lengthy discussion in *De dono perseverantiae* 6.11–13, 7.15, 17.46, 21.56, 22.62, 23.63; PL 45:999–1000, 1001–1002., 1021–1022, 1028, 1030, 1031; and Lesousky, *The Dono Perseverantiae*, pp. 118–119, 124–125, 180–181, 198–199, 206–207.
202. Augustine *De dono perseverantiae* 7.13; PL 45:1001; translation in Lesousky, *The Dono Perseverantiae*, pp. 122–123.
203. Prosper of Aquitaine, *Pro Augustino responsiones, De gratia Dei et libero voluntatis arbitrio contra collatorem*, PL 45 and 51; ACW 32.
204. Prosper of Aquitaine, *Pro Augustino responsiones, De gratia Dei et libero voluntatis arbitrio contra collatorem*; PL 51:185.
205. Jerome, *Dialogus adversus Pelagianos* 3. 14, PL 23:583; translation in FC 53, p. 369. For the story behind this letter, see Augustine, *De gestis Pelagii* 6.16; PL 44:329. For Jerome's Letter to Demetrius, the son of Juliana, see his Letter 130.
206. Jerome, *Dialogus adversus Pelagianos* 3.14; PL 23:583.
207. Jerome, *Dialogus adversus Pelagianos* 3.15; PL 23:585; translation in FC 53, p. 371.
208. Jerome, *Dialogus adversus Pelagianos* 3.15; PL 23:585; translation in FC 53, p. 372.
209. Jerome only made one other brief mention of the LP in *Dialogus adversus Pelagianos* 1.27. Here, Atticus accused Critobulus and the Pelagians of relying too much upon their own wills and not upon the will of God, which is prayed for in the third petition. The problem is that the Pelagians are unwilling to seek the help of God and even ascribe the grace of God to the power of creation, law, and free will.
210. Jerome, *Dialogus adversus Pelagianos* 3.16; PL 23:586–587.
211. Norman Russell, *Cyril of Alexandria* (London: Routledge, 2000), 3–58.
212. Cyril of Alexandria, *Commentary on the Gospel of St. Luke,* Homily 77.
213. Augustine, *De Sermone Domini in Monte* 1.1.2 and 2.5.15–16.
214. Cassian, *Conlationes* 9.2, SC 42, p. 39; translation in Cassian, *Conferences*, trans. Colm Luibheid (New York: Paulist Press, 1985), p. 101: cf. Cassian, *The Conferences*, translated by Boniface Ramsey (New York: Paulist Press, 1997).

215. John Cassian, *Conferences*, Luibheid, p. 11.

216. Cassian, *Conlationes* 9.8.

217. Cassian, *Conlationes* 9.9–17; SC 42, pp. 49ff.; translation in Cassian, *Conferences*, Luibheid, pp. 107ff.

218. Cassian, *Conlationes* 9.17; SC 42, pp. 53ff.; translation in Cassian, *Conferences*, Luibheid, pp. 110–111. Cassian quoted the following biblical passages where Jesus ordained the four types of prayer: 1. supplication—Matthew 26:39; 2. prayer—John 17:4, 19; 3. plea—John 17:24 and Luke 23:24; and 4. blessing—Matthew 11:25f and John 11:41–42.

219. Cassian, *Conlationes* 9.15, SC 42, pp. 50ff.; translation in Cassian, *Conferences*, Luibheid, p. 110.

220. Cassian, *Conlationes* 9.17; SC 42, pp. 53–54; translation in Cassian, *Conferences*, Luibheid, p. 111.

221. Cassian, *Conlationes* 9.18, SC 42, p. 55; translation in Cassian, *Conferences*, Luibheid, pp. 111–112.

222. Cassian, *Conlationes* 9.25, SC 42, pp. 61–62; translation in Cassian, *Conferences*, Luibheid, p. 116.

223. Cassian, *Conlationes* 9.25; SC 42, pp. 61–62; translation in Cassian, *Conferences*, Luibheid, pp. 116–117.

224. Cassian, *Conlationes* 9.18.

225. Cassian, *Conlationes* 9.19; SC 42, pp. 56–57; translation in Cassian, *Conferences*, Luibheid, pp. 113–114.

226. Cassian, *Conlationes* 9.21.

227. Cassian, *Conlationes* 9.22.

228. Cassian, *Conlationes* 9.22; SC 42, pp. 59–60; translation in Cassian, *Conferences*, Luibheid, pp. 114–115; Cf. Caesarius of Arles, who hints at a similar problem in his Sermons 35 and 202.

229. Much more could be said here, and indeed, something could be said about Saint Benedict, who died around 550, and falls just outside the timeframe of these chapters. However, since other modern scholars have written clearly about this, I encourage the reader to look at the excellent works of by Terrence Kardong and Columba Stewart on this topic, especially Columba Stewart's "Prayer among the Benedictines" in Roy Hammerling, ed., *A History of Prayer: The First to the Fifteenth Centuries* (Leiden: Brill, 2008), pp. 201–222.

Conclusion

1. Cyprian, *De dominica oratione* 8; Theodore of Mopsuestia, *Liber ad Baptizandos*, Part 2, Chapter 1; John Chrysostom, Homily 29 on Matthew; Coelius Sedulius, *Paschale Operibus* 2.2; *Opus Imperfectum in Matthaeum*, Homily 14; Pseudo-Fortunatus, *Expositio orationis dominicae*.

2. Peter Chyrsologus, Sermon 67 and 70; Pseudo-Quodvultdeus, PLS 3:299ff; Coelius Sedulius, *Carmen Paschale* 2.231 and *Paschale Operibus* 2.2. Note that in this summary section, some of the references to sources will go beyond the time period of this book, some down to the eighth century.

3. Theodore of Mopsuestia, *Liber ad Baptizandos*, Part 2, Chapter 1.
4. Tertullian, *De Oratione* 2; Cyprian, *De dominica oratione* 8; Chromatius of Aquileia, *Tractatus in Matthaeum*, CCL 9:429ff. and the *Praefatio Orationis Dominicae* CCL 9, p. 445; Peter Chyrsologus, Sermon 69; Pseudo Augustinus, Sermon 65.
5. Cyprian, *De Dominica Oratione* 1–2; Juvencus, *Evangeliorum Libri IV* 1.58–604; Augustine, Sermon 57; Cassian, *Conlationes* 9–10; Pseudo-Chrysostom, Sermon 28; Ildefonsus of Toledo, *Liber de cognitione baptismi* 133.
6. Cyprian, *De dominica oratione* 10; Ambrose, *De Sacramentis* 5.4; Theodore of Mopsuestia, *Liber ad Baptizandos*, Part 2, Chapter 1; Augustine, *De Sermone Domini in Monte*, 2.4; Chromatius of Aquileia, *Tractatus in Matthaeum*, CCL 9:429ff; Peter Chyrsologus, Sermon 71; Pseudo-Quodvultdeus, PLS 3:299ff; Pseudo-Chrysostom Sermon 28; Ildefonsus of Toledo, *Liber de cognitione baptismi* 133.
7. Cyril of Alexandria, *Commentary on the Gospel of St. Luke*, Homily 71.
8. Pseudo Augustinus, Sermon 65.
9. Cyril of Alexandria, *Commentary on the Gospel of St. Luke*, Homily 71.
10. Tertullian, *De Oratione* 8; Augustine Sermons 56 and 57.
11. For more on this, see Joseph C. Plumpe, *Mater Ecclesia: An Inquiry into the Concept of the Church as Mother in Early Christianity*, (Washington, D.C.: Catholic University Press, 1943).
12. Tertullian, *De Oratione* 8; Augustine Sermons 56 and 57.
13. Cyprian, *De dominica oratione* 12; Ambrose, *De Sacramentis*, 5.4; Chromatius of Aquileia, *Tractatus in Matthaeum* 2.1; Cyril of Alexandria, Commentary on the Gospel of St. Luke, Homily 72; cf. Leviticus 11:44; 19:2; 20:7, "Be holy for I am holy."
14. Ambrose, *De Sacramentis* 5.4.
15. Augustine, *Enchiridion* 116; CCL 46, p. 111. Cf. Moffatt, *Augustine*, p. 260. Origen, *On Prayer* XVIII.2–3 and XXVI.1.
16. Tertullian, *De Oratione* 3. Cf. Cyprian, *De dominica oratione* 12; Origen, *On Prayer* XXIV.1; Gregory of Nyssa, *De Oratione Dominica*, Sermon 3; Cyril of Jerusalem, *Mystagogic Catecheses* 5.12; Augustine, *De Sermone Domini in Monte*, 2.5; Cyril of Alexandria, Commentary on the Gospel of St. Luke, Homily 72.
17. Cyprian, *De dominica oratione* 13; Augustine, Sermons 56–57, 59; Cyril of Alexandria, *Commentary on the Gospel of St. Luke*, Homily 73; Caesarius of Arles, Sermon 147.
18. Tertullian, *De Oratione* 4; Cyprian, *De dominica oratione* 14; Augustine, Sermons 56–57; Chromatius of Aquileia, *Tractatus in Matthaeum*; Cyril of Alexandria, *Commentary on the Gospel of St. Luke*, Homily 74; Pseudo Augustinus, Sermon 65; *Opus Imperfectum in Matthaeum*, Homily 14.
19. Clement of Alexandria, *Adumbrationes in Judam II*; Tertullian, *De Oratione* 3; Cyprian, *De dominica oratione* 12; Origen, *On Prayer* XXIV.1; Juvencus, *Evangelica Historia* 1.58–604; Gregory of Nyssa, *De Oratione Dominica*, Sermon 3; Ambrose, *De Sacramentis* 5.4; Theodore of Mopsuestia, *Liber ad*

Baptizandos, Part 2, Chapter 1; Augustine Letter 130; Augustine, *De Sermone Domini in Monte*, Book 2.5, 2.11; Augustine, *De dono perseverantiae* 2.4; Augustine, Sermons 56–59; Cyril of Alexandria, Commentary on the Gospel of St. Luke, Homily 72; Jerome, *Commentariorum in Mathaeum bibri IV*, 6.10; Jerome, *Dialogus adversus Pelagianos* 3.15; Chromatius of Aquileia (d. 407) *Tractatus in Matthaeum* 2.2; Peter Chyrsologus, Sermon 67, 69 and 72; Pseudo-Quodvultdeus, PLS 3:300; Coelius Sedulius, *Carmen Paschale* 2.231; Coelius Sedulius, *Paschale Operibus* 2.2; *Opus Imperfectum in Matthaeum*, Homily 14; Caesarius of Arles, Sermon 147; Pseudo-Fortunatus *Expositio orationis domincae* 14–18; Ildefonsus of Toledo, *Liber de cognitione baptismi* 133.

20. Cyprian, *De dominica oratione* 13.
21. Tertullian, *De Oratione* 4; Cyprian, *De dominica oratione* 14; Origen, *On Prayer* XXVI.1; Gregory of Nyssa, *De Oratione Dominica*, Sermon 4; Augustine, Sermon 56; Cassian, *Conlationes* 9.20; Chromatius of Aquileia, *Tractatus in Matthaeum*; Cyril of Alexandria, *Commentary on the Gospel of St. Luke*, Homily 74; *Opus Imperfectum in Matthaeum*, Homily 14; Pseudo-Fortunatus, *Expositio orationis dominicae* 30–51.
22. Tertullian, *De Oratione* 3. Cf. Cyprian, *De dominica oratione* 12; Origen, *On Prayer* XXIV.1; Gregory of Nyssa, *De Oratione Dominica*, Sermon 3; Cyril of Jerusalem, *Mystagogic Catecheses* 5.12; Augustine, *De Sermone Domini in Monte*, 2.5; Cyril of Alexandria, Commentary on the Gospel of St. Luke, Homily 72.
23. Cyprian, *De dominica oratione* 12; Augustine, *De dono perseverantiae* 2.4; Augustine, Sermon 59; Chromatius of Aquileia, *Tractatus in Matthaeum* 2.2; Chromatius, *Praefatio Orationis Dominicae*; Caesarius of Arles, Sermon 147; Pseudo-Fortunatus *Expositio orationis domincae* 14–18.
24. Pseudo-Fortunatus, *Expositio orationis dominicae* 19–29.
25. Tertullian, *De Oratione* 4.
26. Cyprian, *De dominica oratione* 12. Cf. Augustine, Sermon 59; Caesarius of Arles, Sermon 147.
27. Pseudo Augustinus, Sermon 65.
28. Coelius Sedulius, *Carmen Paschale* 2.231.
29. Cyprian, *De dominica oratione* 12; Theodore of Mopsuestia, *Liber ad Baptizandos*, Part 2, Chapter 1; Augustine Letter 130; Peter Chyrsologus, Sermon 67;; Jerome, *Commentariorum in Mathaeum bibri IV*, 6.10; Cassian, *Conlationes* 9–10; John Chrysostom, Homily 29 *In Matthaeum*; Cyril of Alexandria, *Commentary on the Gospel of St. Luke*, Homily 72; Peter Chyrsologus, Sermons 67, 69–72; Coelius Sedulius, *Paschale Operibus* 2.2; Pseudo-Fortunatus *Expositio orationis domincae* 14–18.
30. While most authors make this argument, see Origen's *On Prayer* XXVI.2 as a representative example.
31. Tertullian, *De Oratione* 6.
32. Cyril of Alexandria, *Commentary on the Gospel of St. Luke*, Homily 75; Isidore of Seville, *De ecclesiasticis officiis* 15; cf. Cyprian, *De dominica oratione* 18;

Juvencus, *Evangeliorum Libri IV* 1.58–604; Augustine, *De Sermone Domini in Monte* 2.7; Peter Chyrsologus, Sermon 70.

33. Theodore of Mopsuestia, *Liber ad Baptizandos*, Part 2, Chapter 1; cf. Cyril of Alexandria, *Commentary on the Gospel of St. Luke*, Homily 75.

34. Chromatius of Aquileia, *Tractatus in Matthaeum* 5.1.

35. Tertullian, *De Oratione* 7; Cyprian, *De dominica oratione* 22.

36. Pseudo-Fortunatus, *Expositio orationis dominicae* 58–61.

37. Theodore of Mopsuestia, *Liber ad Baptizandos*, Part 2, Chapter 1.

38. Tertullian, *De Oratione* 7; Cyprian, *De dominica oratione* 22; Gregory of Nyssa, *De Oratione Dominica*, Sermon 5; Ambrose, *De Sacramentis* 5.4; Augustine, *De Sermone Domini in Monte* 2.8; Augustine Sermons 56–59; Peter Chyrsologus, Sermon 68; Pseudo-Augustine, Sermon 65; Coelius Sedulius, *Carmen Paschale* 2.231ff.; Coelius Sedulius, *Paschale Operibus* 2.2; Prosper of Aquitaine, *Expositio Psalmorum*; Caesarius of Arles, Sermon 147; Pseudo-Fortunatus, *Expositio orationis dominicae* 58–61.

39. Cyprian, *De dominica oratione* 22; John Chrysostom, *Homiliae XC in Matthaeum,* Homily 19.

40. Augustine, Sermon 213; *Enchiridion*, chapters 70–80. For a more detailed analysis of this, see Chapter 2, the section entitled "The Lord's Prayer in Theological Education," the section on Augustine.

41. Augustine, *In Johannis Evangelium Tractatus CXXIV* Sermons 57, 58, 59.

42. Augustine, Sermon 56.

43. Clement of Rome, *First Epistle to the Corinthians* 13.2; Tertullian, *De Oratione* 7; Clement of Alexandria, *Stromatesis* 7.13; Cyprian, *De dominica oratione* 23; Cyril of Jerusalem, *Mystagogic Catechesis* 5.16; Ambrose, *De Sacramentis* 5.4.

44. Cyril of Jerusalem, *Mystagogic Catechesis* 5.16.

45. Theodore of Mopsuestia, *Liber ad Baptizandos*, Part 2, Chapter 1.

46. Cyprian, *De dominica oratione* 24; Augustine, Sermon 56.

47. Tertullian, *De Oratione* 8; Gregory of Nyssa, *De Oratione Dominica,* Sermon 5; Ambrose, *De Sacramentis* 5.4; Augustine, *Enchiridion* 114–116; Augustine, *De dono perseverantiae* 116–117; Chromatius of Aquileia, *Tractatus in Matthaeum*; Pseudo-Quodvultdeus; *Opus Imperfectum in Matthaeum,* Homily 14; Caesarius of Arles, Sermon 147; Pseudo-Fortunatus, *Expositio orationis dominicae* 62; Ildefonsus of Toledo, *Liber de cognitione baptismi* 133.

48. Augustine, *Enchiridion* 114–116; cf. Cyril of Alexandria, *Commentary on the Gospel of St. Luke*, Homily 77.

49. Tertullian, *De Oratione* 8.

50. Augustine, Sermon 56; Augustine, *In Johannis Evangelium Tractatus CXXIV* Sermon 52.

51. Cf. especially, Tertullian, *De Oratione* 8; Cyprian, *De dominica oratione* 25; Juvencus, *Evangelica Historia* 1.58–604; Augustine, *In Johannis Evangelium Tractatus CXXIV* Sermon 52; Augustine, Letter 130; Augustine, *De Sermone Domini in Monte* 2.9–11; Augustine, Sermons 57–58; Cassian, *Conlationes*

9.23; John Chrysostom, *Homiliae XC in Matthaeum* Homily 19; Chromatius of Aquileia, *Tractatus in Matthaeum*; Peter Chyrsologus, Sermons 67–68, 70–72; Pseudo-Quodvultdeus; Pseudo-Augustine, Sermon 65; Caesarius of Arles, Sermon 147; Pseudo-Fortunatus, *Expositio orationis dominicae* 62; Ildefonsus of Toledo, *Liber de cognitione baptismi* 133.

52. Peter Chyrsologus, Sermon 67; cf. Origen, *On Prayer* XXIX.1–2.
53. Tertullian, *De Oratione* 8; Cyprian, *De dominica oratione* 25. Cf. Chromatius of Aquileia, *Praefatio Orationis Dominicae*; Cyril of Alexandria, *Commentary on the Gospel of St. Luke*, Homily 77; Peter Chyrsologus, Sermon 70.
54. Gregory of Nyssa, *De Oratione Dominica*, Sermon 5.
55. Augustine, *In Johannis Evangelium Tractatus CXXIV* Sermon 124; Cyril of Alexandria, *Commentary on the Gospel of St. Luke*, Homily 77.
56. Augustine, *De dono perseverantiae* 116–213.
57. Cyprian, *De dominica oratione* 27.
58. Pseudo-Augustine, Sermon 65.
59. Peter Chyrsologus, Sermon 72.
60. Helmut Thielicke, *Our Heavenly Father* (New York: Harper and Row, 1953), 14.

Selected Bibliography

Primary Sources

Ambrose of Milan. *De Sacramentis, De Mysteriis.* Ed. Josef Schmitz. Freiburg: Herder, 1900. CSEL 73; SC 25 and 29.

———. *Epistolae.* Patralogia Latina PL 16.

———. *Expositio Psalmi CXVIII.* PL 15.

———. *On the Sacraments and On the Mysteries.* Trans. and ed. T. Thompson and Notes by J. H. Srawley. Father's of the Church. Vol. 44. London: SPCK, 1950.

———. *Sancti Ambrosii Opera, pars vii.* Ed. O. Faller. CSEL 73. Vienna: Hoelder-Pichler-Tempsky, 1955.

———. *Traité sur l'Évangile de S. Luc.* SC 45 and 52.

Anderson, Stanley, Sterling Bjorndahl, Shawn Carruth, and Christoph Heil, eds. *Documenta Q: Reconstructions of Q through Two Centuries of Gospel Research Excerpted, Sorted and Evaluated.* Leuven: Peeters, 1996.

Andrieu, Michel. *Les Ordines Romani du Haut Moyen Age.* Spicilegium sacrum lovaniense. Etudes et documents, Vols. 11, 23, 24, 28, 29. Louvain: 1931–1961.

Angenendt, Arnold. *Monachi peregrini.* Münstersche Mittelalter-Schriften, Vol. 6. Munich: 1972.

Bradshaw, Paul F., Maxwell E. Johnson, and L. Edward Phillips, eds. *The Apostolic Tradition.* Minneapolis. MN: Fortress Press, 2002.

Holy Transfiguration Monastery (trans.). *The Ascetical Homilies of Saint Isaac the Syrian*, Homily Two. Boston: 1984.

Augustine. *Contra Duas Epistolas Pelagianorum.* PL 44; CSEL 60.

———. *Contra Faustum Manichaeum Libri Triginta Tres.* PL 42; LNPF 4.

———. *De catechizandis rudibus.* PL 40; CCSL 46; ACW 2.

———. *De Civitate Dei.* PL 41; CSEL 40; CCSL 47–48.

———. *De Correptione et Gratia.* PL 44; FC 2.

———. *De Doctrina Christiana.* PL 34; CSEL 89; CCSL 32.

———. *De dono perseverantiae.* PL 45; LPNF 5; Lesousky, Mary Alphonsine. *The Dono Perseverantiae of St. Augustine: A Translation with an Introduction and a Commentary.* A Dissertation. Washington, D.C.: Catholic University of America, 1956.

———. *Enchiridion.* PL 40; CCSL 46; Augustine. *The Enchiridion on Faith, Hope, and Love.* Trans. Henry Paolucci. Washington, D.C.: Gateway Books, 1961.

———. *De Gestis Pelagii.* PL 44.

———. *De Gratia et Libero Arbitrio.* PL 44.

———. *De Natura et Gratia.* PL 44; CSEL 60; LNPF 5.

———. *De Nuptiis et Concupiscentia.* PL 44; CSEL 42.

———. *De Peccatorum meritis et remissione.* PL 44; CSEL 60; LNPF 5.

———. *De perfectione iustitae hominis.* PL 44; CSEL 42; LNPF 5.

———. *De praedestinatione sanctorum.* PL 44.

———. *De sancte uirginitate.* CSEL 41; FC 26.

———. *De Sermone Domini in Monte.* PL 34; CCSL 35; ACW 5.

———. *De spiritu et littera.* PL 44; CSEL 60.

———. *Epistolae.* PL 33; CSEL 34, 44, 57, and 58; CCSL 46; FC 18; Leinenweber, John ed., *Letters of Saint Augustine.* Liguoiri, MO: Triumph Books, 1992.

———. *In Evangelium Joannis Tractatus Centum Viginti Quatuor.* PL 35; CCSL 36.

———. *Regula Sancta Augustina* [a.k.a. *Regula ad servos Dei*]. PL 32; Verheijen, L., ed., *Le Règle de Saint Augustin.* Paris: 1967; Lawless, George. *Augustine of Hippo and His Monastic Rule.* Oxford: Clarendon, 1987.

———. *Retractiones.* PL 32; CSEL36; CCSL 57.

———. *Sermons: The Works of Saint Augustine.* Trans. and ed. Edmund Hill, Vols. 1–7. Brooklyn: New City Press, 1990. Morin, G. *Augustini tractatus.* Kempten, 1917; PLS 3:299-303.

Benedict, The Rule. *La Règule de saint Benoît,* ed. and comment Adalbert de Vogüe and Jean Neufville, SC 181–186 with Vol. 7. Paris: Les Éditions du Cerf, 1977, not included in the SC series. *RB 1980,* Latin and English Edition. Collegeville, Minnesota: Liturgical Press, 1981. Cf. PL 66:447; PL 103:896.

Boniface. Sermons. *Opera Omnia,* ed. J. A. Giles, 2 vols. London: 1844. PL 139; MGH, *Epistolae* 3; and the updated edition of the same work by M. Tangl in MGH, *Epistolae Selectae,* 1 (1916).

Caesarius of Arles. Sermons. SC 175, 243, 330; CCSL 103–104; CPL. 1008–1009; FC 31.

Chavasse, Antione. *Le Sacramentaire gélasian.* Tournai, 1957.

Chromatius of Aquileia. *Praefatio orationis dominicae,* SC 164; CCSL 9A; CCSL 9, p. 445; cf. Gelasian Sacramentary 36, *Liber Sacramentorum Romanae Aeclesiae Oridinis Anni Circuli,* pp. 51f.; translation in Whitaker, *Documents of the Baptismal Liturgy,* pp. 177ff.; and the *Ordo XI* chapter 69 in Michel Andrieu, *Les Ordines Romani du Haut Moyen Age.* Spicilegium sacrum lovaniense. Ettudes et documents. Louvain: 1931–61, vol. 2.

———. *Tractatus in Matthaeum.* PL 20; SC 154 & 164; CCSL 9A.

Clement of Alexandria. *Adumbrationes in Judam II.* GCS 17.

———. *Paedagogus.* 12.

———. *Stromatesis.* GCS 15.

Coelius Sedulius. *Paschale carmen* and *Paschale opus.* PL 19; CSEL 24; Schefs, N. *Sedulius Paschale Carmen,* Boek I en II. Delft: 1938; Sigerson, George. *The Easter Song.* Dublin: Talbot Press Ltd., 1922.

Council of Toledo 633, Canon 10; J.D. Mansi. *Sacrorum Conciliorum nova et amplissima collectio.*

Cross, J. E., and T. D. Hill translators and eds. *The Prose Solomon and Saturn and Adrain Ritheus*, McMaster Old English Studies and Texts, Vol. 1. Toronto: 1982.

Cyprian. *De Dominica Oratione.* PL 4; CSEL 3; CCSL 3A.

———. *De unitate ecclesiae.* PL 4; CSEL 3; CCSL 3A.

Cyril of Alexandria. *Commentary on the Gospel of Saint Luke*, trans. R. Payne Smith. New York: Studion Publishers, Inc., 1983.

Cyril of Jerusalem. *Catechesis Mystagogica.* PG 23; SC 126; FC 61.

———. Edward Yarnold, S. J., trans. and ed. *Cyril of Jerusalem.* London: Routledge, 2000.

Didascalia Apostolorum 15. Trans. Arthur Vööbus. *The Didascalia Apostolorum in Syriac* II, CSCO, vols. 179–180. Louvain: 1979.

Didymus. *De Trinitate.* PG 39.

Eligius of Noyon. *Vita.* PL 87; MGH, SSRM, Vol. 4.

———. *Epistolae.* PL 87; MGH, *Epistolae*, 3.

———. *Predicacio.* MGH SSRM, Vol. 4.

Eugippius. *Excerpta ex operibus s. Augustini*; *Eugipii Opera.* PL 62; CSEL 9.

Evangelical Lutheran Worship. Minneapolis, MN: Augsburg, Fortress, 2006.

Fulgentius of Ruspe. *Epistolae.* PL 65; CCSL 91.

The Gelasian Sacramentary. *Liber Sacramentorum Romanae Aeclesiae.*

Oridinis Anni Circuli, eds. Leo Cunibert Mohlberg in cooperation with Leo Eizenhöfer and Petrus Siffrin. Rome: Casa Editirce Herder, 1960.

Gregory the Great. *Epistolae.* MGH *Epistolae*, II.

———. *Moralia in Iob.* PL 75-76; CCSL 143-143B.

———. *Homilae in Evangelium.* PL 76.

Gregory of Nyssa. *The Lord's Prayer.* ACW 18.

———. *Gregorii Nysseni: De Oratione Dominica, De Beatitudinibus*, Johannes F. Callahan, ed., Leiden: E.J. Brill, 1992.

Halitgar of Cambrai. *Penitential*, Herman J. Schmitz, ed. *Die Bussbücher und die Bussdisciplin der Kirche*, Vol. 1. Mainz: 1883.

Heinimann, Siegfried. *Oratio Dominica Romanice.* Tübingen: Max Niemeyer Verlag, 1988.

Heliand. Edward Sievers, ed. 1935 reprint of his 1878 edition.

The Heliand: The Saxon Gospel. Trans. G. Ronald Murphy. New York: Oxford University Press, 1992.

Hilary of Poitiers. *Commentary on Matthew;* PL 9; CSEL 65; SC 254 and 258.

Hippolytus. *The Apostolic Tradition of Hippolytus.* Trans. Burton Scott Easton. Cambridge: Archon Books, 1962.

Homilia de sacrilegiis in C.P. Caspari, ed. *Eine Augustine Fälsch beilegte Homilia de sacrilegiis.* Christiana, 1886.

Ildefonsus. *Liber de cognitione baptismi.* PL 96.

Irenaeus. *Adversus Haereses.* PG 7.

Isidore of Seville. *De ecclesiasticis officiis*. CCSL 113.

——. *De viris illustribus*. PL 83.

——. *Sententiae*. PL 83.

Jerome. *De viris illustribus*. LNPF 3, ser. 2.

——. *Dialogus adversus Pelagianos*. PL 23; FC 53.

——. *Epistolae*. CSEL 54; ACW 33.

——. *In Mattheum*. SC 242 and 259; CCSL 77.

John Cassian. *Conlationes*. SC 42, 54, 64; *Conferences*, Trans. Colm Luibheid. New York: Paulist Press, 1985. ACW 57.

——. *Institutiones*. SC 109; Institutions, ACW 58.

John Chrysostom. *Baptismal Instructions*. Trans. Paul W. Harkins. New York: Newman Press, 1963. ACW 31.

——. *Homilies on Matthew*. PG 58; LNPF 10.

——. *In epistoalam ad Colossenses homiliae 1-12*. PG 62.

——. *The Divine Liturgy of Our Father Among the Saints: John Chrysostom*. Oxford: Oxford University Press, 1995.

——. *The Liturgy of Baptism in the Baptismal Instructions of St. John Chyrsostom*. Trans. Thomas M. Finn. Washington, D.C.: Catholic University of America Press, 1967.

Julian of Toledo. *Prognosticon futuri saeculi*. PL 96.

Juvencus. *Evangeliorum Libri IV*. PL 19; CSEL 24; CPL 1385.

Kemble, J. M. *The Dialogue of Solomon and Saturnus*. Ælfric Society Vols. 8, 13, and 15. London: 1848.

Leo I. Sermons and Letters. CCSL 138, 138A; PLS 3:329-500; PL 54-56; SC 22, 49, 74, 200; LNPF 12, series 2; FC 34.

Lutheran Book of Worship. Minneapolis, MN: Augsburg, Fortress, 1977.

Martin of Braga. *De Correctione Rusticorum*. PL 72:17–52; PL 84:575–586; FC 62; Martin of Bracara, *De correctione rusticorum. A Commentary with an Introduction and Translation*, Harold F. Palmer, ed. Washington, D.C.: Master's Thesis, Catholic University of America, 1932.

——. *Martini Episcopi Bracarensis: Opera Omnia*. Claude W. Barlow ed. New Haven, Conn.: Yale University Press, 1950.

——. *Martin von Baraccaras Schrift* De Correctione Rusticorum, C. P. Caspari ed. Christiana, 1883.

Martyrium Polycarpi. SC 10; ACW 14.

Maximus Confessor. *Expositio orationis Dominicae*. PG 90.

——. *The Four Hundred Chapters on Love*, in *Maximus Confessor: Selected Writings*. Trans. George Berthold. New York: 1985.

McNeill, John T. and Helena M. Gamer. *Medieval Handbooks of Penance*. New York: Octagon Books, 1979.

Menner, Robert, ed. *The Poetical Dialogues of Solomon and Saturn*. New York: The Modern Language Association of America, 1941.

Optatus of Milevis. *De schismate Donatistarum*, a.k.a. *Valentiniano et Valente principibus* or *Adversus Parmenianum Donatistam*. CSEL 26; PL 11; PLS 1.

Opus Imperfectum in Matthaeum. Joseph van Banning, ed. PG 56; CCSL 87B.

Origen. *De oratione*, trans. from Eric G. Jay, *Origen's Treatise on Prayer*. London: 1954; also Origen, *On Prayer*. Trans. Rowan A. Greer. New York: 1979; Origen, *On Prayer*, P. Koetschau, ed. *Die Griechischen Christlichen Schriftsteller der ersten drei Jahrhunderte*. Berlin: 1899.

———. *On Prayer* XXIV.5; Origen, *An Exhortation to Martyrdom, Prayer and Selected Works*, Classics of Western Spirituality. New York: Paulist Press, 1979.

Paenitentiale Bobbiense. *Paenitentialia Franciae, Italiae, et Hispaniae Saeculi VIII-XI*. Ed. Raymund Kottje. Turnholt, Belgium: Brepols, 1994; CCSL 156.

Paschasius Radbertus. *De partu virgine*. PL 120.

———. *Expositio in Mattheo Libri XII*. CCSL 56.

Peter Chyrsologus. Sermons. PL 52; CCSL 24A; FC 17.

Pirminius. *Dicta abbatis Pirminii de singulis libris canonicis scarapsus*. PL 89; G. Jecker ed., *Der heilige Pirmin und sein Pastoralbüchlein*. Sigmarigen: 1976.

Poenitentiale Merseburgense b. CCSL 156.

Poenitentiale Hubertense. F. W. H. Wasserschleben ed. *Die Bussordnungen der abendländischen Kirche*. Graz, 1958.

Prosper of Aquitaine. *Expositio Psalmorum*. CCSL 67A.

———. *Pro Augustino responsiones, De gratia Dei et libero voluntatis arbitrio contra collatorem*. PL 45 and 51; ACW 32.

Pseudo-Augustine. Sermon 65. PL 39.

Pseudo-Chrysostom. Sermon 28. PLS 4:825–831.

Pseudo-Quodvultdeus. *De dominica oratione*. PLS 3.

Quodvultdeus. *De haeresibus*. PL 42.

———. *De promissionibus Dei*. SC 101; CCSL 60.

Rabanus Maurus. *De institutione clericorum*. PL 107.

Tertullian. *Adversus Marcionem*. SC 365 (Book 1), SC 368 (Book 2), and SC 399 (Book 3); Ernest Evans. *Tertullian's Adversus Marcionem*, 2 Vols. Oxford: Oxford University Press, 1972. ANF 3; Meijering, E. P., ed. *Tertullian Contra Marcion: Gotteslehre in der Polemik: Adversus Marcionem I-II*. Leiden: E.J. Brill, 1977.

———. *Adversus Praxean* 5. CSEL 47; Ernest Evans. *Treatise against Praxeas*. London: SPCK, 1948.

———. *Apologeticum*. CSEL 69; CCSL 1.

———. *De Baptismo*. CSEL 20; CCSL 1.

———. *De Oratione*. CSEL 20; CCSL 1; FC 40; Ernest Evans. *Tertullian's Tract on The Prayer*. London: SPCK, 1953.

Theodore of Mopsuestia. *Commentary of Theodore of Mopsuestia on the Lord's Prayer and on the Sacraments of Baptism and the Eucharist*. Trans. and ed. A. Mingana, Woodbrooke Studies, Vol. 6. Cambridge: W. Heffer & Sons. Limited, 1933.

———. *Les homélies catéchétiques de Théodore de Mopsueste*. Studi e Testi 145. Eds. Raymond Tonneau and Robert Devresse. Vatican: Biblioteca Apostilica Vaticano, 1949.

Venantius Fortunatus. *Fortunat. Etude sur un dernier représentant de la poésie latine dans la Gaule mérovingienne*. Ed. D. Tardi. Paris: 1927. PL 88:313–322; MGH, AA 4:1–2.

Vogel, Cyrille. *Les "Libri Paenitentiales."* Turnhout, Beligium: Brepols, 1978.

Vulgate. *Biblia Sacra: Iuxta Vulgatam Versionem.* Stuttgart: Deutsche Bibelgesellschaft, 1969.

Whitaker, E. C. *Documents of the Baptismal Liturgy.* London: SPCK, 1970.

Wilmart, André. *Analecta Reginensia,* Vol. 50. *Studi e Testi.* Rome: Biblioteca Apostolica Vaticana, 1933.

Secondary Sources

Bahr, Gordon J. "The Use of the Lord's Prayer in the Primitive Church." *Journal of Biblical Literature* 84 (1965): 153–159.

Banning, Josef van. "The Critical Edition of the *Opus Imperfectum in Matthaeum*: An Arian Source." *Studia Patristica* (17/1): 382–387.

Barnes, Timothy David. *Tertullian: A Historical and Literary Study.* Oxford: Clarendon Press, 1971.

Barré, H. "Sermons marials inédits 'in Natali Domini'." *Marianum* 25 (1963): 71ff.

Bastiaensen, A. A. R. "Obserations sur le vocabulaire liturgique dans l'Itinéraire d'Egérie." *Latinitas christianorum primaeva* 17. Nijmegen and Utrecht, 1962.

Beck, Henry G. J. *The Pastoral Care of Souls in South-East France During the Sixth Century.* Rome: Apud Aedes Universitatis Gregorianae, 1950.

Bedard, Walter. *The Symbolism of the Baptismal Font in Early Christian Thought.* Washington, D.C.: Catholic University Press, 1951.

Betz, Hans Dieter. *The Sermon on the Mount.* Minneapolis, MN: Fortress Press, 1995.

Bieler, Ludwig, *The Irish Penitentials.* Dublin: Dublin Institute for Advanced Studies, 1963.

Bornkamm, Günter. "Der Aufbau der Bergpredigt." *New Testament Studies* 24 (1978): 419–432.

Bouché-Leclercq, A. *Histoire de la divination dans l'antiquité,* Vol. 1. Paris: 1879.

Bouhot, Jean-Paul. "La collection homilétique pseudochrysostomienne découverte par Jean-Paul Bouhot, 'Le sermon *'Dominus et Salvator'* Première forme dérivée d'un sermon perdu de saint Césaire'." *Revue Bénédictine* 80 (1970): 201–212.

———. "Une ancienne homélie catéchétique pour la tradition de l'oraison dominicale." *Augustinianum* 20 (1980): 69–78.

———. "Alcuin et le 'De catechizandis rudibus' de saint Augustine." *Recherches augustiniennes* 15 (1980): 176–240.

Bradshaw, Paul F. *Daily Prayer in the Early Church: A Study of the Origin and Early Development of the Divine Office.* New York: Oxford University Press, 1982.

———. *Poverty and Leadership in the Later Roman Empire.* The Menahem Stern Jerusalem Lectures. Hannover, 2002.

———. "Prayer, Morning, Noon, Evening, and Midnight—an Apostolic Custom?" *Studia Liturgica* 13 (1979): 57–62.

———. The Gospel and the Catechumenate in the Third Century," *Journal of Theological Studies* 50.1 (1999): 143–152.

Braegelmann, Athanasius. *The Life and Writings of Saint Ildefonsus of Toledo, A Dissertation.* Washington, D.C.: Catholic University of America Press, 1942.

Brown, Michael Joseph. *The Lord's Prayer through North African Eyes: A Window Early Christianity.* New York: T & T Clark, 2005.

Brown, Peter. *Poverty and Leadership in the Later Roman Empire.* The Menahem Stern Jerusalem Lectures. Hannover, 2002.

Brown, Raymond. "The Pater Noster as an Eschatological Prayer." *Theological Studies* 22 (1961): 175–208.

Brunhölzl, Franz. *Geschichte der Lateinischen Literatur des Mittelalters.* Louvain: Brepols, 1990.

Brusselmans, Christiane. *Les fonctions de parrainage des enfants aux premiers siécles de l'Eglise (100–550),* Ph.D. Dissertation. Washington, D.C.: Catholic University of America, 1964.

Capps, D. "The Psychology of Petitionary Prayer," *Theology Today* 39 (1982): 130–141.

Charlesworth, James H. "A Caveat on Textual Transmission and the Meaning of Abba: A Study of the Lord's Prayer," *The Lord's Prayer and Other Prayer Texts from the Greco-Roman Era.* Valley Forge, Pennsylvania: Trinity Press International, 1994.

Chavasse, Antoine. *Communion Solemnele et Profession de Foi,* Lex Orandi, 14. Paris: 1952.

Congar, Yves. *A History of Theology.* New York: Doubleday, 1968.

Coraro, F. *Sedulio poeta.* Catina, 1956.

Creed, J. M. *The Gospel According to St. Luke.* London: Macmillan, 1930.

Cullmann, Oscar. *Prayer in the New Testament* Trans. John Bowden, London: SCM Press, 1997.

Curtius, E. R. *European Literature and the Latin Middle Ages.* Trans. Willard Trask. London: Routledge and Kegan Paul, 1953.

Dahan, Gilbert. *Les intellectuels chrétiens et les juifs au moyen âge.* Paris, 1990.

———. *The Christian Polemic Against the Jews in the Middle Ages.* Notre Dame, University of Notre Dame Press: 1998.

Daly, Emily Joseph. *Tertullian: Disciplinary, Moral and Ascetical Works.* New York: Fathers of the Church, Inc., 1959.

Daniel, Robert and Maltomini, Franco. *Supplementum Magicum* I, Papyrologica Coloniensia. Opladen: Westdeutcher Verlag, 1990.

Delahaye, Karl. *Ecclesia Mater: Chez les Péres des Trois Premieres siécles.* Paris: Latour-Maubourg, 1964.

de Lange, N. R. M. *Origen and the Jews: Studies in Jewish-Christian Relations in Third- Century Palestine.* Cambridge: 1976.

De Latte, R. "Saint Augustin et le baptême: etude liturgico-historique du ritual baptismal des adultes chez Saint Augustin", *Questions Liturgiques* 56, no. 4 (1975): 177–224.

———. "Saint Augustin et le baptême: etude liurgico-historique du ritual baptismal des adultes chez Saint Augustin." *Questions Liturgiques* 57, no. 1 (1976): 41–55.

Denis-Bôulet, Noele-Maurice. *La Maison-Dieu.* Paris, 1966.

Dibelius, O. *Das Vaterunser: Unrisse zu einer Geschichte des Gebets in der Alten und Mittleren Kirche.* Gießen, 1903.

Dix, Gregory. *The Shape of the Liturgy.* London: Dacre Press, 1964.

Dondeyne, A. "La discipline des scrutins dans l'Église latine avant Charlemagne." *Revue d'Histoire Ecclesiastique* 28 (1932): 5–33, 751–788.

Dorneich, Monica. *The Lord's Prayer: A Bibliography.* Freiburg in Breisgau: Herder, 1982.

Doval, Alexis James. *Cyril of Jerusalem, Mystagogue: The Authorship of the Mystagogic Cathecesis.* Washington, DC: Catholic University of America Press, 2001.

Drobner, Hebertus and Viciano, Albert. *Gregory of Nyssa: Homilies on the Beatitudes.* Leiden: E.J. Brill, 2000.

Dujarier, Michel. *A History of the Catechumenate: The First Six Centuries.* New York: William H. Sadlier, 1979.

———. *Le Parrianage des adultes aux trois premiers siècles de l'Egliese. Recherche historique sur l'évolution des garanties et des étapes catéchuménales avant 313.* Paris: 1962.

Dyer, Joseph. "Observations on the Divine Office in the Rule of the Master," in Margot E. Fassler and Rebecca A. Baltzer, eds, *The Divine Office in the Latin Middle Ages: Methodology and Source Studies, Regional Developments, Hagiography: Written in Honor of Professor Ruth Steiner.* New York: 2000.

Esser, Kajetan. "Die dem hl. Franziskus von Assisi zugeschriebene 'Expositio in Pater Noster.' " *Collectanea Franciscana* 40 (1970): 241–271.

Étaix, R. "Sermon pour la féte des Apôtres Jacques et Jean attribuable à Saint Césaire." *Revue Bénédictine* 72 (1957): 3–9.

———. "Nouvelle collection de sermons raissemblée par saint Césaire." *Revue Bénédictine* 87 (1977): 7–33.

———. "Nouveau sermon pascal de Saint Césaire d'Arles." *Revue Bénédictine* 75 (1965): 201–211.

Euringer, S. "Das Sator-Arepo-Quadrat." *Historiches Jahrbuch* 71 (1952): 334ff.

Evangelical Lutheran Worship Book. Minneapolis: Augsburg Fortress, 2008.

Ferreiro, Alberto. " 'Frequenter Legere' The Propagation of Literacy, Education, and Divine Wisdom in Caesarius of Arles." *Journal of Ecclesiastical History* 43 (1992): 5–15.

Finkel, Asher. "The Prayer of Jesus in Matthew" In *Standing before God: Studies on Prayer in Scriptures and in Tradition with Essays in Honor of John M. Oesterreicher*, Eds. Asher Finkel and L. Frizzell, 131–70. New York: KTAV, 1981.

Finn, Thomas. *Early Christian Baptism and the Catechumenate: Italy, North Africa and Egypt.* Collegeville: Liturgical Press, 1992.

Fischer, J. D. C. *Christian Initiation: Baptism in the Medieval West.* London: S.P.C.K., 1965.

———. *Die Psalmen als Stimme der Kirche. Gesammelte Studien zur christlichen Psalmenfrömmigkeit.* Trier: 1982.

———. *Die Psalmenfrömmigkeit der Märtyrekirche.* Freiburg: 1949.

Fishwick, Duncan. "On the Origin of the Rotas-Sator Square." *Harvard Theological Review* 57 (1964): 39–53.

Folkemer, Lawrence D. "A Study of the Catechumenate." *Church History* 15 (1946): 286–307.

Fontaine, J. *Naissance de la poésie dans l'occident chrétien. IIIe-VIe siècles.* Paris: 1981.

Froehlich, Karlfried. "The Lord's Prayer in Patristic Literature," *The Princeton Seminary Bulletin,* Supplemental Vol. 2 (1992): 71–87. Reprinted in Roy Hammerling, *A History of Prayer: The First to the Fifteenth Century.* Leiden: Brill, 2008.

Fuchs, Harald. "Die Herkunft der Sator-Arepo-Formel," in *Heimat und Humanität. Festschrift für K. Meuli.* Basel: Krebs, 1951.

Fulton, Rachel. "Praying with Anselm at Admont: A Meditation on Practice," *Speculum* 81 (2006): 700–33.

Furberg, Ingemar. *Das Pater Noster in der Messe.* Lund: CWK Gleerups Förlag, 1968.

George, Judith W. *Venantius Fortunatus: A Latin Poet in Merovingian Gaul.* Oxford: Clarendon Press, 1992.

Göttler, J. *Geschichte der Pädagogik.* Freiburg: Herder, 1935.

Grant, Michael. *Greek and Latin Authors: 800 B.C.-A.D. 1000.* New York: The H.W. Wilson Company, 1980.

Green, H. Benedict, C. R. *Matthew, Poet of the Beatitudes.* Sheffield: Academic Press, 2001 (*Journal of the Study of the New Testament Supplement Series 203*).

Greer, Rowan. *Theodore of Mopsuestia: Exegete and Theologian.* London: Faith Press, 1961.

Grisbrooke, W. Jardine. ed. and trans. *The Liturgical Portions of the Apostolic Constitutions: A Text for Students.* Alcuin/GROW Liturgical Study 13–14, Bramcote: Grove, 1991.

Hamman, Adalbert. *Early Christian Prayers.* London: Regnery, Longmans, Green, 1961.

———. *Le Pater expliqué par les Pères.* Paris: Éditions franciscaines, 1952.

Hammerling, Roy, ed. *A History of Prayer: The First to the Fifteenth Century.* Leiden: Brill, 2008.

———. "Gregory of Nyssa's Sermons on the Lord's Prayer: Lessons from the Classics." *Word and World* 22 (Winter 2002): 64–70.

———. "The History of the Lord's Prayer during the Middle Ages" in *Proceedings of the Patristic Medieval Renaissance Conference*, Villanova University (1993–1994): 1–24.

Hanssens, Jean Michel. "Deux documents carolingiens sur le baptême." *Ephemerides Liturgicae,* 41 (1927): 74ff.

———. *La liturgie d'Hippolyte: Documents et études. Orientalia christiana analecta*, Vol. 155. Rome: 1970.

Harmless, William. *Augustine and the Catechumenate*. Collegeville, MN: Liturgical Press, 1995.

Hauck, F. *Das Evangelium des Lukas*. Leipzig: Hinrichs'sche Buchhandlung, 1934.

Herzog, Reinhart. *Die Bibelepik der lateinischen Spätantike*. Vol. 1. Munich, 1975.

Hillgarth, J. N. "El Prognosticon futurui saeculi de S. Julián de Toledo." *Analecta Sacra Tarraconensia* 30 (1957): 5–61.

Höfer, A. "Zwei unbekannte Sermones des Caesarius von Arles." *Revue Bénédictine* 74 (1964): 44–53.

Jackson, M. G. "The Lord's Prayer in St. Augustine," in E. A. Livingstone, ed., *Studia Patristica*, vol. xxvii (Louvain: Peeters, 1993): 311–321.

Jeremias, Joachim. *New Testament Theology*. New York: Charles Scribner's Sons, 1971.

———. *The Lord's Prayer*. Philadelphia: Fortress Press, 1964.

———. *The Prayers of Jesus*. London: Alec R. Allenson, Inc., 1967.

Jones, Cheslyn, Wainright, Geoffrey, and Yarnold, Edward, eds. *The Study of the Liturgy*. New York: Oxford University Press, 1978.

Jungmann, Josef Andreas. "Altchristliche Gebetsordnung im Lichte des Rebelbuches on 'En Fescha,' " *Zeitschrift für katholische Theologie* (1952).

———. *Handing on the Faith*. New York: Herder and Herder, 1959.

———. *The Early Liturgy*. Notre Dame: University of Notre Dame Press, 1959.

———. *Christian Prayer through the Centuries*. Trans. John Coyne, S.J. New York: Paulist Press, 1978.

Kavanagh, Aidan. "Eastern Influences on the Rule of Saint Benedict," in Timothy Verdon, ed., *Monasticism and the Arts*, ch 2. Syracuse: 1984.

———. *The Shape of Baptism: The Rite of Christian Initiation*. New York: Pueblo Pub. Co., 1978.

Kelly, J. N. D. *Early Christian Creeds*. London: Longmans, 1960.

Kiley, Mark, ed. *Prayer from Alexander to Constantine: A Critical Anthology*. London: Routledge, 1997.

——— "The Lord's Prayer and Matthean Theology," in James H. Charlesworth, Mark Harding, and Mark Kiley, eds., *The Lord's Prayer and Other Prayer Texts from the Greco-Roman Era*. Valley Forge, PA: Trinity Press International, 1994.

Kloppenborg, John S. *Q Parallels: Synopsis, Critical Notes, and Concordance*. Sonoma, California: Polebridge Press, 1988.

Kuhnmuench, Otto J. *Early Christian Latin Poets from the Fourth to the Sixth Century*. Chicago: Loyola University Press, 1929.

Labriolle, Pierre de. *History and Literature of Christianity*. New York: Barnes & Noble, 1968.

Lagrange, M. J. *Évangile selon Saint Luc*. Paris: Libraire Lecoffre, 1921.

Lambert, M. von. "Édition d'une collection latine découverte par Dom Morin." *Revue Bénédictine* (1969): 255–58.

Lampe, Gordon W. *Studies in the Gospels, Essays in Memory of R.H. Lightfoot.* Oxford: Basil Blackwell, 1955.

Latte, Robert de. "Saint Augustin et le baptême. Etude liturgico-historique du rituel baptismal des enfants chez Saint Augustin." *Questions liturgiqes et paroissiales* 56 (1975): 177–223.

Leaney, A. R. C. *A Commentary on the Gospel According to Luke.* London: Adam & Charles Black, 1958.

———. "The Lucan Text of the Lord's Prayer (Lk xi 1–4)." *Novum Testamentum* 1 (1956): 104ff.

Lehmann, Paul. *Die Parodie im Mittelalter.* Stuttgart: Anton Hiersemann, 1963.

Lewis, J. P. *A Study of the Interpretation of Noah and the Flood in Jewish and Christian Literature.* Leiden: E.J. Brill, 1968.

Lohmeyer, Ernst. *Our Father.* New York: Harper and Row, 1965.

Luz, Ulrich. *Matthew 1–7: A Commentary.* Minneapolis, MN: Augsburg Publishing House, 1985.

Lynch, Joseph. *Godparents and Kinship in Early Medieval Europe.* Princeton, NJ: Princeton University Press, 1986.

MacMullen, Ramsay. *Roman Social Relations 50 B.C. to A.D. 284.* New Haven: Yale University Press, 1974.

Maertens, Theirry. *Histoire et pastorale du rituel du catéchuménat et du baptême*, Paroisse et liturgie, Collection de pastorale liturgique, Vol. 56. Bruges: 1962.

Manitius, Max. *Geschichte der lateinischen Literatur des Mittelalters*, Vol. 1. München: C.H. Beck'sche Verlagsbuchhandlung, 1911.

Manson, T. W. "The Lord's Prayer." *Bulletin of the John Rylands University Library of Manchester* 38 (1956): 105ff.

Marshall, I. H. *The Gospel of Luke: A Commentary on the Greek Text.* Grand Rapids, MI: Eerdmans, 1978.

Martène, Edmond. *De antiquis ecclesiae ritibus libri quatuor*, 4 vols. Antwerp: 1736–1738.

Martimort, Aimé-Georges. "La Lecture patristique dans la liturgie des heures," in Giustino Farnedi, ed., *Traditio et Progressio.* Studi liturgici in onore del Prof. Adrien Nocent, Studia Anselmiana 95. Rome: 1988.

———. *Les lectures liturgiques et leurs livres*, Typologie des sources du Moyen Âge occidental 64. Turnhout: 1992.

McDonald, A. D. "The Iconographic Tradition of Sedulius." *Speculum* 8 (1933): 150–156.

McKenna, Stephen. *Paganism and Pagan Survivals in Spain up to the Fall of the Visigothic Kingdom*, A Dissertation. Washington, D.C.: The Catholic University of America, 1938.

Meer, Frederic van der. *Augustinus der Seelsorger: Leben und Wirken eines Kirchenvaters.* Köln: J.P. Bachem, 1951; in English, trans. G. Battershaw and G.R. Lamb, *Augustine the Bishop.* London: Sheed & Ward, 1961.

Meier, John. *A Marginal Jew. Rethinking the Historical Jesus*, Vol. 2, *Mentor, Message, and Miracles.* The Anchor Bible Reference Library. New York: Doubleday, 1994.

Meyer, Kuno. "An Old Irish Treatise *De arreis.*" *Revue celtique* 15 (1894): 485–498.

Mitchell, Leonel L. *Baptismal Anointing.* Notre Dame, IN: Notre Dame Press, 1978.

———. "Ambrosian Baptismal Rites." *Studia Liturgica* 1 (1962): 241–253.

Moeller, W.O.. "The Mithric Origin and Meanings of the Rotas-Sator Square." *Études préliminaires aux religions orientales* 38 (1973): 44–52.

Moffat, James. "Augustine on the Lord's Prayer." *The Expositor* 106 (1919): 259–72.

———. "Cyprian on the Lord's Prayer." *The Expositor* 105 (1919): 176–89.

———. "Tertullian on the Lord's Prayer." *The Expositor* 103 (1919): 24–41.

Morin, G. "Étude sur une série de discours d'un évêque (de Naples?) du VIᵉ siècle." *Revue Bénédictine* 11 (1894): 385–402.

———. *Revue des Études Augustiniennes* 16 (1970): 139–146.

Mullins, Patrick Jerome. *The Spiritual Life According to Saint Isidore of Seville,* A Dissertation. Washington, D.C.: Catholic University of America Press, 1940.

Murphy Center for Liturgical Research. *Made, Not Born: New Perspectives on Christian Initiation and the Catechumenate.* Notre Dame, IN: University of Notre Dame Press, 1976.

Norton, M. A. "Prosopography of Juvencus" in J. M. F. Maricq, ed., *Leaders of Iberian Christianity.* Boston: 1962.

Olivar, A. "Trois nouveaux fragments en onciale du Commentaire de Jérôme sur l'Evangile de Matthieu." *Revue Bénédictine* 92 (1982): 76–81.

O'Neill, J. C. "The Lord's Prayer." *Journal for the Study of the New Testament* 51 (1993): 3–25.

Opelt, I. "Die Szenerie bei Iuvencus." *Vigiliae Christianae* 19 (1975): 191–207.

Pelikan, Jaroslav. *The Emergence of the Catholic Tradition (100–600).* Chicago: University of Chicago Press, 1971.

Penn, Michael. "Performing Family: Ritual Kissing and the Construction of Early Christian Kinship." *Journal of Early Christian Studies* 10 (2002): 151–174.

Petit, Fr. "Sur les catéchèses post-baptismales de saint Ambroise. A propos de *De sacramentis* IV, 29." *Revue Bénédictine* 68 (1958): 156–265.

Phillips, L. Edwards. *The Ritual Kiss in Early Christian Worship.* Cambridge: Grove Books Limited, 1996.

Plaine, F. "Nouvelles Remarques sur les homèlies attribuèes à saint Éloi." *Revue des Questions Historiques* 65 (1899): 235–242.

Plummer, A., *A Critical Study and Exegetical Commentary on the Gospel According to St. Luke.* Edinburgh: T&T Clark, 1896.

Plumpe, Joseph C. *Mater Ecclesia: An Inquiry into the Concept of the Church as Mother in Early Christianity.* Washington, D.C.: Catholic University Press, 1943.

Puniet, Pierre de. "Les trois homélies catéchétiques du sacramentaire gélasien pour la tradition des évangiles, du symbole et de l'orason dominicale." *Revue d'Histoire Ecclisiastique* 5 (1904):. 505–521, 755–786; 6 (1905): 15–32, 170–179, 304–318.

———. "La liturgie baptismale en Gaule avant Charlemagne." *Revue des questions historiques* 72 (1902): 396–397.

Quasten, Johannes. *Patrology*, Vols. 1–4. Westminster, Maryland: Christian Classics, Inc., 1990.

———. *Der Psalm vom Guten Hirten in den altchristlichen Baptisterien und in den Taufliturgien des Ostens und Westens* in Pisciculi Festschrift Dölger. Munster: 1939.

Raby, F. J. E. *A History of Christian Latin Poetry from the Beginnings to the Close of the Middle Ages*. Oxford: Clarendon Press, 1953.

———. *A History of Secular Latin Poetry in the Middle Ages*, Vol. 1. Oxford: Clarendon Press, 1957.

Riché, Pierre. *Education and Culture in the Barbarian West*. Columbia, SC: University of South Carolina Press, 1978.

Riley, Hugh M. *Christian Initiation*. Washington, D.C.: Catholic University of America Press, 1974.

Robbers, Michael. *Biblical Epic and Rhetorical Paraphrase in Late Antiquity*. Liverpool: Francis Cairns, 1985.

Rordorf, Willy. *Der Sonntag*. Zurich: Zwingli Verlag, 1962.

———. "The Lord's Prayer in the Light of its Liturgical Use in the Early Church." *Studia Liturgica* 14 (1980/81): 1–19.

———. "Wie auch wir vergeben *haben* unsern Schuldnern (Matth. VI, 12b)," in F. L. Cross, ed., *Studia Patristica*. Vol. 10. Berlin: 1970.

Rowlandson, Jane, ed., *Women and Society in Greek and Roman Egypt: A Sourcebook*. Cambridge: Cambridge University Press, 1998.

Russell, Norman. *Cyril of Alexandria*. London: Routledge, 2000.

Salmon, Pierre. "La composition d'un *libellus precum* à l'époque de la réforme grégorienne," *Benedictina* 26 (1979): 285–322.

———. *L'Office divin au Moyen Âge. Histoire de la formation du bréviaire du IXe au XVIe Siècle*. Paris: 1967.

Saxer, V. *Saints anciens d'Afrique du Nord*. Vatican City: 1979.

Schnurr, Klaus Bernhard. *Hören und handeln*. Freiburg: Herder, 1985.

Sickenberger, Joseph. *Titus von Bostra: Studien zu dessen Lukas-homilien*. Leipzig: Hinirich, 1901.

Simonetti, Manlio, ed. *Matthew 1-13*. Ancient Christian Commentary on Scripture Series. Downers Grove: 2001.

Scott, E. F. *The Lord's Prayer*. New York: 1951.

Spidlik, Tomas. *The Spirituality of the Christian East*. Kalamazoo: Cistercian Studies, 1986.

Springer, Carl P. E. *The Gospel as Epic in Late Antiquity: The Paschale Carmen of Sedulius*. Leiden: E.J. Brill, 1988.

Steinmann, Jean. *Saint Jerome and His Times*. Notre Dame, IN: Fides Publishers, 1959.

Stenzel, A. "Die Taufe. Eine genetische Eklärungder Taufliturgie." *FGTh* 7/8 (1958): 177.

Stevenson, Kenneth W. Abba, *Father Understanding and Using the Lord's Prayer*. Norwich: Canterbury Press, 2000.

——. *The Lord's Prayer: A Text in Tradition*. Minneapolis, MN: Fortress Press, 2004.

——. "The Six Homilies of Peter Chyrsologus on the Lord's Prayer," in Maxwell E. Johnson and L. Edward Phillips, eds, *Studia Liturgica Diversa: Essays in Honor of Paul F. Bradshaw*. Portland: Pastoral Press, 1986.

Steweart-Sykes, Alistair. "Manumission and Baptism in Tertullian's Africa: A Search for the Origin of Confirmation," *Studia Patristica* 31 (2001): 129–149.

——. "Prayer Five Times in the Day and at Midnight:Two Apostolic Customs," *Studia Liturgica* 33 (2003): 1–19.

Stewart, Columba. *Prayer and Community: The Benedictine Tradition*. Maryknoll, NY: 1998.

Stritzky, Maria-Barbara von. *Studien zur Überlieferum und Interpretation des Vaterunsers in der frühchristlichen Literatur*. Münster: Aschendorff, 1989.

Swanson, R. A. "Carmen Paschale I." *Classics Journal* 52 (1957): 289–298.

Szövérffy, Joseph. *A Concise History of Medieval Latin Hymnodi. Religious Lyrics between Antiquity and Humanism*. Leyden: 1985.

Taft, Robert F., SJ. "The Lord's Prayer in the Eucharist: When and Why?" *Ecclesia Orans* 14 (1997): 137–155.

Thurston, Bonnie. *The Widows: A Women's Ministry in the Early Church*. Minneapolis, MN: Fortress Press, 1989.

Thielicke, Helmut. *Our Heavenly Father*. New York: Harper and Row, 1953.

Tuilier, A. "Didache," in *Theologische Realenzyklapädie*, Vol. 8. Berlin and New York: Walther de Gruyter, 1981.

Vacandard, E. "Les Homélies attribuées à saint Élois." *Revue des Questions Historiques* 64 (1898): 471–480.

——. "Rèponse aux remarqes de Dom Plaine." *Revue des Questions Historiques* 65 (1899): 243–255.

Vallin, P. " 'Prex Legitima': Pseudo-Augustine, Sermon 65.1." *Revue des études Augustiniennes* 26 (1980): 303ff.

Van Ro, William A. *The Christian Sacrament*. Rome: Pontificia Universita Gregoriana, 1992.

Verbraken, Pierre Patrick. "Les sermons CCXV et LVI de saint Augustin 'De symbolo' et 'De oratione domica.' " *Revue Bénédictine* 68 (1958): 5–40.

Vokes, F. E. "The Lord's Prayer in the First Three Centuries." *Studia Patristica* 10 (1970): 253–260.

Vries, J. de. *Altgermanische Religionsgeschichte: Die Religion der Südgermanen*, Vol. 1. Berlin: 1935.

Wagner, Johannes, ed. *Adult Baptism and the Catechumenate. Concilium: Theology in the Age of Renewal Vol. 22*. New York: Paulist Press, 1967.

Walker, J. H. "Terce, Sext, and None, and Apostolic Custom?" *Studia Patristica* V (1962): 206–212.

Walsh, P. G. "Venantius Fortunatus." *The Month* 120 (1960): 292–302.

Walther, H. "Versifizierte Paternoster und Credo." *Revue du Moyen Age Latin* 20 (1964): 45–64.

Ward, Benedicta (trans.). *The Sayings of the Desert Fathers: The Alphabetical Collection*. Kalamazoo: Cistercian Studies, 1975.

Warr, George C. W. *Teuffel's History of Roman Literature*, Vol. 2. New York: Burt Franklin, 1967.

Westerhoff III, John H. and Edwards Jr., O. C. eds. *A Faithful Church: Issues in the History of Catechesis*. Wilton, Connecticut: Morehouse-Barlow Co., Inc., 1981.

Willis, G. G. "The Lord's Prayer in the Irish Gospel Manuscripts," in *Studia Evangelica* III (Texte und Untersuchungen 88). Berlin: Akademie-verlag, 1964.

———. "St. Gregory the Great and the Lord's Prayer in the Roman Mass," in *Further Essays in Early Roman Liturgy*. London: SPCK, 1968.

Wilmart, André. "Pour les prières de dévotion," in his *Auteurs spirituels et textes dévots du Moyen Age latin: Études d'histoire littéraire*. Paris: 1932.

Wlosok, A. "Vater und Vatervorstellungen in der römischen Kultur," in H. Tellenbach, ed., *Das Vaterbild im Abendland*, vol. 1. Stuttgart: 1976.

Woolfenden, Graham. "Daily Prayer: Its Origin in its Function," in E. A. Livingstone, ed., *Studia Patristica* 30. Leuven: 1997.

Wright, Charles D. *The Irish Tradition in Old English Literature*. Cambridge: Cambridge University Press, 1993.

———. "The Three 'Victories' of the Wind: A Hibernicism in the Hisperica Famina, Collectanea Bedae, and the Old English Prose Solomon and Saturn Pater Noster Dialogue." *Ériu* 41 (1990): 13–25.

Wright, Tom. *The Lord and His Prayer*. London: SPCK, 1996.

Yarnold, Edward. *The Awe-Inspiring Rites of Initiation*. London: St. Paul Publications, 1971.

Zahn, T. *Das Evangelium des Lucas 3. und 4. durchgeshene Aufl.* Leipzig: A. Deichert, 1920.

Zeiller, J. *Les origines chrétiennes dans les provinces danubiennes de l'Empire Romain*. Paris: 1918.

Index